W9-CFK-667

OTHER BOOKS BY SUZAN CAROLL

Becoming ONE, People and Planet
Volume Two

(for free versions of many of the meditations in the book or to purchase the audio CD, please go to Multidimenisons.com)

The Thirty Veils of Illusion

Visions from Venus

Reconstructing Reality

Seven Steps to Soul
A Poetic Journey of Spiritual Awakening

Becoming ONE
People and Planet

A Manual for Personal and Planetary Transformation

Volume One

Text, Poems, Stories and Art
By
Suzan Caroll PhD

ISBN 978-0-9799862-1-5

Multidimensional Publishing
http://www.multidimensions.com

DEDICATION

I dedicate this book to my seven grandchildren, (chronologically) Brittany, Miles, Taylor, Olivia, Tristan, Andrew, and Jade. May they have a safe and healthy planet on which to live, learn, and love.

In fact, I dedicate this book to *all* the children of the world, encouraging every adult to cherish and protect the great light that shines within them.

THE CHILDREN

These children come from Heaven.
Their wings are newly clipped.
Their memories are awake still.
Their halos have not slipped.

How long can they remember
the places they came from?
How long can Soul live in their hearts
and warm them like the sun?

Can others that come near them
know this child will lead the way
then guide them to remain them SELF,
so innocence can stay?

The glory of a newborn
matures into a child,
but as the child becomes adult,
that innocence turns wild.

If we help them to remember
the purpose of their birth,
they'll know the meaning of their life
and acknowledge their self-worth.

The leaders of our future
have bodies very small,
but if we listen with our hearts,
then they can guide us all.

Love them with a love that's true
and see their inner glory,
then they'll know that they are safe
to share their lives-long story.

For fresh in their remembrance
is the truth we seek to find,
but pain has made us deaf
and fear has made us blind.

We'll protect them from the fate
that we ourselves have suffered
then know that from the harm of life
our love has kept them buffered.

We welcome all our children
for they know much more of life
than those of us who have been lost
in illusions of our strife.

Lead us please, dear children.
We follow now your light.
We hear the vision of your words
and see with your clear sight.

For, as these children take the lead
their love will show the way
to open up our hearts and minds
to see a brand new day.

TABLE OF CONTENTS

SECTION ONE

We are not just *living on* the planet; we are *part of* the planet.

SECTION TWO

Not only are we a *part of* the planet, we are a *part of* our SELF.

SECTION THREE

If we are going to *heal* the planet, we must also *heal* ourselves.

SECTION FOUR

When we look into the *face of SELF,*
we see all that stands in the way of *being SELF.*

APPENDIX

BIBLOGRAPHY

(Please visit Multidimensions.com
for free, accompanying audio meditations)

SECTIONS FIVE THROUGH SEVEN IN VOLUME TWO

SECTION FIVE

When we *love* all creation,
we can *create* love.

SECTION SIX

As we become *ONE* with our SELF
we become *ONE* with the Planet.

SECTION SEVEN

The reality we choose to *perceive*
is the reality we choose to *live*.

ACKNOWLEDGMENTS

I would like to acknowledge my first spiritual teacher, Mrs. Reed, who brought me into her Faerie-filled home to give me a much-needed foundation. I would also like to thank the many great pioneers in consciousness whose books are mentioned in the bibliography. Their education created a lifeboat in a sea of spiritual confusion.

I also thank Wyn Saunders for being a wonderful sounding board, as well as for her editing, and re-editing and re-editing... Her constant support was much needed and greatly appreciated. I thank Estrella Jones for formatting the book, creating the book's website, and putting many details under the scrutiny of her Virgo mind to bring order and structure. I also thank Wendy Horwitch for creating and maintaining my multidimensions.com website, which was the foundation for this book.

Thanks to Anne Marie Geyer for touching up my art work and for her fantastic graphics, which were delivered in a timely and perfect manner. Her creative eye was of great assistance. I would also like to thank Eric Cygiel for the inspired creation of the book cover. I also want to thank Katy Koontz for the final editing and some great conversations. I also wish to thank Milton Kahn, who served as the catalyst for the book and whose constant support and patience were invaluable.

I thank my daughter, Julie Roussel, for her support, camaraderie, and help with the finishing touches, as well as my husband Terje Lie, who is always on my side and encouraging me to be my true SELF. Last, but not least, I thank my granddaughter Jade for being born just as the book was finished to remind me that pure innocence still exists.

FOREWORD

Becoming ONE People and Planet is a blend of ecology, psychology, metaphysics, science, art, poetry, and storytelling. This combination is meant to encourage whole brain thinking—the ability to simultaneously use the analytical/sequential thinking of our left brains and the holistic/creative thinking of our right brains.

This synchronized and unified thinking can allow us to access more than the usual 10 to 15 percent of our brains to discover what latent potentials lie hidden from our conscious awareness. As we expand our brains, we open our minds to concepts and ideas that once seemed impossible. This expansion allows us to rise above the doldrums of daily survival to discover not only our hidden qualities, but also our multidimensional selves, the part of us we have forgotten.

Not only are we not using the vast majority of our brain cells, but we're also not using the bulk of our DNA. The latest studies show that up to 95 percent of our DNA has no known function; scientists actually refer to it as "junk DNA." Where in nature is an organism only 10 to 15 percent functional? The respond is, when the organism is in chrysalis form. If we are in chrysalis form, then who or what are we becoming? This answer may be so complex that it's simply not available to our mundane mind.

Fortunately, as our right and left brains communicate with each other, our egos and our Souls also communicate, this expanded communication extends our consciousness beyond the confines of what we think of as ordinary reality. With this expansion, multidimensional realities from the quantum world to the higher dimensions become available for our exploration. What is constant in all of these realities is Gaia, the consciousness of planet Earth. With this realization, we understand that we are not only merging with our expanded potentials and our multidimensional selves, we are also merging with Earth, the planet of which we are a part.

These concepts may seem unfeasible now, but our everyday lives have greatly changed in a very short time. Only one generation ago, the world seemed very large. Letters and newspapers could take days, weeks, or even months to travel from sender to receiver. Due to the difficulty in communication, the different areas of the world were very separate. It was a time when everyone could safely feel as though his or her personal reality was protected from the problems and strife far, far away.

Now, there is no "far away" in communication. Through the internet, we can communicate instantly with just about anyone, anywhere. Every area of the world is a click away, and we can view events the instant they happen—no matter where on the globe they are occurring. Because of this, the planet no longer seems so large; nor do we feel as safe, for now our problems are planetary. Humanity is finally realizing that the Earth, not just our neighborhood or even our country, is our home—and *our home* is in trouble!

When the planet seemed so big and we all felt separated from each other, we believed we were limited in our ability to change planetary situations. Besides, we thought that as humans, we were the most evolved species and nothing could end our reign over this Earth that we thought of as a thing. Fortunately, our consciousness has expanded enough for many of us to realize that the Earth is a living being whose ecosystem is vital to our survival.

Because of these realizations, the collective consciousness of humanity experiences immense fear. Many people will ask, "I am only one person. What can I do?" Indeed, one person seemingly does not have much power to make an impact on our currently grave situation, that same situation about which we were repeatedly warned back when we felt safe.

Yet if we pull our heads out from under the covers and use our collective voice, we can make a difference. In the children's story *Horton Hears a Who!*, by Dr. Seuss, *all* the Whos in Whoville had to raise their voices in order to save their world. In the end, it was the contribution of the small voice of one child who had been playing alone who saved Whoville from sure disaster.

What if our *individual* voice is the *one* voice that will save our planet, and we do not speak up? Maybe our singular contribution is the one that will move our collective consciousness into the critical mass that will wake up the sleeping masses from millennia of separation to manifest planetary unity. However, whether we wish to recognize it or not, the planet is already a unified, living being and her consciousness, Gaia, calls us to awaken *now*. We must release old illusions of being separated within our thinking, from our expanded selves, from each other, and from our planet.

Up until now, we have all been caterpillars whose entire universe was a single branch. But we, like Earth, are great multidimensional beings who are on the verge of expansion into the greater expression of self. Now we are becoming butterflies, and like the monarch, we can travel vast distances within our lifetime. Amazingly, the greatest distance we will travel is from our caterpillar (ego/self) to our butterfly (Soul/SELF). Yes, the situation on our planet seems impossible to cure. However, a caterpillar can only crawl, whereas a butterfly can travel huge distances on wings that can be dismantled by a simple touch.

We do not have to look far to find the miracle that will save us. Myriad miracles are right here on the very planet we have thought of as a thing. What if we instead viewed the planet as a life form named Gaia? What if we saw ourselves as a part of this life form, just like our fingers are a part of our hands? What if we awakened from millennia of illusion to find the truth that the people and the planet are *one*? If we are indeed one with Gaia, then healing our own fear and darkness would heal a portion of the planetary fear and darkness. Then, we would no longer be talking about being one person but instead about *being one planet*.

SECTION ONE

We are not just *living on* the planet.
We are actually *part of* the planet.

CHAPTER ONE

AWAKENING TO SELF

In our modern times, not only have we separated ourselves from our planet, we seem to be on a mission to destroy it, with tribulations such as global warming, unchecked pollution, and overpopulation. However, if the planet is destroyed, where are we to live? This question strikes such fear in us that many try to ignore it, as it seems that one person is not enough to stop the tide of total planetary destruction. At the same time, most of us are having challenges of our own, such as our health, finances, an increasing disillusionment with institutions of all kinds and a nagging sense that something is about to happen. No wonder we often feel exhausted and confused.

Could these two events—planetary destruction and personal crises—be connected? Is it possible that this impending "disaster" is the chaos that precedes great transformation? What can one person do? Perhaps the answer lies in the possibility that the person we appear to be today has vast, untapped potential which has been lost in the daily struggle for survival. This latent potential could also connect us to each other and to the planet. After all, we are currently using only 10 to 15 percent of our brain, and scientists have told us that at least 90 percent of our DNA is "junk DNA," or DNA with no identified function.

If we can rise above our fear and live in the unity of love, perhaps we can awaken the vast, untapped abilities of our greater, true SELF. After all, where in nature is an organism only 10 percent functional? The answer is, when an organism is in its chrysalis form. We have been programmed by the world around us to believe that change is frightening. However, we can look into our lives and remember times of great challenge when we were frightened that we might not make it through, yet we later found that that period of change actually lead to great improvements in our lives.

Could it be that the devastation for which we seem to be headed could also be a powerful transition for the better? Many ancient prophecies attest to that fact. If, indeed, we are in a time of great transformation, we need to activate our inner resources and combine forces with like-minded others. These "others" include our planet, the living being with whom we are a part. It is time now that we awaken to our true SELF, because we will need more than 10 percent of our potential to face the task at hand.

As we awaken to our true SELF, our consciousness will expand to encompass concepts that have long been forgotten. When we were "primitive humans," we believed that everything was filled with the light of Spirit and part of our Great Mother Earth. However, as we became "civilized," we separated from our environment, from other humans and from the light of our Spirit, our true SELF. Instead, we identified our "self" with the physical body that carried our light and with the ego that has been its captain.

This separation has created many innovations and inventions, but it has also created great fear. No longer is Earth our mother and the living being who protects us and affords us a place to live and evolve. In our separation, not only have we forgotten how to communicate with the planet of which we are a part, we have also become her enemy and treated her as poorly as we treat other humans. In fact, we treat our planet as badly as we often treat ourselves. It is fear that creates this misconduct, because when we are afraid, adrenaline fills our body and our body then goes into survival mode.

Unfortunately, fear is far too natural to many, many people. How can it not be? We have to protect ourselves and our loved ones from a world that is constantly in flux. On the other hand, what if we could spend one day, or even one hour, perceiving *everything* as alive and an element of our SELF who, in turn, is an element of the planet? Would we behave differently than we do under the present paradigm of separation?

What reality would we create in a world where everything is alive and a portion of our total SELF? This SELF is actually already inside of us, waiting to be activated with our "conscious intention." Conscious intention is often something we don't have time for in our busy lives. Nonetheless, with practice, conscious intention can be just as familiar as fear is now.

In reality, if we are not consciously intent on living in love, fear (which is a natural reaction to today's changes) will take over. Two antidotes to fear are information, as fear thrives on ignorance, and love, especially love for ourselves. For how can we give away what we do not have within ourselves? Through remembering our true, Multidimensional SELF, we can experience the unconditional love that constantly flows from the SELF that we have forgotten and from the planet whom we have made into a thing. Love is free and infinite, for love is a vibration that resonates to the light of the ONE from whence we came and the ONE that we are becoming.

AWAKEN

The early morning light
shines through the window
glistening and dancing
across the table

Now is the time to remember,
remember our SELF

Now, when the light is near
we must allow it to enter deep within
to reveal ourselves and
awaken ancient memories

that know all
feel all
think all
love all

For only in
knowing our SELF
can we truly know another

Only in
trusting our SELF,
can we truly trust another

Only in
receiving comfort from our SELF
can we truly comfort another

Only in
loving our SELF
can we truly love another

We have many "selves," for we are the sum total of everyone we have ever been and everything we have ever experienced. Most of our many selves are unconscious to our everyday life, which is fortunate because otherwise we would be completely overwhelmed. On the other hand, each of us has some extremely evolved people who are lost inside our unconscious mind, as well as some very wounded people whom our powerful selves could love into healing. Love is the healing force of the universe. Love is an energy field that expands and unites. Hence, it is the perfect balance for fear, an energy field that constricts and separates.

It is time *now* to release the illusions of separation from our true SELF, so that we can be free of the illusionary limitation that we have been taught by a world filled with fear. One of the first aspects of our self that we need to recover is our inner child so that we can regain our wonderful imagination. Imagination is the brick and mortar for creating the life that is just beyond our belief in limitation, for how can we create that which we cannot imagine? Imagination is the core of creativity because it allows us to embrace that which is so different that it seems impossible.

Wake up now from the dream that you believed was reality, and your true SELF will be revealed like the parting clouds reveal the sun.

THE DREAM

I gazed upon the glorious being floating just before me. Its light filled the entire room with a warm radiation.

"Who are you?" I asked within my heart.

"I am you, Beloved," was the unexpected reply.

I did not understand what the beautiful being had said. I was not glorious. I could not float in the air as the being before me did, and I definitely did not have enough light to fill the entire room.

I was just a regular person with a regular life. Some days I felt good, even peaceful. But some days I felt bad, even tormented. I did my job as well as I could and tried to pay my bills on time.

I was a good citizen. I had a family that I loved and friends who I cared for and who cared for me. However, sometimes I was frightened, annoyed, or sad.

No, I was not special. I was just regular.

"Oh, but my one," the being interrupted my thoughts, "just regular IS special."

"What?" I responded in a somewhat angry and disrespectful voice. Quickly, I covered my mouth and muttered an apology.

"You needn't apologize to me, my dear. I am you!"

"No, I'm sorry," I replied, almost to myself. "I can't believe that. I cannot accept that. If I were you, then why would I ever want to be me?"

"I am very proud to be you. I am very proud of how you have maintained your life under difficult circumstances. Life upon the physical plane can be, and usually is, challenging. And you/I have maintained a heart that loves."

"A heart that loves?"

"Yes, and a mind that thinks. You, that is you and I together, have kept our bond, our promise to remain our SELF in the face of many temptations that could pull us out of 'being regular,' out of 'being special.'"

"Well yes," I replied as I scratched my chin. "I must say that there are a million temptations, from choosing to walk to the recycling bin to remembering to think before I speak. I guess I do try, most of the time, to be the best person that I can be."

"Yes, and all of the time, you are special. You are special not just because you try to do your best, but because you have chosen to leave the form that you see before you/myself/ourselves and enter into the experience of physical life."

Now I was confused. I did not remember making such a choice. In fact, if I could have chosen to, I would have instantly become the glorious being before me.

"Are you sure?" responded the being, reading my thoughts. "What about your family, your friends, your work, your planet? Would you not miss them?"

"Well, yes, I would. I would miss them all very much. But if I am also a being like you, then they must also have a part of them that is like you. Don't they?"

"Most certainly," replied the being with a smile so bright that the radiance extended beyond the walls of the room until there were no walls and no floor. There was only light.

At first, I was a bit frightened. Standing in the middle of blazing light was not a regular occurrence in my experience.

The being gently laughed, saying, "Be not concerned. The room around you, in fact your entire physical world, still exists. However, your attention is now on my world, which is of a higher vibration.

"Follow me," said the being. "There is something I would like you to see."

The being led me to a door that seemed to appear from nowhere. It opened wide as we approached it.

The being stepped through the door and beckoned me to follow. It took a moment for my sight to clear. Then I saw it.

Before me was a vision of my house, my family, and my friends joining together in friendly communion, except that everything and everyone was emanating radiant light. They all turned towards me and smiled. Their smiles lit the room even brighter.

"You have brought your physical awareness," they said as one voice. "We are trying to bring our physical consciousness here as well. Wouldn't it be beautiful if we all could meet here, physical with spiritual, and then return to earth? Think of it! Can you imagine the impact it would make if we could link our physical and spiritual essences to create a continuous flow from Spirit into matter?"

"I must be dreaming," I thought out loud. I reached to pinch my arm, but it looked different. It was not hard. It was more like a cloud, a golden cloud. My hands were as radiant as the glorious being's. I looked around to ask the being what had happened and found that it had gone.

"No," replied the being's voice from inside my heart and mind. "I am not gone. I am inside of you. Now, please take me into your physical world and don't forget that I am you-inside."

I sat up in my bed with a start. My body was drenched with sweat and my mate was sleeping beside me.

"It was just a dream after all," I thought.

"Oh, but what a glorious dream!" came the now familiar inner voice.

Fortunately, it was still responding to my every thought.

CHAPTER TWO

DIMENSIONAL CONSCIOUSNESS

We the people, as well as our planet, are multidimensional beings. However, when we were born, our great, multidimensional light passed through the prism into the third dimension to enter our physical body, and we forgot our SELF. If we can awaken to the fact that we are more than our earth vessel and remember that "we" are really the light that fills this vessel—and much, much more—we can remember our true, Multidimensional SELF.

Actually, one person at a time, we are beginning to remember that we were always ONE and we just forgot. To activate our memory, each of us must go into the depths of the person who we are now to find our roots in the core of the planet, and then share our great, multidimensional light with her. Mother Earth, in turn, will share her planetary light with us to assist in expanding our consciousness to remember our SELF.

Once we remember our Multidimensional SELF, we are free of the illusion that we are separate from our SELF, from others, and from our planet. It is through expanding our consciousness to encompass our Multidimensional SELF that we remember why our light has come through the third-dimensional filter of our present state of consciousness and also what we have promised to do for ourselves, for others and for our planet. To begin the activation of our multidimensional consciousness, let's take a look at all five dimensions—one dimension at a time.

FIRST-DIMENSONAL CONSCIOUSNESS

First-dimensional consciousness is awareness as a point. The consciousness that resonates to this dimension is the Mineral Kingdom that both people and planet both in their bodies. Current third-dimensional science has not proven that minerals have any awareness as we recognize it, but healers and shamans have been using crystals as healing tools for many centuries.

As humans, our first-dimensional consciousness is unconscious—it is in fact a state of not being conscious of our five physical senses. However, the first dimension is a portion of our bodies and represents the minerals, water, cells, and genetic codes that are the foundation of all physical forms. If we could access this level of our unconscious, we could connect with Gaia and all her creatures via the most basic common denominator, the individual molecules. Perhaps we could even consciously access our own genetic coding.

> Visualize yourself as a first-dimensional being. You are an atom of carbon, a drop of water, and an imprint upon a strand of DNA. However, you cannot perceive the strand or the other molecules of water and carbon. You are only conscious of the exact point of your awareness. However, as you look inside you, you find that another world exists, a world of electrons, protons, nuclei, and quarks. You are the gateway between the macrocosm and the microcosm.

SECOND-DIMENSIONAL CONSCIOUSNESS

Second-dimensional consciousness is awareness as point and line. The consciousness that resonates to this dimension is biological matter, such as the Plant Kingdom, which covers our beautiful planet, and the lower Animal Kingdom, such as reptiles and fish. The consciousness of this dimension does not possess self-awareness. These beings are only conscious of their species' identity and their need for feeding, fighting, and procreation. Their consciousness is based upon survival of the fittest and they live solely within the awareness of the moment.

Human second-dimensional consciousness is centered in the lower brain, also known as our "reptilian brain," which directs the autonomic nervous system to regulate and maintain life support functions. Our five physical senses are largely unconscious of this component of ourselves, but with training (such as biofeedback and meditation) we can establish some conscious awareness and control. Yogis, for example, are known to achieve enough conscious control of their autonomic nervous system to regulate their heartbeat and metabolism.

"Primitive" peoples are much more aware of this "animal" portion of their physical form and, therefore, have conscious access to their basic instincts and an awareness of how they are a portion of a greater whole. Unlike "civilized" man, they have a constant respect for all life and the balance of nature.

> As you expand your consciousness to perceive the second dimension, you become aware of your environment. However, your demands from your environment are simple: you must survive, and you live only to continue the existence of your species. You will protect yourself and procreate in the proper season, but you look neither forwards nor backwards, and you dwell only in the present. You are what you are and where you are. You do not plan or reflect. Your perceptions are confined to what you can eat, use, fight, mate with, or rear. However, your herd and you are one. Your instincts guide you, and you are a part of nature.

THIRD-DIMENSIONAL CONSCIOUSNESS

Third-dimensional consciousness is awareness of point, line, length, breadth, height, and volume. The primary consciousness of this dimension is the higher Animal Kingdom (including humans). Just like our third-dimensional planet, our third-dimensional body is composed of all the elements of the first and second dimension: water, minerals, genetic coding, and biological matter, as well as an individual Soul. It is this individual Soul that distinguishes humans from the other members of the Animal Kingdom who mostly have a group Soul.

The name Gaia is the Greek noun for “land.” In Greek mythology, Gaia was the primordial element from which all the gods originated. Gaia was worshiped throughout early Greece but later fell into decline and was supplanted by other gods. Like the ancient Greeks, we have stopped revering the land that gives us a home and we have instead turned to worshiping power and money. However, what good will those gods do us if we have no land on which to live? As we remember our multidimensional consciousness, we will no longer need to worship anything or anyone. Our consciousness will expand to embrace all the dimensions from the first to the twelfth, and we will be united with *all* life.

Our third-dimensional Earth is locked in a time/space and cause/effect paradigm. This dimension is a schoolroom that our higher-dimensional Souls attend by inhabiting humanoid, physical bodies to learn more about creation. In the third dimension, life mirrors all that we are seeking to understand. Therefore, the process of creating via our thoughts and feelings is slowed down so that we can track the circumstances of what we hold in our consciousness.

There are different stages of human consciousness aligned in a hierarchical manner, which often, but not always, coincide with our age:

FIRST LEVEL OF THIRD-DIMENSIONAL CONSCIOUSNESS

In the first level of consciousness, we are dependent on others for our survival. In this state of dependency, we do not realize that our consciousness holds the seeds of the lives we are creating. We believe that we are powerless over our environment and that we are victims to the circumstances of our lives. Our goal in this level is to gain enough self-awareness, as we mature beyond this child-state, to become independent.

SECOND LEVEL OF THIRD-DIMENSIONAL CONSCIOUSNESS

In the second level of consciousness, we are independent. This independence develops as we learn that we can control our own life. Through our choices and experiences, we gain trust in our ability to be responsible because we respect ourselves. This respect is based upon our sense of personal power. Without this sense of personal power, we are filled with fear, which reduces us to surviving. Although age is a factor in gaining our independence, it is certainly not the only way we gain independence. It is the ability to self-reflect and learn from life's experiences that pushes us on to the third level of consciousness.

THIRD LEVEL
OF THIRD-DIMENSIONAL CONSCIOUSNESS

In the third level of consciousness, we are dependable. This dependability develops as we gain enough trust and respect for ourselves that we can become responsible for others. Through life's experiences, we have learned that we definitely have an impact, not only on our own life, but also on the lives of others. Because of our earned self-esteem, we feel confident that we are reliable. We have "earned" our self-esteem by taking the time to recognize our victories, no matter how small.

EXPANDING THIRD-DIMENSIONAL CONSCIOUSNESS

As humans, we have the ability to remember the past and the future while remaining aware of the present. However, much of our true SELF becomes lost in our unconscious mind. This loss leaves us with a feeling of separation from the whole, a fear that we are limited in our ability to achieve our desires, and a belief that we have to work hard to accomplish our goals.

Both third-dimensional society and science seek to prove that the only reality that exists is the one we perceive with our five physical senses, urging us to believe that our third-dimensional perceptions of reality *are* the only reality. From this state of consciousness, spirit congeals into matter and our thinking is limited to our ego. Hence, the need for the development of a strong sense of ego is often gained at the cost of losing our sense of group identity and sense of responsibility to others and to our planet. This ego limitation is especially predominant in the Western world where individual achievement and possessions often become the most important parts of our lives.

Awareness of our Multidimensional SELF is best remembered when we have expanded our consciousness beyond the confines of mundane life to take some time for inner reflection. It is with the brave journey into our unconscious mind that we can find our greatest power, as well as our deepest wounds that have barred us from our power.

When we become aware of the many aspects of our forgotten SELF, our consciousness expands to encompass more than our ego and third-dimensional reality.

> Imagine your "self" from the perspective of your inner imagination. How do you look to yourself from here? How do you *feel* about you from your inner being? Do you feel grounded in the Earth and connected to all life? Perhaps now that you have directly experienced your first- and second-dimensional selves, you feel a greater unity with the life around you that resonates to the lower vibrations of your physical body and planet. Perhaps a crystal can heal, and a plant can respond to your voice and personal attention. Your mundane thoughts tell you that that is ridiculous, but a primitive instinct seems to have been jarred in your consciousness. You are no longer so very different from the world around you. Maybe, you *are* a portion of the planet.

FOURTH-DIMENSIONAL CONSCIOUSNESS

Fourth-dimensional consciousness is awareness of point, length, breadth, height, volume, and time. The laws of time and space are different here than in the third dimension, as it is an octave up in frequency from our physical world. Because of this, fourth-dimensional perceptions of past, present, and future are fluid. From your third-dimensional self, your fourth-dimensional self may seem like your "higher human," as it is the last dimension where physical vehicles are used to contain individual consciousness. However, our Multidimensional SELF expands far beyond this reality.

Fourth-dimensional consciousness encompasses our group identity without the loss of our personal ego. However, because of the fluid nature of time and space, our fourth-dimensional forms naturally morph. Hence, there is great mobility of form here, and this is the realm of the mythological shape shifters. A shaman or holy person who can shape-shift has learned to ground his or her fourth-dimensional form into the third dimension so completely that he or she can temporarily change shape.

Much of our third-dimensional life also exists on the fourth dimension in the format of a higher vibration, but we are not aware of it because that reality is not in sync with our physical time and space. We can have a dream of an entire lifetime and wake up to find that only five minutes of our physical time has passed. Our fourth-dimensional reality is not perceivable to our third-dimensional self until we have expanded our consciousness.

The fourth dimension is the realm which holds the awareness of our body's first- and second-dimensional components, as well as all past experiences of our entire life. We can expand our third-dimensional consciousness into the fourth dimension through gaining an awareness of the inner-workings of our physical body, remembering our dreams, and having intense experiences of passion, emotion, creativity, and/or spirituality.

The Astral Plane, also known as the Emotional Plane, is the lowest octave of the fourth dimension and is the realm of dream life. When we are asleep, we are unconscious in the third dimension, but we are conscious in the fourth dimension. Our fourth-dimensional astral body possesses advanced dreaming, imagination, psychic ability, intuition, magic, and creativity. As we expand our mind to the frequency of the fourth dimension, we can experience more and more of these qualities while in our physical form.

Some people are born with an innate connection to their fourth-dimensional self and must work to ground their consciousness in a third-dimensional world that often feels foreign and hostile. Others are born without this awakened connection, and they usually feel more comfortable and at home within the third-dimensional paradigm. These people often feel cut off from the higher-dimensional portions of themselves and may not even believe that their higher selves exist.

However, our fourth-dimensional body does exist and its highest vibration is known as our Spiritual Body. Much as a person upon a mountaintop can observe and guide the residents of the valley below, our Spiritual Body observes us on the third dimension and can give us guidance. However, the fourth dimension still has the polarization of light and dark, and this realm is not necessarily more loving, especially on the lower sub-planes. On the fourth dimension, thought and feelings create reality much more quickly than on the third dimension, and fear can create evil as easily as love can create beauty and joy.

FOURTH-DIMENSIONAL PLANES

The fourth dimension encompasses several different sub-planes, which we can perceive with our expanded consciousness. The Lower Astral Plane, which is actually a lower octave of the Astral/Emotional Plane, holds the invisible emanations of all the fear and negativity that is projected into it from the physical plane. The Lower Astral has been known as Hell, with Purgatory being above that. Fourth-dimensional consciousness feeds into and amplifies third-dimensional emotions. Therefore, it is often known as the realm of emotion. Because the Lower Astral holds the third dimension's negative emotions, it is not a pleasant experience and a path must be forged through it into the higher sub-planes, such as Faerie.

The Land of Faerie is also an octave of the Astral/Emotional Plane. Faerie, which we read about as children in our fairy tales, actually exists in the fourth dimension. Faerie acts as respite after we have forged our pathway through the fear and darkness of the Lower Astral Plane. After we have experienced Faerie, we can travel in our fourth-dimensional consciousness into the higher vibrations of the Astral/Emotional Plane to learn about balancing our emotions.

From there, we can travel up into the Mental Plane to learn how to choose our thoughts and into the Higher Mental Plane to learn how to expand our consciousness. In the Causal Plane we can learn the cause and effect of how thoughts and feelings create our world. The Spiritual Plane is next and shows us how to connect with our spiritual guidance and I AM presence, the highest frequency of all our fourth-dimensional bodies. It is our I AM Presence who stands at the threshold to the fifth dimension, waiting to guide us back into the ONE of the fifth dimension and beyond.

The fourth dimension is like a river that flows between the higher dimensions and the physical body. The mouth of the river is where the physical and astral bodies overlap, much like the brackish water of a river's delta, where salt and fresh water mix. This area is known as the Etheric Body, where the third and fourth dimensions intermingle. This body encompasses the physical body and extends beyond it a few inches.

We navigate our travel into and through the fourth dimension with our desires, thoughts, and emotions. A metaphor of this would be sailing. We are the boat, the water is the fourth dimension, the location we wish to reach is our desire, our thoughts are the sail and the steering, and the wind is our emotions. If our emotions are fearful and tumultuous we will have an uncomfortable ride. Even though our desire is for the higher planes of the fourth dimension, our personal imbalance will limit our entry to the Lower Astral Plane, where fear—which is the lack of emotional balance—rules.

If we wish to journey to the higher planes of the fourth dimension, we must keep our thoughts harmonious and our feelings centered in the infinite balance of love. In that manner, eventually, we can experience all the planes of the fourth dimension. Then our I AM presence can lead us across what is known as the Rainbow Bridge into the fifth dimension and beyond.

> In order to imagine your fourth-dimensional body, you remember the many adventures of your dreams. Yes, you did change locations instantly, and yes, you also changed forms. You begin to ponder the possibility that your dreams are actually a part of your total SELF trying to talk to you. But why can't the communication be clearer? Why doesn't your fourth-dimensional self just speak directly to you? Then you remember how isolated your first and second-dimensional selves felt from your third-dimensional self, for you feel just as isolated from your fourth-dimensional self. If you can imagine being a cell or a plant, surely you can imagine being your "dream self."

FIFTH-DIMENSIONAL CONSCIOUSNESS

Fifth-dimensional consciousness is awareness of length, breadth, height, time, and spirit. All life on the fifth dimension lives in the unity consciousness of Spirit, but there is still an experience of "I" as an individual member of the group.

All is ONE in the fifth dimension. There are no polarities of male-female, good-bad, pretty-ugly, and linear time and space do not exist. Hence, there is *no* illusion of separation (across empty space) or limitation (due to time constraints). Since there is no separation into polarities, such as here/there (space) or past/future (time), there is a constant experience of the *here* and the *now*.

The primary consciousness of this dimension is in androgynous, stellar beings living in bodies of light. These lightbodies are light-based rather than carbon-based. Lightbodies have the conscious awareness of their lower selves, our third-dimensional physical selves, without the physical limitations. All actions on this plane are based on unconditional love and divine compassion. Unconditional love is the higher octave of the polarity of love/fear and divine compassion is the higher octave of judgment/acceptance.

If we were to experience fear or judgment while in the fifth dimension, our vibration would drop and our consciousness would instantly plummet to the lower sub-planes of the fourth dimension. Our complete Multidimensional SELF who resonates to the fifth dimension and beyond, constantly projects unconditional love and divine compassion into our consciousness. Unfortunately, we are usually unconscious of this gift until we expand our consciousness to encompass the fifth dimension.

In this expanded consciousness, we can travel with the flow of the ONE in harmony with all life. Within this flow, every being, place, situation, or location that is desired becomes instantly manifest. If we do choose the experience of movement, it feels like a combination of flying and treading water. Our fifth-dimensional lightbodies, like our fourth-dimensional bodies, are mutable and can easily change form. Just as we can change our location or experience with our desire in the fourth dimension, we can also change the form of the "body" that surrounds our fifth-dimensional consciousness.

Just as we can observe the lower dimensions while in our third-dimensional consciousness, we can observe all the lower dimensions from our expanded fifth-dimensional consciousness. It is natural to view the dimensions below us, as we can easily perceive the second and first dimensions. However, in order to perceive a higher dimension than the dimension we are currently experiencing, we must raise our consciousness to encompass that dimension. Because there is no sense of limitation while in this consciousness, we can perceive many different vibratory rates in the ONE moment of the fifth-dimensional *now*.

The fifth dimension also has sub-planes, but awareness of, and therefore writings about, these sub-planes is minimal. It has been my experience that there is a threshold upon which we wait for our divine complement (also known as our twin flame), the opposite polarity of our androgynous lightbody that was split off from us when we took embodiment in the lower dimensions.

In order to imagine our fifth-dimensional self, who is our Multidimensional SELF, we would need to release the feelings of separation and the many limitations of our physical world. Our fully realized SELF could have anything or be anyone by joining thoughts and emotions with conscious intention and perceive the subatomic particles that connect each illusion of matter. Yes, from this state of consciousness all matter is indeed revealed as an illusion, an elaborate hologram, which we can easily edit with a mere thought or emotion. Are you ready for that responsibility? If not, any action that is taken towards another will instantly return to us, via those very subatomic particles.

THE STAIRWAY

I awaken to find myself on a stairway. Above me the stairs are brighter and of a loose form. Below me the stairs become darker and appear to be more constricted.

I look at the stairs above me and feel a sparkle of love calling me to climb them. But when I try, I find that an inner pull urges me to go down the stairs below me. As I turn to look down the stairway, fear chills my heart.

“Why would I want to go down there?” I say to myself.

"Because you already have," whispers a voice that seems to emanate from the sparkle of love above me.

"If I have been to that place," I ask, "why would I ever want to return?"

"You do not need to return," the voice breathes into my heart. "You have never left."

"No, that is not possible. I feel myself only here, upon this step."

"But you are on other steps as well. There is a ‘you’ (in fact, there are many of ‘you’) on every step. You see, each step is like a dimension, a plane of existence."

"If there are so many fragments of myself, why don't I know about them?"

"Do you feel the pull from the steps beneath you?"

"Yes, I do."

"That pull is coming from the portions of your self that are lost in the lower dimensions. They are lost because they believe they are alone. Because you have not freed them, you believe that you are alone."

"How can I free them when I feel as though I am lost myself?"

"Oh my one, you are not lost. You have found your higher voice; you have found *me*! Your 'lost' fragments of self have sent you up this stairway, like a scout, to see if there is another way. Now you have found it. Go back and share your experience with them."

"Please don't make me leave. I remember it down there now, and I want to stay here."

"You shall stay where you are, just as you will stay where you have been. You will not move; instead, you will expand."

"Expand?"

"Yes. You see yourself now as a single point of awareness. Can you extend that awareness to imagine that you are standing on every step?"

I close my eyes and call upon my imagination. I have always had a vivid imagination. Oh yes, there they are. There is a person on every step. Each one has the same amount of light and density as the step that they are standing on. They all look very different, but there is something about them that feels the same, as well.

"Yes," the voice replies to my thoughts. "They all are of one consciousness. Can you feel how you and I are the same?"

It seems difficult for me to imagine that I could be the same as this wise and loving voice, but I close my eyes and try to make the connection. At first all I can perceive are the many voices of doubt, ridicule, and fear calling from the stairs below me. But gradually, I also feel the love and support flowing from the stairs above me, as well.

With this feeling, my consciousness and perception begin to expand more and more. I feel pulled like a rubber band being stretched so tight that it is ready to break. Tighter and tighter I feel the pull until I can barely stand the tension.

Then, with a sudden *snap*, I understand. **I** am the loving voice that has guided me. **I** am the pull of fear and doubt. **I** am each person upon each step. In fact, **I** am each step and the imagination that created them. **I** am *all in all*.

"Yes," resonates the loving voice from every person, every step, and every dimension. "*We* are a multidimensional being. It is *our* expansion from a singular consciousness to multidimensional consciousness that allows us to *know* who we are."

CHAPTER THREE

UNCONSCIOUS AND CONSCIOUS DIMENSIONAL BODIES

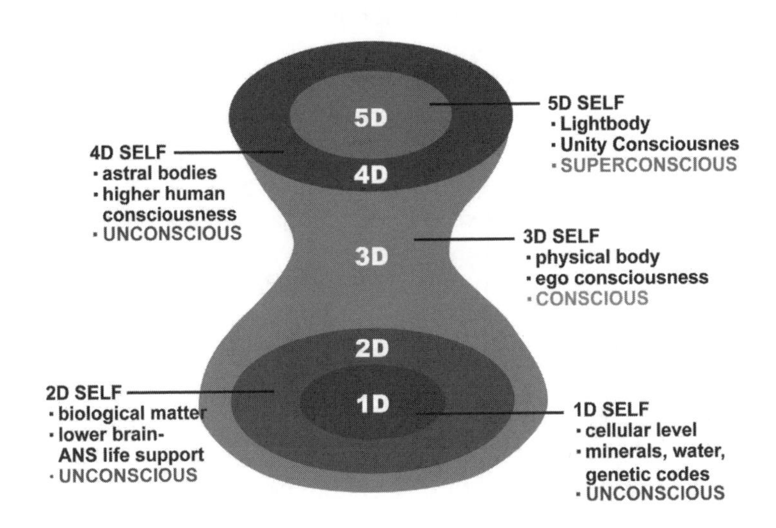

UNDERSTANDING DIMENSIONS

All five dimensions exist within, are a portion of, and emanate from our third-dimensional body. We are a vessel that we fill with our own multidimensional universe. As we become aware of the five dimensions of our self, we can become conscious of the inter-relationship between all of our many aspects. Through this awareness we can begin to integrate our unconscious first- and second-dimensional selves and our superconscious fourth- and fifth-dimensional selves into our third-dimensional conscious self.

We accomplish this integration by collapsing the lower first- and second-dimensional selves, as well as our higher fourth- and fifth-dimensional selves, into our third-dimensional self. Think of a travel cup with the smallest bottom section of the cup being your lower-dimensional, unconscious self, the middle section of the cup being your third-dimensional self, and the largest, top section of the cup being your higher-dimensional, superconscious self.

If you were to partially collapse the cup, the bottom section would be surrounded by the middle with the top section just above it. However, if you were to completely collapse the cup, you would see the bottom section (lower-dimensional self) surrounded first by the middle section (third-dimensional) and then by the top (higher-dimensional) section.

How can we remain conscious of this process? How can we help both ourselves and others? Perhaps if we can each take personal responsibility for expanding our own consciousness, we can assist in expanding the consciousness of our group, nation, and planet. Could one person have that much power? As we raise our individual consciousness, we will realize that we are not just one person. Our third-dimensional Earth is suffering from our disregard for her body. We are running out of unpolluted space and running out of time to repair the damage we have done. If we remain unconscious of our physical, destructive behavior and unconscious of how *we* create our world, we may not have a third-dimensional Earth on which we can be conscious. Our first- and second-dimensional bodies are usually ruled by our unconscious mind.

OUR UNCONSCIOUS DIMENSIONAL BODIES

OUR FIRST-DIMENSIONAL BODY

We have a body in all five dimensions. Each dimension holds a resonant frequency, which is the primary vibration of that dimension. The first dimension is the lowest frequency, but it is the foundation for all physical life. For example, the single cell, which has a first-dimensional consciousness, is the core of all life on our planet and in our physical body. A single cell also carries the threshold to another universe, the subatomic world.

Before quantum physics, we were less interested in the subatomic reality, although science had delved deeply into the single cell. Metaphysics talks about our first eight cells. The first eight cells represent the pattern for our essence. Our essence is our entire persona, which our parents noticed in our infancy and watched develop into our adulthood.

In Jungian psychology, this essence is called our Divine Child. Our Divine Child is the crystal core of our true SELF, which is gradually and steadily covered with the dust of our many life experiences. Our Divine Child represents our Multidimensional SELF, and he or she has a consciousness that expands from our first-dimensional, cellular self to our highest-dimensional, Spirit SELF. Just as all the atoms on our planet hold the threshold into the subatomic reality, our Divine Child holds the threshold to our multidimensional world. Our Divine Child does not forget our multidimensional being. However, we forget our Divine Child.

Some of us are fortunate enough to have had parents who encourage and reward this core of our essence. More often, however, our parents and society squelch our beautiful, multidimensional being and try to mold us into the person that they want us to be. In the far extreme, some parents are even abusive. In whatever the scenario, our Divine Child (and the glorious being that he or she protects) resides deep in our unconscious and superconscious mind.

OUR SECOND-DIMENSIONAL BODY

Our second-dimensional self correlates to the less evolved animals and the plant kingdom. Animals have an instinct for self-protection, and plants have innate protective devices. Second-dimensional beings take in food, procreate, and survive, much like the organs of our body. Just as nature provides food and shelter for plants and animals, each of our organs has a special dietary need, which they are dependent on our body to supply. If the proper food is not given, these second-dimensional beings will cease to function.

Within our innate second-dimensional consciousness, we also have an instinct, a knowing, that tells us what food we need, when we are safe, and when we need to seek protection. Unfortunately, most of these skills—which were prized, survival tactics to our primitive self—have been lost to our modern, city self. However, just like our Divine Child, our primitive self is latent in our unconscious, waiting for us to recognize and use it.

Unfortunately, our unconscious is also filled with the many painful experiences that we did not feel strong enough to confront. Therefore, like a ball of tangled yarn, our unconscious mind is filled with our deepest pain and our greatest glory. This agony and ecstasy is sealed off from our mundane self. Hence, many of our latent abilities are lost, while our repressed trauma and unhappiness become our inner saboteur, who stops us from being our true Multidimensional SELF.

OUR CONSCIOUS DIMENSIONAL BODIES

OUR THIRD-DIMENSIONAL BODY

Our third-dimensional body is usually ruled by our conscious mind, but when we have the courage to dip into the shadows of our unconscious mind, we begin to heal our wounded child. This healing creates a powerful catalyst for change. It does not matter how we change, for each one will change in his or her own way according to his or her own directions. What matters is that as we heal our wounded child, we slowly begin to connect with our Divine Child, who holds the memory of our true, Multidimensional SELF. With the awakening of our Divine Child, we gradually become conscious of some of the innate abilities of our true SELF.

Unfortunately, many of us may feel as though we must hide our new abilities for fear of judgment from others. On the other hand, if we are courageous enough to come out of the closet and say things such as, "I met an angel in my dreams last night," or "I knew you were going to say that," or to openly admit that we have awakened to our multidimensional powers (such as precognition, telepathy, empathy, instincts, telekinesis, or clairvoyance), we make it safer for others to come out as well. Many of these abilities have been shrouded with superstition and disbelief, but as more and more of us come forward, what has formerly seemed different will become normal.

This fear of being different began long ago with the superstition unleashed by the Dark Ages. At that time, anything that was different was bad. Hence, if someone accidentally remembered his or her Multidimensional SELF and openly expressed it, that person was considered different. Worse yet, the person was considered evil. With luck, we have evolved enough in this passage of time that fear is no longer the first reaction to a unique experience. Psychic powers are not evil or even magic. They are natural abilities of our Multidimensional SELF.

We are on the verge of a paradigm shift. Once we thought the world was flat and the sun rotated around the Earth. As we expand our consciousness beyond the strict confines of the third dimension, our perceptions also expand so that we can consciously perceive beyond the limits of our third-dimensional reality. Some of the multidimensional, expanded perceptions that we will regain are:

Empathy

n. Direct identification with, understanding of, and vicarious experience of another person's situation, feelings, and motives.

Empathy is the ability to feel another person's emotions. It is a second-dimensional ability shared by "primitive" tribal societies, herd animals, and birds in a flock. An example of this is when our pet comes up and nudges us in an attempt to comfort our sadness. Other examples are a mother's understanding of what her nonverbal infant needs and a healer's deep knowing of how a patient feels.

Instinct

n. An inborn pattern of behavior that is characteristic of a species and is often a response to specific environmental stimuli: *the spawning instinct in salmon; altruistic instincts in social animals.* A powerful motivation or impulse, or an innate capability or aptitude: *an instinct for tact and diplomacy.*

Instinct, which is an innate knowing, is another second-dimensional ability based on our "primitive self" who has the ability to tune into the planet to know where water is, what food will heal us or poison us, and the location of our tribe. If we give a horse his head, he will find water. Animals in the wild know what food they are meant to eat and what food will hurt them. Animals know when a predator is staking them or simply sharing the waterhole. If humans are more evolved than these animals, why would we loose that ability?

Intuition

n. The act or faculty of knowing or sensing without the use of rational processes; immediate cognition. Knowledge gained by the use of this faculty; a perceptive insight, a sense of something not evident or deducible; an impression.

Intuition, another form of second-dimensional knowing, gives us answers or gut feelings without the need for thought. Intuition is the ability to combine the perceptions of the fourth dimension and beyond, such as vision, hearing, proprioception (our location in space), and smell. All these abilities are derived from our brain's functioning beyond the 10 to 15 percent range that is considered normal. Many people use their intuition everyday, but they call it luck.

Telepathy

n. Apparent communication from one mind to another without using sensory perceptions

Telepathy is the ability to read, or have a knowing of another person's thoughts. An example would be when we answer a question that another person has not yet asked. It is a fourth- and fifth-dimensional ability, which is a natural consequence of either moving beyond the constraints of third-dimensional time and into the more fluid fourth-dimensional time, and/or moving into fifth-dimensional consciousness where all life is blended in unity with the ONE.

Precognition

n. Knowledge of something in advance of its occurrence, especially by extrasensory perception.

Precognition, seeing into the future, is the fourth-dimensional ability to move beyond the constraints of third-dimensional time and into the mutable time of the fourth dimension. Once we have practiced our sense of precognition, we can even discriminate between a possible reality and a probable reality. A possible reality is a choice of the ego, and a probable reality is a directive from our fifth-dimensional SELF. If we are in tune with our SELF, we will likely welcome and choose to experience that reality by filling it with our desire and conscious intention.

Telekinesis
n. The movement of objects by scientifically inexplicable means.

Telekinesis is a fourth and fifth-dimensional ability that allows us to move objects through space without the workings of our physical body. In our fourth- and fifth-dimensional selves, our mind, emotions, and intentions are more powerful than our muscles. Therefore, we can displace objects by combining our thoughts and emotions with our conscious intention.

Clairvoyance
n. The power to see objects or events that cannot be perceived by the senses; acute intuitive insight or perceptiveness.

Clairvoyance is the ability to see objects that resonate to the fourth dimension and beyond. As we expand our consciousness, our perceptions expand beyond the confines of the third-dimensional spectrum of light. Hence, we can see objects and beings in the fourth dimension and beyond that we couldn't see before.

Clairaudience
n. The power to hear things outside the range of normal perception.

Clairaudience is the ability to hear sounds from the fourth dimension and beyond. With practice, we can all communicate with realities that resonate to frequencies beyond the third dimension.

Clairsentience
This term is not found in traditional dictionaries.

Clairsentience is the umbrella term for all psychic senses together. When we are clairsentient, we can access our expanded senses to smell, see, and touch another person's aura, hear another person's thoughts, or feel another person's emotions.

Illumination
n. A condition of spiritual awareness; divine illumination; "follow God's light." The degree of visibility of your environment, an interpretation that removes obstacles to understanding.

Illumination arises as we surrender our ego to our fifth-dimensional Soul/SELF to become ONE with the *now* of the higher dimensions. Just one third-dimensional moment of such union can set us on a path that takes most of our life to journey.

As we connect with our Multidimensional SELF, we feel an inner urge to expand our abilities beyond the limitations of the society in which we live. Our SELF gives the courage to come out with our latent abilities and to ignore the fear and judgments of others. The world is uniting, thanks to the few who have the vision to forge ahead where others are afraid to change. It is the unperceived influence of our Multidimensional SELF that is creating this change. Imagine the change that will occur as we consciously recognize and unite with our greater SELF.

THE CONSCIOUS MIND

What does it mean to be conscious in the physical plane? Does it mean simply to be alive or does it mean also to be aware? And of what are we aware? Actually, the more precise question is to which of the myriad perceptions do we choose to consciously attend? Our physical life is not just what we hold in our daily, conscious mind. It is also the ability to be conscious of what we try to hide deep inside ourselves. We all have many memories hidden in our unconscious minds, as well as in our superconscious minds.

To be truly conscious in our mundane life, we must also be aware of these hidden portions of our total consciousness. Otherwise, we will not have access to all of our possible choices of perception. While we are limited to the logical, sequential processing of our third-dimensional consciousness, we cannot attend to the constant bombardment of multidimensional stimuli. Therefore, we must filter out most of what we perceive and remain aware of only a small portion of our total life experience. All that we have chosen to ignore is then stored in our unconscious and superconscious minds.

These perceptual filters are created by our beliefs. Our beliefs influence our expectations, and in turn our expectations influence our perceptions. For example, if we believe that the world is a hostile place, we will expect to see an enemy around every corner. Then since we believe that the world is hostile, when someone comes around that corner—a normal someone with a vast and paradoxical range of thoughts and emotions—we expect to see an angry threatening person.

Therefore, we are aware of only the portions of that complex person that are expressing anger, as we have filtered out the portions of that person that are kind and loving. Then because we have chosen to perceive this complex person as being angry, we feel a need to defend ourselves against this "angry" person. With our fear and anger, we amplify the fear and anger in this stranger. Voila! We have created an enemy, and we have also reaffirmed our belief that the world is a hostile place.

On the other hand, let us say that our belief is that the world is generally a loving place and that most people are of good nature. Now on the very same day, at the very same time, we walk around the same corner and meet that same complex person. Because we believe the world is generally a loving place, we expect the approaching person to be friendly. Therefore, we smile warmly and say hello.

Since we are warm and friendly, we amplify the portion of this stranger that is also warm and friendly. Also, we expect a friendly reply, so we filter out the portion of this person that is frightened or angry and choose to perceive the portion that is friendly. In this scenario, it is likely that the person will respond in the same manner in which he or she was addressed. Again, we have affirmed our belief by unconsciously choosing to perceive that which is consistent with the expectations of that belief.

CREATION OF BELIEF FILTERS

How were the belief filters formed? Belief filters are custom-made based on a hierarchical system. In other words, what is most important comes first. And, what is most important of all is survival. Inherent in all species is the fear for survival. Once this fear is activated, we create systems that provide a primary coping mechanism so that we can survive. For example, if we believe that the world is a hostile place, we were likely raised in a frightening environment. In order to survive to adulthood, we learned to believe that everyone and everything was a possible threat.

Therefore, we expected an enemy everywhere and were constantly prepared for battle. This preparation for battle became a primary coping mechanism, and even though the external danger eventually left, our preparation for war was stored in our unconscious self. This unconscious belief system then directs our expectations and eventual perceptions. Hence, we are now recreating our childhood environment.

On the other hand, if we believe that the world is a loving place, we were likely raised in a safe and caring environment. Or perhaps we worked through our early fear and anger and have found a way to believe in love. Either way, we have learned to believe that the world is a loving place or at least we have learned to believe in the power of love. Therefore, we are now able to filter out the surrounding negativity and be aware of the positive.

The fact is, not many of us are able to come into adulthood without some fear, anger, loss, or pain. However, if we are somehow able to find love, we can use our past trauma to recognize real, not perceived, danger so that we can protect ourselves. All of us are now experiencing or have experienced a reality that was created for us by our families, our past, and our society. These realities are based on beliefs that were programmed into our consciousness.

Some of these beliefs have assisted us, but some of them have created great limitations in our ability to expect, and perceive, the positive and loving aspects of our third-dimensional life. Our beliefs can be changed, but habit is powerful. The reality that is familiar brings comfort, even if it hurts. Therefore, how can we break out of the habitual beliefs of the familiar and dare to step into an unknown and unfamiliar reality?

CHANGING OUR REALITY

To change our reality, we must transmute our belief in fear and limitation into a belief in love and freedom. When our belief system is based on fear, we feel separate from the world around us because our view is that everyone and everything may try to harm us. However, when we learn to believe in love, we feel united with the world. Everyone and everything can then be viewed as a new opportunity to experience love.

Belief in fear and limitation creates a self-image of being a victim: "The world is my enemy, and I am its victim." On the other hand, belief in love and freedom creates a self-image of empowerment: "Somehow I created my reality and since I created it, I can change it." It is in switching from living in fear to living in love that we can alter the basis of our belief systems. Only then can we begin to change the reality that we experience. This change takes time and understanding, but if we can recognize that our experiences are lessons, we can begin our transformation from a dependent victim to a dependable leader.

This transformation has three phases: being dependent, being independent, and being dependable. Everyone moves through these stages of consciousness. Since we are all complex people, we often move through these phases more quickly in some areas of our life and more slowly in others. Usually, it is in the areas of our life where we have known love that we can transform quickly, and the areas that have caused us fear that transform more slowly. Unfortunately, these fear-filled areas of our life often become our personal nemeses, and we return again and again to address the same old issues in a new way. Fortunately, we each have only a few of these stuck places. These areas of our life are our greatest challenge, yet they also provide the greatest opportunity for personal growth.

AWARENESS

The flower opened slowly
because I thought it must
the labor was so painful
because it seemed unjust

The sky was dark and dreary,
for tears had blurred my sight
but love returned and called
the Sun
to turn me towards the light

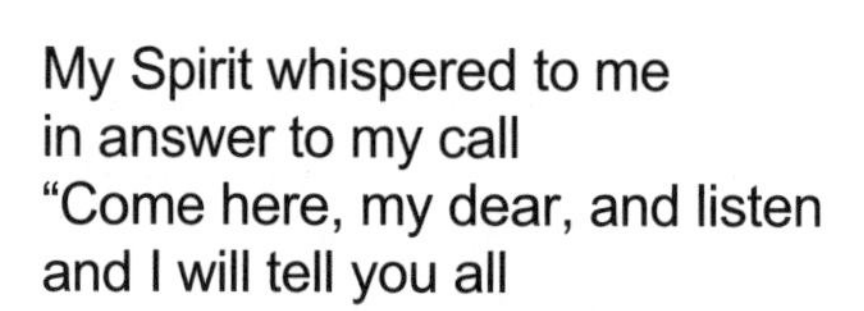

My Spirit whispered to me
in answer to my call
"Come here, my dear, and listen
and I will tell you all

"You are creator of your life
in each and every way
by the actors you perform with
and the dramas that you play

"What moment are you choosing?
What torment are you losing?

"Open up your heart, my dear
fill it full of love, not fear
the journey is beginning
your freedom you are winning

"Live life in surrender
allow your Soul to choose
walk upon the path of love
there's nothing you can lose."

At last I know, I am aware
I remember what I knew
I welcome in a brand new life
The old one now is through!

CHAPTER FOUR

SUPERCONSCIOUS AND EARTH'S DIMENSIONAL BODIES

Our fourth and fifth-dimensional bodies are usually ruled by our superconscious mind.

OUR FOURTH-DIMENSIONAL BODY

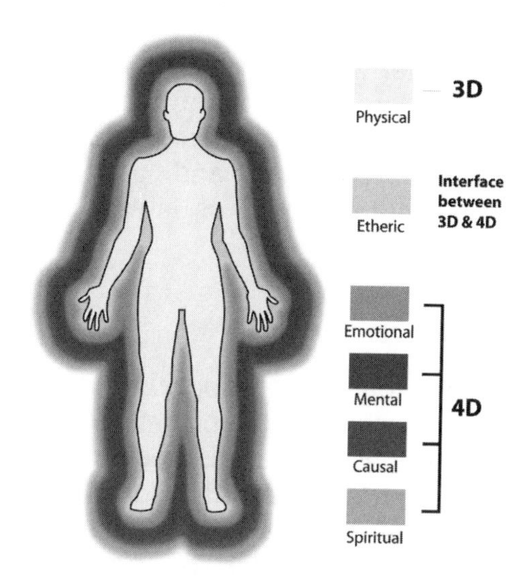

Each of the sub-planes of the fourth dimension has a correlate body, with every body resonating to a higher vibration than the one it precedes.

The Emotional Body, also known as the Astral Body, is higher in vibration than the etheric and physical bodies and extends beyond them.

Overlaid on the lower-frequency bodies is the Mental Body, which is also of a higher vibration and extends beyond the Emotional Body. The Higher Mental Body is overlaid on our Mental Body and extends beyond it.

Then the Causal Body, with its higher vibration, overlays the other bodies and extends beyond the Mental Body.

Finally, there is the Spiritual Body, the "I AM Presence," which is the highest in vibration and extends beyond all the other bodies. The "I AM Presence" is the guardian of the Rainbow Bridge, which is an energetic bridge that spans across the void that lies between the fourth and fifth dimensions.

All the fourth-dimensional bodies exist over, under, around, and through the physical body, but they cannot be seen by our five physical senses. Our fourth-dimensional self, an octave above the frequency of our third-dimensional body, is the aura of our physical body. All our thoughts and emotions drift into our fourth-dimensional body to be stored in our aura. Eventually, they drift back into our conscious mind and physical body to greatly influence health, choices, and behavior.

An appropriate analogy would be the ocean. Just as we might throw something into the ocean, and it would return with the next wave, what we release into our aura eventually returns to our physical reality. Unfortunately, we are usually as unconscious about what we throw into our aura as we are about what we throw into the ocean.

Earth has sub-planes in her aura, just as we do. The sub-planes in Earth's aura (or atmosphere) are the troposphere, the stratosphere, the mesosphere, and the ionosphere, with each sphere overlapping and projecting beyond the first. In fact, our planetary body is as multilayered as our physical body.

OUR FIFTH-DIMENSIONAL BODY

Our fifth-dimensional body, our superconscious SELF or Soul/SELF is fully aware that we are part of the planet because it is the body of our Multidimensional SELF. This body forever resonates to the ONE, and thus it is beyond the confines of time and space, as well as free of the illusions of separation and limitation that stem from the polarities of the fourth dimension and below.

Our superconscious self (who is often called our higher guidance, spirit guide, and/or higher self) resonates above the limitations of our mundane reality because it is not separated from the ONE. Fortunately, our conscious self is a great integrator and has the innate ability to assimilate messages received from our unconscious and superconscious selves while simultaneously being aware of our everyday physical reality.

To explain the body of our Multidimensional SELF demands a new vocabulary to understand it, as well as an awakened imagination to experience it. Therefore, suffice it to say for now that the fifth dimension is the realm with which we are becoming ONE.

EARTH'S MULTIDIMENSIONAL BODY

Everything in Earth's system can be placed into one of four major subsystems: land, water, living things, or air. These four subsystems are called spheres. Specifically, they are the lithosphere (land), the hydrosphere (water), the biosphere (living things), and the atmosphere (air). Each of these four spheres can be further divided into sub-spheres.

Earth's lithosphere, or its land, correlates to the physical matter of our bodies. Earth's hydrosphere, its water, correlates to the fluids in our bodies. Earth's biosphere, the living things, correlates to the etheric life force and our emotions, and Earth's atmosphere, the air, correlates to our aura and to our thoughts.

LITHOSPHERE

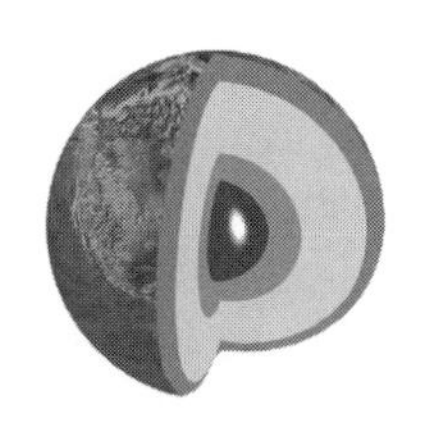

The lithosphere, which correlates to our physical body, contains all of the cold, hard, solid land of the planet's crust (or surface), the semi-solid land underneath the crust, and the liquid land near the center of the planet. The surface of the lithosphere is very uneven, as there are tall mountains, huge plains and deep valleys along the ocean floor.

Much of these landed areas are made up of the same elements as our physical earth vessel. The major elements, making up more than 96 percent of the human body, are oxygen (65 percent), carbon (18.5 percent), hydrogen (9.5 percent), and nitrogen (3.2 percent). The remaining four percent is other elements. In our planetary body, the elements of the solid crust are 62 percent oxygen, 22 percent silicon and 6.5 percent aluminum.

HYDROSPHERE

The hydrosphere contains all the solid, liquid, and gaseous water of the planet and correlates to our Etheric Body. It ranges from 10 to 20 kilometers in thickness. The hydrosphere extends from Earth's surface downward several kilometers into the lithosphere and upward about 12 kilometers into the atmosphere.

The percentage of Earth's water is similar to the percentage of water in our bodies. Seventy percent of the Earth's surface is covered by water, and about 60 to 70 percent of our physical bodies are comprised of water. Babies are born with 78 percent water, which drops to 65 percent by the time they are one year old, and women tend to have more water than men, as they have more adipose (fat) tissue.

BIOSPHERE

The biosphere contains all the planet's living things, including all of the microorganisms, plants, animals, and humans. Within the biosphere, living things form ecological communities based on the physical surroundings of an area. This sphere correlates to our fourth-dimensional Emotional Body. Our Emotional (or Astral) Body is an echo of how we are emotionally responding to our environment, to other people, and to our own physical body.

Our challenge as the people of this planet is to learn to live within Earth's biosphere in a cooperative, constructive manner, rather than the dominating, destructive manner that has marked our behavior for too many decades. The planet that we call home has suffered from our actions, yet Earth will survive. It is humanity that will suffer when our home is no longer habitable.

ATMOSPHERE

The atmosphere contains all the air in Earth's system. The atmosphere extends from less than one meter below the planet's surface to more than 10,000 kilometers above the planet's surface. The upper portion of the atmosphere protects the organisms of the biosphere from the sun's ultraviolet radiation. It also absorbs and emits heat. When air temperature in the lower portion of this sphere changes, weather conditions follow. As air in the lower atmosphere is heated or cooled, it moves around the planet. The result can be as simple as a breeze or as complex as a tornado.

The atmosphere, which is comprised of many layers, correlates to our fourth-dimensional self, our aura. The fourth dimension does not have the same degree of separation as the third dimension. Therefore, personal auras and planetary atmosphere intermingle so that people respond to the planet's aura and the planet responds to our aura. In this manner, we can serve to either calm planetary conditions or exacerbate them.

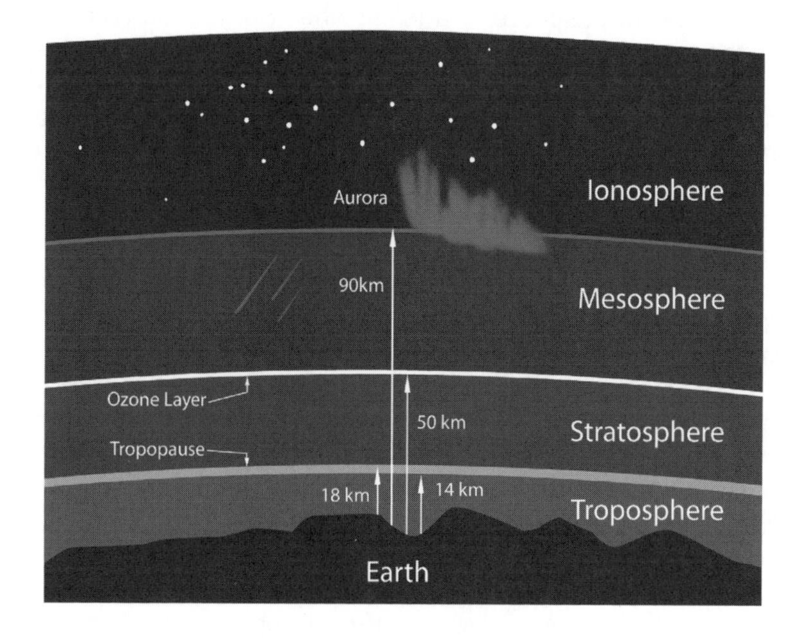

LAYERS OF EARTH'S ATMOSPHERE

The Earth is surrounded by a blanket of air, which reaches over 560 kilometers, or 348 miles, from the surface of the Earth. The envelope of gas surrounding the Earth changes from the ground up. Four distinct layers have been identified using thermal characteristics, chemical composition, movement, and density. The chemical composition of the atmosphere is 78 percent nitrogen, 21 percent oxygen, and one percent other gases.

Life on Earth is supported by the atmosphere, solar energy, and our planet's magnetic fields. The atmosphere absorbs the energy from the sun, recycles water and other chemicals, and works with the electrical and magnetic forces to provide a moderate climate. The atmosphere also protects us from high-energy radiation and the frigid vacuum of space. The four layers of the atmosphere are: (1) the troposphere; (2) the stratosphere; (3) the mesosphere; (4) the thermosphere or ionosphere; and (5) the exosphere.

TROPOSPHERE

The troposphere starts at the Earth's surface and extends 8 to 14.5 kilometers high. This part of the atmosphere is the densest. As you climb higher in this layer, the temperature drops from about 17 to -52 degrees Celsius. Almost all weather is in this region. The tropopause separates the troposphere from the next layer. The tropopause and the troposphere are known as the ***lower atmosphere***. The troposphere is where all the weather takes place due to the regions of rising and falling pockets of air. The air pressure at the top of the troposphere is only 10 percent of that at sea level.

The troposphere layer of atmosphere correlates to the Mental Plane of the fourth dimension and to our fourth-dimensional Mental Body. Our Mental Body is a reflection of our thoughts and our communication with others and our self. Again, it behooves us to consciously attend to the thoughts that we allow to linger in our consciousness and our daily communications. Just as fluorocarbon compounds pollute the atmosphere, our negative, fearful thoughts and emotions pollute the collective consciousness.

If we can free our mind of fearful thoughts and worry, we can more easily tap into our multidimensional abilities of clairvoyance, clairaudience, telepathy, and telekinesis. With these abilities at our conscious disposal, our inner knowing will calm our fears and guide us so that we can make a difference in these changing times.

STRATOSPHERE

The stratosphere starts just above the troposphere and extends to 50 kilometers high. Compared to the troposphere, this part of the atmosphere is dry and less dense. The temperature in this region increases gradually to -3 degrees Celsius, due to the absorption of ultraviolet radiation. The ozone layer, which absorbs and scatters the solar ultraviolet radiation, is primarily in this layer. Ninety-nine percent of air is located in the troposphere and stratosphere. The stratopause is in between the stratosphere and the next layer.

The stratosphere layer of the atmosphere correlates to the Upper Mental Plane of the fourth dimension and to the frequency of the consciousness of our inner, Divine Child. Our Divine Child, who is an intelligent being of light, is also known as our Guardian Angel. We often think of our Divine Child as being in our body and our Guardian Angel as being in our aura. However, both beings hold our Christ consciousness, which is the frequency of our purest essence. Our Divine Child/Guardian Angel serves as a silent watcher and acts as a transformer to step-down the higher frequencies of our Multidimensional SELF into the awareness of our physical self.

The airflow in the stratosphere is mostly horizontal, and the thin ozone layer in the upper stratosphere has a high concentration of ozone. Ozone (O_3) is a molecule consisting of three oxygen atoms. It is an allotrope of oxygen, which means that it is possessed by specific, pure elemental substances that can exist with different crystalline structured atoms. Hence, it is much less stable than oxygen, (O_2), which has two oxygen atoms. Ozone is present in low concentrations throughout the Earth's entire atmosphere. The pure consciousness of our Divine Child/Guardian Angel also exists in every dimension of our SELF with differing structures and functions.

The formation of the ozone layer is a delicate matter. Only when oxygen is produced in the atmosphere can an ozone layer form and prevent an intense flux of ultraviolet radiation from reaching the surface, where it is quite hazardous to the evolution of life. There is considerable recent concern that manmade fluorocarbon compounds may be depleting the ozone layer, with dire consequences to the Earth. In the troposphere, bad ozone is an air pollutant that is a key ingredient of urban smog. The troposphere extends upward to the stratosphere, which is where good ozone protects life on Earth by absorbing some of the sun's UV rays.

A healthy ozone layer filters 99 percent of the ultraviolet radiation so that only UVA reaches the Earth's surface. UVA ultraviolet light is primarily absorbed within the lens of the human eye with no documented eye disorders. In the same manner, our Divine Child/Guardian Angel protects us from being overwhelmed by the high frequency light of the higher dimensions and maintains a reference point of purity for which we can strive.

MESOSPHERE

The mesosphere starts just above the stratosphere and extends to 85 kilometers high. In this region, the temperatures fall as low as -93 degrees Celsius as we increase in altitude. The chemicals of the mesosphere are in an excited state, as they absorb energy from the sun. The mesopause separates the mesophere from the thermosphere, also known as the ionosphere. The regions of the stratosphere and the mesosphere, along with the stratopause and mesopause, are called the *middle atmosphere*.

This layer of atmosphere correlates to the Causal Plane of the fourth dimension and to the frequency of our Causal Body. When we are consciously connected to our Causal Body we have a superlative sense of cause and effect. Hence, we can look at any situation and know how it will echo out into the collective reality to be either destructive or constructive. In other words, we awaken our precognitive abilities. In this manner, we can monitor our decision-making and resulting behavior from the perspective of our higher SELF, who is able to see the big picture. From the detached perspective of our Causal Self, we can be of great assistance to others, to our planet, and to our physical self.

THERMOSPHERE or IONOSPHERE

The thermosphere, also known as the ionosphere, starts just above the mesosphere and extends to 600 kilometers high. The temperatures go up as we increase in altitude due to the sun's energy. Temperatures in this region can go as high as 1,727 degrees Celsius. Chemical reactions occur much faster here than on the surface of the Earth. This layer is known as the ***upper atmosphere***. The thermosphere is where many atoms are ionized, which means that they have gained or lost electrons so that they have a net electrical charge. The ionosphere is very thin, but it is where the shimmering colors of the aurora take place.

The ionosphere is responsible for absorbing the most energetic photons from the sun. It also reflects radio waves, which makes long-distance radio communication possible. The structure of the ionosphere is strongly influenced by the charged particle wind from the sun, known as the solar wind. The solar wind, in turn, is governed by the level of solar activity.

The ionosphere layer of the atmosphere correlates to the Spiritual Plane of the fourth dimension and to the frequency of our Spiritual Body. Just as the sun communicates, nourishes, and gives life to our Earth, our Spiritual Body patiently waits to communicate, nourish, and assist us in transforming our life. It is through communication with our Spiritual Self that we move into the fifth-dimensional *now* of the ONE. Eventually, we can download our fifth-dimensional Soul/SELF into our physical body, as well as our physical planet.

EXOSPHERE

The exosphere starts at the top of the thermosphere and continues until it merges with interplanetary gases, or outer space. In this region of the atmosphere, hydrogen and helium are the prime components and are present only at extremely low densities. The exosphere correlates to the fifth dimension and to the frequency of our fifth-dimensional body.

CHAPTER FIVE

RELEASING FEAR

Fear is a constrictive energy field. When we feel it in our body, we have an urge to curl up in order to protect ourselves. Fear is initially felt in our bodies, and we have many sayings to attest to this, such as, "I was so frightened my knees shook," or "that scared the ___ out of me." Fear is a very visceral emotion and often makes us feel we can't stand on our own or we want to move our bowels. The problem is that fear feeds itself. Once we feel fear in our bodies, it frightens us, and then we feel more fear. Unfortunately, we have developed behaviors that actually exacerbate our fear, when what we want to do is release it.

One of these behaviors is to try to hide from fear by receding further and further into whatever appears to offer us safety. This could be staying home, isolating ourselves, eating too much, or taking drugs. On the other hand, some of us try to attack fear by lashing out at it with anger. However, fear is only an emotion, and fighting it merely combines it with anger making the fear especially toxic. Also, once the anger dissipates, the fear is still there because we have not directly confronted it or released it.

Remember, fear in itself is neither good nor bad. Fear is the waste material of the third dimension. Fear simply *is*, like garbage *is*. It is what is left over once the constant rush of adrenaline from the battles of life is depleted, and our body is trying to clear itself.

Direct confrontation of our fear is possible when we have our higher SELF at our back, and this confrontation is best begun inside of our mind. There are, of course, situations where we are in danger. In these cases, our fear is a valuable warning, and we don't want to release it until the danger is over. After all, if we had no fear, we would have no warning. However, there is also the danger of the "enemy within." This enemy stops us on our path of self-awareness, but fighting with our self will only dissipate our energy and distract us from what we are trying to accomplish. This is the time when we need to feel the fear and do it anyway. But how do we do this once we have allowed the fear into our conscious mind?

Try observing fear in this manner: Take a long, slow, deep breath and feel the feeling of fear. Then, without comment or discussion, take another long, slow, deep breath and release the fear with a long exhale. In this calm state, we can determine the source of the fear—whether it is a warning or merely more anxiety coming from our unconscious or from others. If it is a warning, we can take the warning and proceed with caution.

On the other hand, it might well be coming from a repressed memory that has not been cleared from our unconscious and that we are projecting onto the present. As we focus on our Multidimensional SELF, we often feel strong enough to remember fear that has long been hiding in our unconscious mind. Because of the support and unconditional love we feel from our SELF, we are strong enough to confront this inner saboteur—the forgotten, wounded part of our self that will not allow us to move forward. If we can be conscious of our inner saboteur, we can calmly confront it and give this wounded part of our self the recognition and love that it needs.

Still other times, the fear we feel is not even ours. We live in very challenging times, and many of the people around us, as well as the collective consciousness of our planet, are afraid. Remember, whether we are aware of it or not, we do have telepathy and empathy. Therefore, we can feel fear that is not our own.

Once we have accepted the warning, identified that the fear is not our own, and/or recognized and loved our wounded self, we are ready to release the fear. First we can take a moment to remember that fear is merely what is left over from our many experiences of life. We have done whatever we felt was necessary at the time, so it is time to thank fear for its message and release it. Then we can take a long breath and clear it from our Physical Body, excuse it from our Emotional Body, and push it through our Mental Body—before we have a chance to think about it. We can then allow our Causal Body to see the cause and effect of the fear and ask our Spiritual Body to dissolve it with love.

Eventually, we will learn to identify fear simply by its feel and not attach it to anything external or internal. In this manner, we can learn to allow fear to just *be*, like a flea, a snake, or a sunset. *Fear just is!* If we don't get attached to it, it will merely flow around us. When fear merely *is*, and we do not attend to it, the energy field of fear begins to dissipate. This method of dealing with fear is like swimming with sharks. If we find a shark next to us in the water, and we become hysterical and desperately try to swim away from it, we will look like prey and attract the shark's attention. On the other hand, we don't want to be so unconscious that we bump right into it. Our best plan would be to stay calm and slowly allow the shark (our fear) to pass us by.

Fear is a third-dimensional negative thought that has been highly charged with negative emotion. Too often, fear is thrown out into the fourth dimension where it collects in the Lower Astral Plane, waiting for a chance to be swept back into the third dimension with the next waves of collective fear. If we feed fear with our conscious attention, or even our unconscious attention, it would be like feeding the shark. The best way to stay out of attachment is to remember that fear is a constrictive force, whereas love is an expansive force. If we can think of and feel love for something or someone, even our self, we can *expand* our consciousness and allow the fear to flow through us.

MEDITATIONS TO RELEASE FEAR

BREATHING OUT FEAR

Take three long, slow, deep breaths.
With each exhalation imagine that your consciousness gets larger and larger until it fills the room.

Take three more long, slow, deep breaths.
With each exhalation imagine that your body gets larger and larger until it fills the room.

Take three more long, slow, deep breaths.
With each exhalation imagine that you can see the spaces in between the particles of matter of your expanded body.

Now, see the vapors of fear as they approach you.

Calmly observe them as they move past you and through the spaces in between your expanded form.

Do *not* attach to the fear. Simply allow it to flow through you.

DAILY DEALINGS WITH FEAR

This exercise is to identify whether fear is a reality (a warning of true danger), or a feeling. Rather than constantly pushing fear into your unconscious, take a moment to be aware of it and to differentiate between danger and feeling.

If fear is a danger, ACT ON IT!
If fear is a feeling, LET IT GO!

Go through the day identifying the feel of fear.
Identify the fear and LET IT GO!

Notice, did the fear bubble up from your unconscious self to be released?
Identify the fear and LET IT GO!

Notice, did you have a thought that created the fear?
Identify the thought and LET IT GO!

Gradually, without effort, allow fear to lose its power.
Imagine the fear getting smaller and smaller.

As it moves further and further away from you, tell yourself,
"Fear *is*, but it is *not* me!"

LISTENING TO YOUR THOUGHTS

Since most of us seldom stop our constant activity, choose a moment of mundane action while driving, doing the dishes, waiting on hold on the phone, etc., to *listen to your thoughts*.

What are you saying to your self that is demeaning or frightening?
LET IT GO!

What are you saying about your life that makes you feel out of control and frightened?
LET IT GO!

What are you thinking about the world that makes you frightened?
LET IT GO!

What are you saying about others that gives them power over you?
LET IT GO!

Are you thinking of responsibilities and duties that you are not able to fulfill at this time?
LET IT GO!

MANTRA

I now take *all* power that I have ever given away to any
person
place
situation, or
thing
and I *own* it for my SELF!

IMAGINING A WORLD WITHOUT FEAR

Take a moment to imagine life without fear.
Imagination is fifth-dimensional thought and therefore carries great power.

Imagine a reality free of worry.
Imagine what you would think of.
Imagine what you would feel.
Imagine what you would do instead of worry.

Imagine a reality free of *all* conflict.
Imagine how your life would be.
Imagine how your communications would be.
Imagine how your relationships would be.

Imagine a world without money.
Imagine what the answer to your problems would be when getting more money is no longer a goal.

Imagine a reality where your value system is not based on monetary wealth.

Imagine what you would value then.

Imagine a world without longing.
Imagine what you would long for when you have everything.

Imagine what would make you feel fulfilled.

Imagine a world without separation.

Imagine how you will relate to others when you are united with everyone.

Imagine a reality where you commune rather than communicate.

Imagine a world where you love your body.

Imagine how you would look.
Imagine what you would eat.
Imagine what you would do.

Imagine a world without death.

Imagine how you would feel without the fear of death.

Imagine what you would *do* when there were no time limits.

Imagine a reality where there is *no* beginning and *no* ending.

Imagine a world without fear.

Imagine *how* you will love without fear.
Imagine *where* you will live without fear.
Imagine *what* you will do without fear.
Imagine *who* you will be without fear.
Imagine *when* you will be without fear.

FOCUS ON WHAT YOU WANT

NOT ON WHAT YOU FEAR.

THE CIRCLE OF FEAR

I had a dream, or was it a nightmare? I can't remember much, but I do remember the fear: fear of the unknown. I was somewhere, anywhere. It didn't matter. What mattered was the noise. It was a noise like a loud knock, a knock of something or someone who wanted in.

When I heard this knock, the area around the noise started to decompose. In a circular pattern, the wall or the floor or the furniture began to morph into something different, something that looked like liquid light.

I was terrified and so was everyone around me. Many children needed my protection. Were these the children outside of me or the children inside of my mind? I, too, needed comfort, and I clung to my mate for love and safety.

What was this phenomenon, and what could I do to stop it? Those around me looked to me for intervention, but I, too, was afraid. How could I help anyone when I was so frightened?

Well, of course, I couldn't. First, before I could help anyone else, I would have to confront the fear that I harbored inside myself.

Then it happened again, louder than ever before. The children ran to me for cover. I had to do something. I had to face my fear for them.

The circular pattern of morph opened on the floor just before me. I knew that love could conquer all fear. Could I find the conviction to put that knowledge into action? Could I take the risk to love that which I feared?

I leaned forward and sent all the unconditional love that I could find in my heart to the swirling circle before me. The love that coursed through my body eased my fear and gave me the courage to bend over and tentatively stroke the air above the circle of fear, much like I would stroke a frightened child. In just a few moments, I was actually able to lovingly stroke the circle itself.

Slowly, the circle ceased its swirling, and the ground before me became normal. But what was normal? Was it normal for everything to be hard and dense and filled with fear? Or was it normal for everything to be a swirling vortex of liquid light?

What was it that was trying to enter my reality, and why did it frighten me so? I only know that it changed my world, just for a moment, and made everything that had been dense and hard into a swirling vortex of light. I guess I will find out if my dream was the warning of destruction or the promise of transformation.

Only time will answer my question,
but at least now,
I am *not* afraid.

SECTION TWO

Not only are we a *part of* the planet,
we are a *part of* our SELF.

CHAPTER SIX

WHAT IS CONSCIOUSNESS?

Once we choose to release the constricting, separating energy of fear, we can feel good enough to choose the expanding, unifying energy of love. Love not only opens our hearts, it also expands our minds, as love allows us to release fear's greatest tool of separation—judgment. Once we are freed of the judgment of others, we can stop being who they want us to be and start being our SELF. However, to *be* our Self, we must find our Self.

That search often begins in our unconscious mind, where our forgotten past and hidden thoughts and emotions interfere with our ability to expand our consciousness. Often, the door to the unconscious is in the superconscious, the part of us that surpasses the illusions of time. Once free of the barrier of time, we can travel in our consciousness to find that everyone we have ever been, on every dimension, is still alive and functioning inside of our mind. All of US live inside of US. Not only are we a *part of* the planet, we are also a *part of* our Multidimensional SELF.

DEFINING CONSCIOUSNESS

We will begin our travels in consciousness by defining "consciousness." *Webster's New World Dictionary of the American Language* defines consciousness as: "the state of being conscious; awareness, especially of what is happening around you; and the totality of one's thoughts, feelings, and impressions."

Consciousness, therefore, encompasses our external as well as our internal reality. Cognitive science defines consciousness as a phenomenon that is explained in terms of computational or neural mechanisms such as:

- The ability to discriminate, categorize, and react to environmental stimuli
- The ability to access internal stimuli

- The integration of information by a cognitive system
- The focus of attention
- The difference between wakefulness and sleep
- The deliberate control of behavior

The Western world is more apt to define consciousness as the ability to be aware of external events that are recognized by the five physical senses. On the other hand, the Eastern world is more inclined to say that one is a conscious being if one has the ability to be aware of inner events that are recognized by our higher sense organs.

CONSCIOUSNESS AND PERCEPTION

The next question is: "What is the mind conscious of?" In other words, of the myriad internal and external stimuli, what do we perceive and hold in our conscious mind? Our physical, conscious reality is perceived by our five physical senses: vision, hearing, taste, smell, and touch.

However, our five physical senses are limited to a small segment of the total electromagnetic spectrum, and even this small segment is much more than we can consciously register. Therefore, we must filter out most of our perceptions and send them to our unconscious and/or superconscious minds. Thus relegated, this information can be called upon when needed.

What is this filtering system? Physiologically and anatomically this mechanism is the Reticular Activating System, or "RAS." The word "reticular" means net-like, and the reticular formation itself is a large, net-like diffuse area of the brainstem. Because the brain's Reticular Activating System controls arousal, attention, and awareness (which are core elements of consciousness), it is the first line in managing how we interpret, respond to, and react to both internal and external information.

The RAS acts as a filter, similar to one on a camera or a microphone that filters out certain frequencies of light, sound, or other perceptual stimuli. Most stimuli will be *filtered out* and sent to either the unconscious or the superconscious mind. The stimuli that are *filtered in* will be imprinted on the areas of the cerebral cortex to which we have access in our daily conscious life.

Our physical senses recognize stimuli as frequency and intensity. We cannot consciously perceive a stimulus that is above or below a certain frequency band. For example, we can only perceive light above infrared and below ultraviolet. The stimulus is still there, but we can only perceive it unconsciously through our first-, second-, fourth-, or fifth-dimensional bodies.

Also, we cannot consciously perceive stimuli with intensity below the threshold of our physical receptors. A sound may exist at 5 decibels, but if our threshold of hearing for that sound is 10 decibels, we will not consciously hear it. We also learn to adapt to familiar stimuli. For example, someone who has lived next to a train track for years may not even notice a passing train, whereas someone new to the area may perceive it as being extremely loud.

EXPERIENCE AND CONSCIOUSNESS

Robert Ornstein, in his book *The Psychology of Consciousness,* talks about consciousness as a constructed reality. He believes that in order to create a stable, manageable environment, a sensory-filtering system develops from childhood and is continually adapted by subsequent situations. Therefore, our experience of conscious reality is actually only a representation of that which we choose to experience. It is our personal history of experience that creates a belief system that defines our reality.

Beliefs define our experience because they create our filters. Filters are custom-made, based upon a hierarchal system: what is most important comes first. How do we determine what is most important? The third dimension is based on survival. Therefore, that which is most important is that which will facilitate survival. Survival is a relative term and is dependent upon the circumstances of one's reality. If someone is a street person, survival means finding edible food in the trashcan. On the other hand, if someone is a stockbroker, survival may mean knowing the intricacies of the stock market.

That which is familiar is also important. Therefore, we filter in what is familiar because it brings comfort and a sense of security. This sense of security is vital because it eases our fear. Fear is not overcome by bettering our life. Fear is a key element of third-dimensional life because there is always some possibility of danger. We seek to register what is familiar because it calms our anxieties, and we are startled by what is unfamiliar because it creates a release of adrenalin and a subsequent feeling of fear.

BELIEFS AND EXPECTATIONS

Our belief system, which is based on our history of experience, creates our expectations, and our expectations greatly influence our perception. A street person may not believe that he can survive off the stock market and so would not choose to notice the newspaper article on the stock market. On the other hand, a stockbroker may not believe that he can survive by recycling cans. Therefore, he may not notice the discarded can. Belief creates expectations, and expectations direct perceptions.

Beliefs also create our worldview and worldviews create beliefs. For example, the Western and scientific worldview believes that matter is the ultimate reality, the primary basis of existence. Because of this, consciousness is perceived as a consequence of our having a finite, physical body. Conversely, the Eastern and esoteric worldview believes that consciousness is the ultimate reality, and that the physical universe is our projection of our infinite, inner life.

As a result, those who believe in the Western and scientific worldview believe that only the third dimension exists, and they tune their filters to align with the frequency of the world of matter. On the other hand, those who believe in the Eastern or esoteric worldview believe in multiple dimensions, and they tune their filters to encompass the frequencies of the non-material realities.

Because of their beliefs, the scientific world has focused its primary attention on the intellect with its logical, deductive reasoning powers and the perceptions of the five physical senses of the physical body. Conversely, the esoteric world has focused its primary attention on the inner self and the extrasensory perceptions of the higher selves. In both cases, the belief system dictates expectation, and expectation dictates perception. We have access to both our inner and outer perceptions if we can expand our belief system to encompass both viewpoints.

ATTENTION AND PERCEPTION

"Where your attention is, there you are also." But what is attention? We can perceive things without attending to them. Many events make up our conscious experience of life, yet most of them form a backdrop that is the environment in which we live. It is not until we observe our "self" focusing our attention on inner or outer stimuli that we become intimately aware of it. For example, we can hold a book on our lap and know that it is filled with letters. We know that those letters create words and sentences. However, until we take the initiative and choose to focus our attention upon those letters, we do not know what they say.

Perception is a triangular circuit. The first point of the triangle is our sensory preceptors, which carry the information to our brain. The second point of the triangle is our perceptual filter. Once the perception has been filtered in, it is a part of our conscious environment. In order for this perception to move beyond our perceptual "wallpaper" we must engage the third point of the triangle, which is our attention. It is the conscious focusing of our concentration upon a given stimulus that creates attention.

Attention can also be passive or active. For example:

Knowing that there is music playing is passive attention.
Listening to the music is active attention.

Hearing someone talking is passive attention.
Having a conversation is active attention.

Noticing a birdcall is passive attention.
Bird watching is active attention.

It is active attention that creates learning and intimacy. We will not learn from a person or an experience unless we experience it intimately. Without a conscious sense of self it is difficult, if not impossible, to experience intimacy with others or with our self. From the Western/scientific world-view, "self" would mean Ego. Alternatively, from the Eastern/esoteric world-view "self" would mean Higher Self. As we expand our consciousness to remember our true, Multidimensional SELF, we are able to broaden our attention to encompass both worldviews.

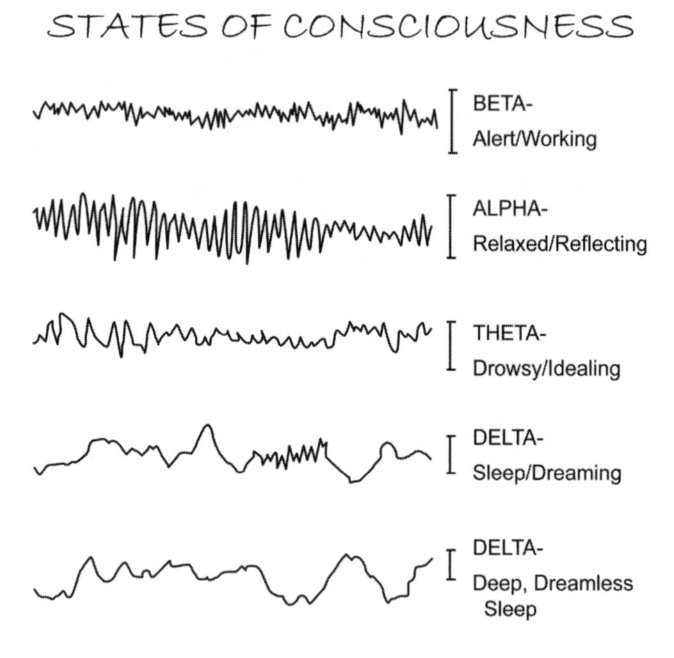

BRAINWAVES AND CONSCIOUSNESS

Brainwaves, which are measured by an electroencephalograph (or EEG), represent the language of the brain. An EEG measures brainwaves of different frequencies within the brain by placing electrodes on specific sites on the scalp to detect and record the electrical impulses of the brain.

Brainwaves, like all waves, are measured in two ways. The first is frequency, or the number of times a wave repeats itself within a second. Thus, frequency is measured in cycles per second (cps, sometimes also called HZ), ranging from .5 cps to 38 cps.

The second measurement is amplitude, which represents the power of electrical impulses generated by the brain. The main categories of brainwaves are Gamma, Beta, Alpha, Theta, and Delta. When we are accessing our Multidimensional SELF we are able to use a combination of all four brainwaves.

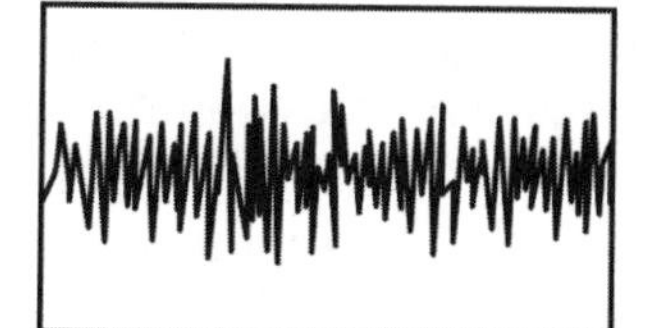

BETA BRAINWAVES
13 to 39 cps

Beta waves, in which our brainwaves pulsate at between 13 and 39 cps, are associated with day-to-day wakefulness. These waves are the highest in frequency and lowest in amplitude and are also more desynchronous than other waves. That is, the waves are not consistent in their pattern. This desynchrony is due to the daily mental activity of our many cognitive, sensory, and motor activities and experiences. Also, it is during Beta Consciousness that our focus is desynchronous, as our daily life has many inner and outer distractions.

Beta waves are seen on both sides of the brain and are most evident in the frontal lobe, where decisions and expressions of our persona are initiated. Beta brainwaves stimulate rational, analytical thinking and the consequent action. In this state, our attention is focused on our external activities, and our brain is primarily accessing the logical, sequential thoughts to process, organize, and act upon the myriad stimuli that arrive through our five physical senses.

If all this information is not put into some kind of order, we will become confused and overwhelmed. The voice of our inner self can still be dimly heard, but as in talking to someone in a loud and busy airport, we can hear it, but we can't always understand what it is saying. Beta waves are the predominant brainwaves in our everyday life. Without Beta Brainwaves, it would be difficult to function effectively in our daily world.

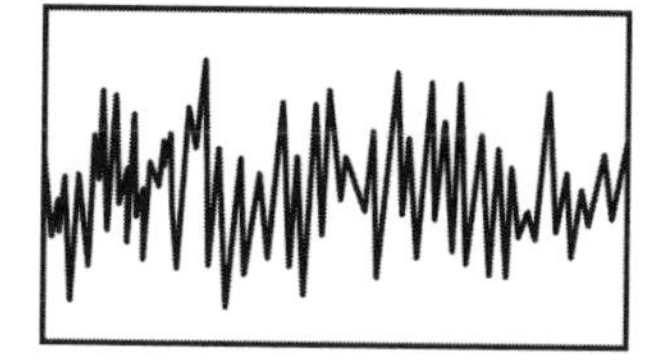

ALPHA BRAINWAVES
8 to 12 cps

Alpha waves, which are between 8 and 12 cps, are slower in frequency, higher in amplitude, and more synchronized than Beta waves. When we take time out of our busy day to have a power nap, reflect, listen to music, read a poem, or meditate, we go into Alpha Consciousness. When we concentrate intently on one thought, emotion, or activity, we have fewer stimuli to process and our brain can move into the intense focus of Alpha waves.

Alpha waves will peak around 10 cps. Alpha wave thinking promotes mental resourcefulness and aids in our ability to mentally coordinate stimuli so that we can quickly and efficiently accomplish whatever task is at hand. When Alpha predominates, most people feel calm and at ease, which serves to manage stress and benefit our health. The vivid imagery and relaxed, detached awareness serves to create conscious links to both our conscious and unconscious minds.

Alpha is the major rhythm seen in normal, relaxed adults, and it is present during most of life, especially beyond age 13. Alpha waves are predominant in the white matter of the brain, which is the part of the brain that connects all other parts with each other. Alpha is a common state for the brain and arises when a person is alert, but not actively processing information. Alpha waves, strongest in the occipital lobe (at the back of the head), cortex and also frontal cortex (the forehead), have been linked to extroversion, active listening and improved problem solving, and creative mental activity.

Whereas Beta brainwaves are predominantly logical, sequential thinking, Alpha brainwaves incorporate holistic, creative functioning. Hence, when in Alpha Consciousness we lose track of time and space. An hour feels like a minute and a mile feels like a few blocks. With the concentrated focus on a creative task in Alpha Consciousness, we experience fewer distractions, and we hear our own inner voice more easily. It is in this state of consciousness that we have our moments of "A-ha." Many performers, artists, scientists, and athletes consciously or unconsciously put themselves into an Alpha state to gain inspiration and to achieve their best performance.

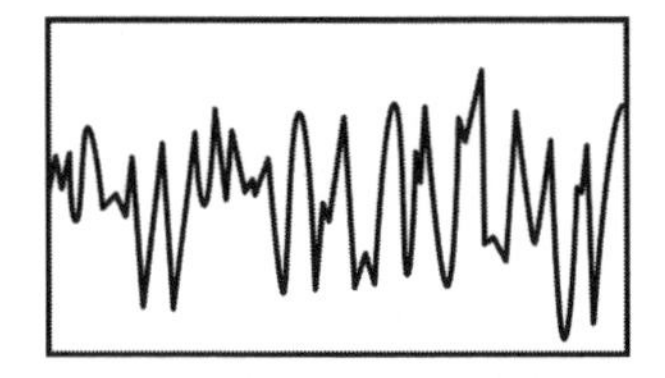

THETA BRAINWAVES
4 to 7 cps

Theta waves allow us to access our innate creativity, inspiration, and spiritual connection. Theta waves, 4 to 7 cps, are even slower than Beta or Alpha waves and are typically of even greater amplitude. When we narrow our focus primarily on our inner self, we can go into Theta waves, which are usually associated with deep meditation or sleep. In this state it is difficult to maintain conscious contact with the outside world. Our bodies need to be in a safe place when we access Theta Consciousness, for to maintain this state, our bodies must be still and our eyes closed.

Even then, the mere act of opening our eyes or listening to the exterior world could bring in too much stimuli and shift our consciousness back to the faster brainwaves, and our Theta wave experiences are lost. In order to bring our Theta state experiences into our conscious mind, we must be able to communicate these experiences to our language centers so that we can "save" them to our cerebral cortex.

Taking time to relax, write, and/or draw after sleep or deep meditation will help us in translating our Theta wave experiences into our Alpha and Beta wave thoughts. Even then, our Theta experiences are usually retrieved by our right brain's symbolic, imagistic language and not by the sequential language area of the left brain. Relaxing into an Alpha state can translate these images onto our language area where we can think about them or write them down.

Theta waves are abnormal in adults who are awake but are perfectly normal in children up to 13 years old. They are normal for all ages during sleep. The Theta state is believed to reflect activity from the limbic system and hippocampus regions deep inside the temporal lobe, which are related to emotions, converting short-term memory to more permanent memory, and recalling spatial relationships. Theta Consciousness promotes adaptive, complex behaviors such as learning and memory.

Theta brainwaves are conducive to profound inner peace, "knowing," feelings of oneness, mystical truths, transformation of unconsciously held limiting beliefs, creating a better quality of life, physical and emotional healing, and finding our purpose. Theta Consciousness provides the "peak" in the peak experience.

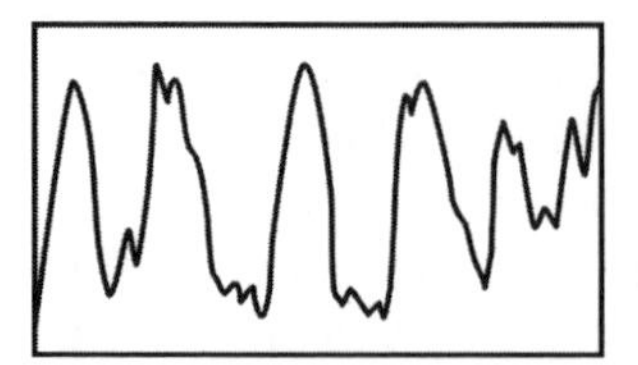

DELTA BRAINWAVES
.5 to 4 cps

Delta waves, usually ranging from .5 to 4 cps, are involved with our empathy as well as with our interaction and connection to our full multidimensional perception. These brainwaves are involved with our ability to integrate and let go. Delta waves are of the greatest amplitude and the slowest frequency and are the dominant rhythm in infants up to one year of age. Delta waves never go down to zero because that would mean that we would be dead. In fact, Delta waves are often associated with being in a coma.

In this state of consciousness, our bodies are in hibernation mode. Practiced yogis can consciously achieve this state. While in Delta Consciousness, they are able to regulate their body temperature and heart rate. They may even appear to be dead, but they are able to revive themselves. Delta waves are the deepest level of dreamless sleep in which our bodies shut down to completely focus on healing and growing.

Peak performers *decrease* Delta waves when high focus and peak performance are required. However, most individuals diagnosed with Attention Deficit Disorder (ADD) naturally *increase* rather than decrease Delta activity when trying to focus. The inappropriate Delta response often severely restricts their ability to focus and maintain attention. It is as if the brain is locked into a perpetual drowsy state. Going into Delta Consciousness is like driving a car and shifting into first gear. We can't go very fast in first gear (Delta), we but have maximum control of the car.

Delta brainwaves are conducive to miracle healing, divine knowledge, inner being and personal growth, rebirth, trauma recovery, oneness with the universe, samadhi, and near death experiences. Delta brainwaves provide profound intuition, empathic attunement, and instinctual insight.

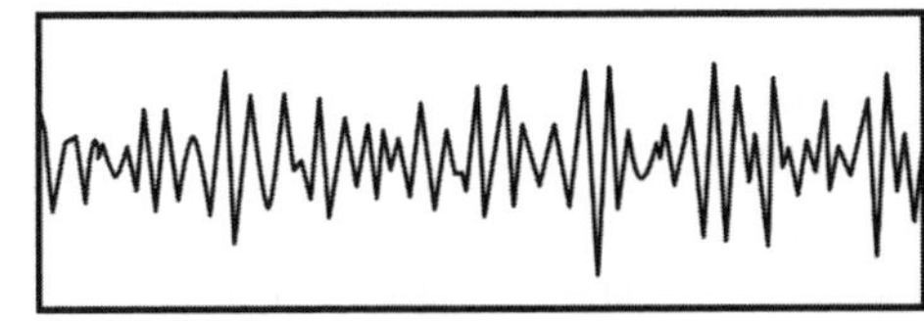

GAMMA BRAINWAVES
36- 40 cps

Gamma waves, 36 to 44 cps, faster than Beta waves, are the only brainwaves found in every part of the brain. It has been hypothesized that when the brain needs to simultaneously process information from different areas that the Gamma activity consolidates the required areas for simultaneous processing. A good memory is associated with well-regulated and efficient Gamma activity, whereas a Gamma deficiency creates learning disabilities. Gamma waves are associated with high levels of information processing and integrative thinking.

CHANGING BRAINWAVES

When we fall asleep, our brain shifts gears and our brainwaves begin slowing down. We start at Beta then go down to Alpha, Theta, and then Delta. When we move towards waking up, our brainwaves move in the reverse order of Delta, Theta, Alpha, and finally Beta. Just as we unconsciously change our brainwaves in sleep, we can learn to consciously change our brainwaves while we are awake.

- To keep our brain in an effective Beta brainwave pattern, we can determine to narrow our focus to a few things at a time and choose not to allow ourselves to indulge in obsessive or fearful thinking.
- We can take time out to relax, contemplate our lives, and enjoy our creativity to induce Alpha brainwaves.
- We can meditate and/or pray and place our total focus upon our inner Self on a regular rhythmic basis to induce Theta brainwaves.
- We can get plenty of sleep, let go, and surrender to our Soul to induce Delta brainwaves.

It is important to set aside a time at least three to five days a week to spend inside our SELF. If we can set aside that special time, we can learn to gain conscious mastery over our consciousness and realize that we choose our consciousness by choosing the thoughts we allow to take residence in our mind and the emotions we allow to linger in our heart.

If we allow fear to dictate our thinking and we give in to fearful emotions, our consciousness will be overwhelmed by the myriad stimuli supporting our choice to focus on fear. Our Beta brainwaves will then become rapid and erratic as our awareness darts from enemy to enemy like a frightened rabbit.

However, we are not rabbits. We have the ability to calm our thoughts and release our fear by focusing on love and calling to our higher guidance for protection and wisdom. This inner focus instantly changes our brainwaves. With practice, we can learn to take a few deep breaths and call on our guidance, chant, and/or visualize our mantra.

A mantra is an inner or outer visual picture and/or a positive sentence that can be used to filter out fear and negative thinking. For example, a visual mantra may be a symbolic picture of a favorite place, a loved one, or a pet that evokes a positive feeling of peace and love. Verbal mantras work best if they are in first person, present tense. For example: I am successfully fulfilling my goal. If the mantra is in the future tense (I will successfully fulfill my goal), it is like a carrot on a stick that is never obtained.

A mantra is used to edit out negative thoughts and feelings by believing in our self enough to remember that we can choose to shift our attention from fear to love. It is best if we choose a mantra that is based on self love and one that is correlated enough to the specific fear we are experiencing so that it can be an effective antidote. For example, if the fear is that we will not achieve our goal, our visual mantra is an imaginary or real picture of us achieving a goal; the verbal mantra is, "I am achieving my goal;" and the feeling is one that is associated with the fulfillment of that goal.

If we can identify the fear before it is amplified by our conscious or unconscious attention, we can take a moment to close our eyes (limit our focus), take a deep breath (breathe through the fear), and visualize a picture that is the antidote for our fear (choose another channel), while we say our verbal mantra and allow the positive feelings of love to override the fear. Once we have regained our footing in love, we can look again at the fear from our objective self. Does this fear carry a warning? If it does, then we can listen to the warning, act appropriately, and release the fear.

TRAVELING IN OUR CONSCIOUSNESS

Traveling in our consciousness is like changing channels on a radio or television. Our MULTIDIMENSIONAL SELF is the broadcast tower, which broadcasts messages to us across many different frequencies.

Our CONSCIOUSNESS is the broadband radio or TV, which receives messages from many different frequencies, and allows us to choose a channel.

Our BRAINWAVES are the channels that calibrate the radio or TV to the frequency of the desired station.

When we calibrate our consciousness (radio or TV) to the different brainwaves (channels), we set our expectation to *filter in* the perceptions within the frequency range of that filter/expectation.

We then *experience* the reality that vibrates at that wavelength/brainwave.

When we dial the Beta Brainwave Channel, we calibrate our consciousness to *filter out* the perceptions that do no pertain to our external third dimensional world. On this channel, our Multidimensional SELF gives us information regarding our conscious ego self in our physical world. Our "beta reality," which is our individual consciousness, is filled with myriad stimuli. It is directed towards survival, thoughts, decisions, and actions. Our individual consciousness directs our attention, and hence our perceptions, toward our individual assessment of reality.

When we dial the Alpha Brainwave Channel, we calibrate our consciousness to *filter-out* any extraneous, third-dimensional perceptions that do not pertain to creative activity. On this channel, our Multidimensional SELF gives us information about our physical world from the perspective of our superconscious fourth-dimensional self, as well as forgotten memories and stimuli regarding our true potential, which we have formerly filtered out. Our "alpha reality," which is our collective consciousness, is one of creativity, artistic focus, relaxation, and imagination. Our collective consciousness directs our attention, and hence our perceptions, to an assessment of reality based on the consciousness of all humanity.

When we dial the Theta Brainwave Channel, we calibrate our consciousness to *filter-out* all third-dimensional frequencies except maintenance of our physical body. On this channel, our Multidimensional SELF relays information from our superconscious self regarding our fifth-dimensional world, our fourth- and fifth-dimensional extra-sensory perceptions, moments of illumination from the past, and new ideas regarding attaining our present goals. We can also experience euphoric feelings and moments of illumination on this channel. Our "theta reality," which is our planetary consciousness, is deeply spiritual and introspective. Our planetary consciousness directs our attention, and hence our perceptions, to an assessment of reality based on the multidimensional consciousness of all planetary life forms.

When we dial the Delta Brainwave Channel, we calibrate our consciousness to *filter-out* all external, third-dimensional frequencies. On this channel, our Multidimensional SELF gives us information from our superconscious mind regarding our fifth-dimensional self and beyond, as well as information from our unconscious mind regarding our first- and second-dimensional earth vessel. Our "delta reality," which is our galactic consciousness, is focused on our cellular and subatomic reality and our inter-dimensional self. Our galactic consciousness directs our attention, and hence our perceptions, to an assessment of reality based on the multidimensional consciousness of our planet, our solar system, and our galaxy.

When we dial the Gamma Brainwave Channel, we calibrate our consciousness to *filter-out* individual stimuli and move beyond *all* time, space, and dimension to integrate the information we have received on the other channels so that we may be conscious of our process. Our "gamma reality" is truly multidimensional, as it is ALL in ALL. This cosmic consciousness directs our attention, and hence our perceptions, to an assessment of reality based on multidimensional consciousness of our universe.

Our first journey in consciousness will be to the fourth dimension. It is not such a foreign experience because we go there every night in our sleep. Remember that:

"Wherever you go, YOU are there!"

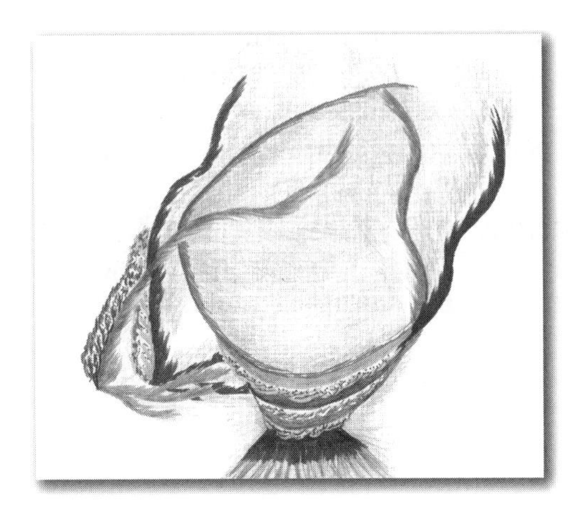

THE CORE OF CONSCIOUSNESS

I AM the core of your consciousness
I live inside of the inside of you
Your eyes are my eyes, and your ears are my ears

Through you, I can see and hear
your physical, third-dimensional world
I can see what you see and hear what you hear

But, I have an advantage that, too often, you do not
I am ALWAYS aware of my Self
I cannot forget that I AM
looking through YOUR eyes and hearing through YOUR ears

I AM of you, but I AM much more
I AM the part of you that looks through yourself
I AM the part of you that is ALWAYS self-aware, ALWAYS awake

While you are asleep to your physical world
I AM awake
While you are asleep to your dream world
I AM awake

I AM ALWAYS awake, and I ALWAYS remember

Always I remember that the world OUTSIDE of you
is a creation of your own illusion

Always I remember that the world INSIDE of you
is a creation of your own illusion

So, if ALL, inside and out, is an illusion
then what is real?

I AM real, for I AM your SELF!

CHAPTER SEVEN

THE FOURTH DIMENSION

One way to understand the fourth dimension is to review the perception of a cube from different levels of consciousness.

Zero Dimension: A point is a zero-dimensional cube that has no width, length, or height. A zero dimensional cube would have no perception of anything outside of itself.

First Dimension: To create a first-dimensional cube, the zero-dimensional point can be pulled in any direction to create a line segment. All line segments are one-dimensional, as they differ in size by only one measurement—length. If we expanded the line infinitely, it would cover one-dimensional space. This picture shows how a cube would be perceived through first-dimensional consciousness.

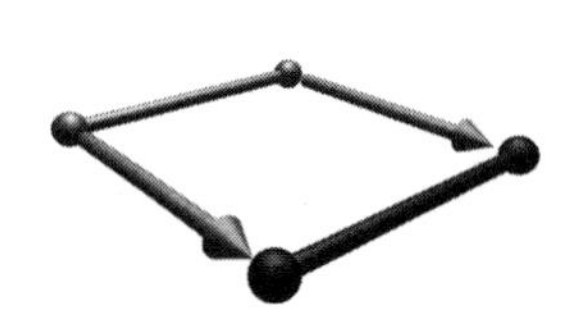

Second Dimension: To create a second-dimensional cube, we would pull the line three times in a direction that is perpendicular to the last direction, to eventually create a square. All squares are two-dimensional because they differ with each other in size by two measurements—length and width. If we expanded the square infinitely, it would cover two-dimensional space. This picture shows how a cube would be perceived through second-dimensional consciousness.

Third Dimension: To create a third-dimensional cube, we would pull the entire square perpendicular to the entire square to create a cube. This process would be like opening an accordion. All cubes are three-dimensional because they differ with each other in size by all of the three measurements of length, width, and height. If the cube was expanded infinitely in all directions, it would cover three-dimensional space. This picture shows how a cube would be perceived through third-dimensional consciousness.

Fourth Dimension: To create a fourth-dimensional cube, a tesseract, we would take the cube and pull it beyond the confines of third-dimensional space and into the fourth dimension. This picture shows how a cube would be perceived through fourth-dimensional consciousness. As this hypercube shows, there appears to be a cube within a cube, much like we have a self within our self. In fact, the way to view the creation of a fourth-dimensional cube is called "inner projection," in which the four-dimensional cube is created by projecting our consciousness beyond the space and time of our physical self and into hyperspace, which is a Euclidean space of dimension greater than three. However, only from hyperspace are we able to perceive a cube as a hypercube.

WHAT IS SPACE-TIME?

The fourth dimension is a vibration range that resonates beyond the confines of the third-dimensional space and time. The *American Heritage Dictionary* defines time as "*a non-spatial continuum in which events occur in apparently irreversible succession from the past through the present to the future.*" The *Oxford English Dictionary* defines time as "*the indefinite continued progress of existence and events in the past, present, and future regarded as a whole.*" These represent two distinct views about the meaning of time.

One view is that time is a part of the fundamental structure of the universe in which events occur in sequence, and the other is that time itself is something that can not be measured. Through our third-dimensional perception, we often think of time as a stream of sequential events, with only the current event being real in the present "time." However, time is very relative. If we are doing something that is creative and our

Alpha brainwaves are activated, time rushes by. When we meditate or dream and our Theta brainwaves are activated, third-dimensional moments can feel like hours. For example, a dream can feel like it takes all night, but when you wake up, you may discover that only a few minutes have passed. In the Beta brainwaves of our mundane life, when we are doing sequential activities that are not of our choice, such as paying bills or driving in traffic, each moment crawls by, feeling like an hour.

Time is often related to space in that it takes a certain amount of time to travel a certain space of territory, or that it takes a certain time to read all the information that covers the space of this page. However, according to Albert Einstein's theory of relativity, our concepts of space and time do not agree with actual reality. Our three-dimensional space and our one-dimensional time are actually two aspects of a four-dimensional "super-space" called "space-time."

Our third-dimensional senses do not perceive space-time directly; but its existence is well verified through decades of scientific experiments, as well as through the objective experiences of experienced meditators who were able to control their brainwaves to activate their fourth-dimensional consciousness. In addition to Einstein's relativity theory, modern physics is based on quantum theory, developed by famous physicists such as Heisenberg, Schrödinger, Bohr, and Dirac.

Relativity theory focuses mainly on the macro world of outer space, quantum theory on the micro world of the atom and its subatomic particles, both of which are beyond our unaided physical perception. Quantum physics also assumes a four-dimensional space in which our third-dimensional space and time are blended into ONE. Just as scientific experiments have afforded scientists with personal experiences that convinced them of the existence of another dimension beyond the third, spiritual meditations have afforded spiritual seekers with the same proof, derived from a different kind of experience.

PARADIGM SHIFT

A paradigm shift is a major shift in the collective consciousness in any given period of time. As more and more scientists, spiritual seekers, writers, and artists document their personal experiences of realities beyond the third dimension in fiction or scientific journals, the collective consciousness of Earth is flooded with the same information from many different channels. This influx of the *same* message coming from *different* places makes the unknown more familiar, and hence, less frightening.

Many movies, television shows, books, and other art forms represent a reality that travels through hyperspace, has great powers of extra-sensory perception, and moves easily from one vision of reality into another. Gradually, we are coming to a paradigm shift about the nature of reality. *We* are on the edge of that paradigm shift. Much as we once believed the sun orbited our Earth and found the opposite to be true, we have believed that our physical world is "real" and our inner worlds were "just our imagination." As our consciousness expands, we will discover that the opposite is true here, as well.

The tesseract, fourth-dimensional cube, shows us that with our expanded consciousness we can see the cube within the cube. Which is the real cube, we might ask? It is the very asking of this question that expands our consciousness further. We have been taught in the Western World that the physical world is real. On the other hand, the Eastern World has taught us that the physical world is an illusion, a mere projection from our inner world—the cube within the cube.

Can our physical world, in fact, be the projection of the real world of the higher dimensions, the "real world" that actually exists inside of our physical body? From within our Multidimensional SELF, we can see through our physical preceptors while simultaneously being aware of myriad worlds of many different dimensions. Of course, the physical world is "real" in that *we* are real and *we* are imagining it. Quantum physics tells us that we can change what we observe by the mere act of observing it. What if our Multidimensional SELF is allowed to observe our third-dimensional life?

We look into a mirror to see the projection of our self and see our *real self* looking back at us. We are the perceiver, the perceived, and the mirror through which we focus our perceptions. What is real? What do we want to be real? In fact, what do we *want*? The fourth dimension is often called our Desire Body, for it is the wellspring of our creativity and our powers of creation. It is time for us to take a long look into the mirror and ask what we really *want* to create, and if we want to create it with fear or with love.

THE MIRROR

I looked into the face of pure wisdom and innocence and felt deep, pure love. Of course, I would not trust it.

"What is love?" I asked with a glint of anger in my eyes and a touch of sadness in my voice.

"Love…," I heard in a clear calm voice, "…lasts."

"And what is that supposed to mean?" I snarled, no longer attempting to disguise my anger.

The face smiled and chose to ignore my anger. It knew that it was really sadness that I felt. I don't know how, but it knew that my sadness was like an anchor in my heart.

Finally, the voice answered me, "What that means is that love, true love, is unconditional. Unconditional love lasts even though you may not understand, even though you may not agree, and even though you may feel differently. Unconditional love lasts through all the fear, all the sorrow, and all the anger. Unconditional love lasts because it is *unconditional*. One does not have to want it, earn it, or even desire it. Unconditional love is free."

"Ha," I smirked. "Now I really don't understand you. I have never received anything for free—*never*." I yelled the final "never."

"Are you sure?"

I tried to lash out at the voice again, but I made the mistake of looking into the clear eyes of the vague form that looked into my heart. Well maybe it was not a mistake. Maybe it was a blessing. Yes, that was it. I looked into the eyes and I received a blessing. It was a blessing of love. This love had no judgment, no restraint and no limitation.

When I looked into the eyes, the love I felt made me completely forget my anger and my pain. My fear was gone and so were all the walls that my fear had created.

I felt naked, vulnerable, open, and alive. I closed my eyes, just for a moment I thought, so that I could drink in the feeling and allow it to enter every atom of my body. But when I broke contact with the gaze, I lost it all—all the love—all the acceptance—all the forgiveness—GONE!

Gone from my experience, but not from my memory!

I tried to be angry, but the memory of that love soothed me like a tender touch.
I tried to be afraid, but the memory of that love protected me like my walls of fear once had.

I tried to doubt the experience, to judge it, criticize it, but for once in my life, my heart was louder than my mind.

My mind tried to doubt, but my heart reassured.
My mind tried to question, but my heart understood.
My mind tried to forget, but my heart remembered.
My mind tried to race ahead, but my heart was calm.

From my heart I asked, "Why did the feeling go when I closed my eyes?"

I saw a smile; or did I just imagine it?

I would get no answer, but I felt gentle wisps of arms around my neck. I didn't resist. In fact, I leaned my head against what might be a heart and melted into the feeling of *unconditional* acceptance, forgiveness and *love*.

And then I was awake. Or maybe I was really asleep and that voice, that angel, was real.

"Huh," my mind said. "Get up. It's time to go to work. You have important things to do, important people to meet. These people will bring you recognition, fame, and money. Forget that dream. It's a distraction."

I was awake now. I forgot the memory in my heart and listened instead to the logic of my mind. That silly dream had made me late. I had to rush through my shower, throw on my expensive suit, grab a cup of coffee, and finish getting ready in the car.

I went through my day in a flurry of activity.

Deals were made, moneys were earned, and contracts were signed.

I was important.
I was successful.
I was rich,
and I was *alone*.

I went through all of my important meetings—alone.
I had a romantic dinner with an attractive companion—alone.
Later I had passionate sex with the person I hardly knew—alone,
and fell asleep wrapped in a stranger's arms—alone.

At 4:00 AM I crawled from the bed and put on my expensive suit, left the penthouse like a thief in the night, got into my BMW, and drove to the ocean. I did not know why, but I had to go to the ocean. I was remembering something, something in my heart.

I parked the car just before the first light of dawn. I took off my Italian shoes, my tailored suit and silk shirt. I grabbed a swimsuit that I kept in the trunk and ran onto the beach. I didn't stop until I had immersed myself in the ocean.

Then I lay on the cold sand and felt it cover my wet skin and get into my hair. I looked up into the sky. It was pale gray and misty. The sun was barely lighting the sky.

I was alone. But wait. Was I?

There was a feeling, yes, a feeling I had had just yesterday. Or was it a lifetime ago?

What was it? It was a feeling I had in my heart, a memory, a desire. I desired something that I could not achieve, or win, or buy. I desired a memory that was lost, lost in a lifetime of anger, sadness, and fear.

Yes I—so Strong, so Smart, so Rich—was afraid.
I knew now that I was afraid. I felt it.

Was that the feeling? Was that the memory?

Depressed and desolate, I dragged myself to my car.
I had left the keys in the ignition.
I did not care. It was only a thing.

I sat my wet and sandy body heavily on the leather seat.
I did not care. It was only a thing.
I slammed the car door so hard that it rattled the windows.
I did not care.

I cared for *nothing*,
NO ONE,
except...
except...there was the feeling, the memory.

A memory of someone—a mystical lover—*no*, an angel.
What was it?
Where was it?

I sighed and reached for the ignition. It seemed to take all my strength to turn the key and put the car into reverse.

"Oh great," I muttered to myself. "I knocked the rearview mirror out of position." I reached up to move it when I realized that not one time in my busy day or busy evening had I looked, really looked, into a mirror.

Not one time had I looked at my SELF.

The light was still dim, and it took a few moments for my eyes to focus on what I saw.

Then, with a gasp and a shot of recognition, I saw, not my eyes, but
the eyes!

Then I remembered the feeling, the feeling of unconditional love.

It was a long moment before I regained my reason.
It was a long moment before I realized that the eyes I looked into actually were my *own*.

But inside my eyes was a glint.
I was not alone!

"I am with you always," I heard the voice inside my heart.

"*We are one*!"

LIFE IN THE FOURTH DIMENSION

Spiritual masters all over the world (such as those from the ancient societies of India, Tibet, Egypt, and Africa, as well as the indigenous peoples of the Americas, Hawaii, Australia, and New Zealand) have traveled in their consciousness into the fourth dimension. Through deep meditation, spiritual leaders of these societies were able to move into their higher Alpha, Theta, and even Delta brainwaves to activate their fourth-dimensional perceptions. These leaders then mapped their inner journey and sought to share their experiences with other members of their community.

At the turn of the twentieth century, the "modern world" was introduced to the fourth dimension by English writers such as H. B. Blavatsky, Alice Bailey, Rudolf Steiner, C. W. Leadbeater, Annie Besant, and others. Through deep meditation and initiation of their innate powers of telepathy, empathy, clairvoyance, clairaudience, and clairsentience, these spiritual vanguards were able to channel with some of the leaders of the ancient world who had gone before them. One of the primary messages received from all these cultures was that there is a higher dimensional reality, which is in fact the "real" world, and that the physical reality is actually an illusion of their own creation.

STORIES AND ANOLOGIES

Plato, in an analogy about prisoners in a cave, also alluded to the concept that the third dimension is an illusion. In his analogy, several prisoners are chained up in a cave for all of their lives and can never see outside of the cave. In fact, they can only see the wall of the cave before them. Sometimes animals, birds, people, or other objects pass by the entrance of the cave casting a shadow on the wall inside the cave. When the prisoners see the shadow of these beings projected on the wall of their cave, they mistakenly view the shadows on the wall as reality.

However, one man eventually breaks free from his chains and runs out of the cave. For the first time, he can see the birds and animals of the real world and realizes that they are far more magnificent than the shadows he saw in the cave. In his amazement and joy he goes back into the cave to inform his fellow prisoners of the wonders of the "real" world. Much to this messenger's dismay, the other prisoners are actually angry with him and accuse him of being crazy. The shadows are all that they had ever known and hence, they are the only "reality" in which they believed.

According to Plato, the world outside the cave represents the world of light, while the shadows on the cave's wall are merely reflections of the objects in the world outside the cave. The escaped prisoner represents philosophical, enlightened ones who have gained the realization that what is seen in the light outside the cave, not the shadows inside the cave, is the true reality. Most people are like the prisoners in the cave, living in darkness, believing that shadows are reality. Philosophers and spiritual seekers are like the man who in search of knowledge escapes the cave and sees the light of the true reality.

Edwin Abbott further added to the spiritual renaissance of the turn of the century with his 1884 novella, *Flatland: A Romance of Many Dimensions*. *Flatland* is respected for its satire on the social hierarchy of the Victorian society. However, what has made it well known to this day is the book's exploration of dimensions. His primary assessment is that we can perceive the dimensions below our own, but not the dimensions of a higher frequency, a higher dimension. In Abbott's book, Flatland is a two-dimensional world, with the narrator being a humble, two-dimensional square. Square dreams of a visit to a one-dimensional world called Lineland. In his dream, Square attempts to convince the realm's monarch of a second-dimensional world.

Square is then visited by a being from a three-dimensional world, which he cannot comprehend until he sees this world for himself. He then dreams that he and his new friend, Sphere, visit Pointland, which comprises a self-aware Point that occupies all space and knows nothing but itself. Even Square and Sphere together cannot rescue Point from his self-satisfaction. However, Square also becomes a messenger when he tells his story to others in Flatland and tries to teach them how they, too, can have his experiences. The final two paragraphs, quoted below, reflect the feeling held today by many of us who are expanding our consciousness and trying to share our experiences with others in the midst of everyday life.

"Hence, I am absolutely destitute of converts and, for aught that I can see, the Millennial Revelation has been made to me for nothing. Prometheus up in Spaceland was bound for bringing down fire for mortals, but I—poor Flatland Prometheus—lie here in prison for bringing down nothing to my countrymen. Yet I exist in the hope that these memoirs, in some manner, I know not how, may find their way to the minds of humanity in Some Dimension, and may stir up a race of rebels who shall refuse to be confined to limited Dimensionality. That is the hope of my brighter moments. Alas, it is not always so. Heavily weights on me at times the burdensome reflection that I cannot honestly say I am confident as to the exact shape of the once-seen, oft-regretted Cube; and in my nightly visions the mysterious precept, "Upward, not Northward," haunts me like a Soul-devouring Sphinx.

"It is part of the martyrdom which I endure for the cause of Truth that there are seasons of mental weakness, when Cubes and Spheres flit away into the background of scarce-possible existences; when the Land of Three Dimensions seems almost as visionary as the Land of One or None; nay, when even this hard wall that bars me from my freedom, these very tablets on which I am writing, and all the substantial realities of Flatland itself, appear no better than the offspring of a diseased imagination, or the baseless fabric of a dream."

(For the online version of *Flatland: A Romance of Many Dimensions*, visit http://www.alcyone.com/max/lit/flatland/index.html.)

In the first chapter, "Worlds Beyond Space and Time," of his book *Hyperspace: A Scientific Odyssey Through Parallel Universes, Time Warps, and the Tenth Dimension*, Michio Kaku, tells of a carp pond that he pondered as a child. Sitting by the pond, he imagined what it would be like to live an entire life in the shallow pond, believing that your entire universe consisted of the murky water and lilies. In this world you would only be dimly aware of life beyond your pond.

One day, a rainstorm created a great turbulence on the surface of the water, with the water lilies being pushed around the pond. He noted that since the water in the pond would be invisible to the carp, just as the air is invisible to us, the fish would have no way of understanding why the water lilies would move all by themselves. This is similar to our wondering what created our weather before we were able to project our awareness into Earth's atmosphere.

Kaku tells of another time when his childhood "imagination" wondered what would happen if he reached down and lifted one of the carp out of the pond. To the other fish in the pond, this carp's disappearance would appear as though the fish simply vanished without leaving a trace. When the carp reappeared a few seconds later, it would seem like a miracle to the other fish. What would happen if the "abducted" fish told how it was miraculously lifted up into another world with blinding lights, strangely shaped objects and a extraordinary creature that didn't look at all like a fish and that held him prisoner? Would the other fish believe him? In the infinite wisdom of a child, his assumption was that they would *not*!

In all the above analogies, the "other" dimensions are separate from us. Hence, we are limited in our ability to experience, or even believe in, their existence. Separation and limitation are markers of our third-dimensional consciousness. The above stories also speak to the great courage it takes to move beyond the illusions of the only world we have ever known to find a greater truth. Furthermore, it takes even greater courage to be the messenger and share our journey with others.

Hence, we must call upon our imagination to allow our belief system to embrace the concept that we are multidimensional beings who have many bodies, some of whom live in the fourth dimension. Once we can believe it is possible to perceive the fourth dimension (which in fact we do every night in our dreams), we can expect to experience it. With our expectation set towards an interdimensional journey to meet more parts of our SELF, we can focus our attention on our superconscious mind and allow our Multidimensional SELF to open the window to a new reality.

WINDOWS OF REALITY

There is a huge tower reaching from
just beneath the surface of the earth
up into the exosphere

All around
and up and down
this tower are windows

You live inside this tower and
interact with the outside world
by looking out the windows

Through each window
you have a different vision
which you have been taught to BELIEVE
is a different reality

Since your beliefs direct your expectations
and your expectations direct your perceptions
when you look through each window
you see something different

Then, you believe that the realities are different
because you have been taught to believe
that what you perceive is the truth

However, TRUTH lives only
within your SELF

Therefore, truth is not something to be believed
It is something to be remembered

The truth you will remember is that
only your SELF is real
And everything “else” is a projection of
your beliefs and expectations

Hence, the only thing that can
TRULY become "different"
is your SELF

If you were to look again through the SAME window
with a DIFFERENT belief
you would have a DIFFERENT expectation
and perceive a DIFFERENT reality

On the other hand
if you would look through DIFFERENT windows
with the SAME belief
you would have the expectation
and perceive the SAME reality, through DIFFERENT windows

The only thing that changes is YOU

When YOU change
your beliefs, expectations and perceptions
change as well

You are different because
your journey up and down the tower
has helped you to remember
the TRUTH inside your SELF
When you remember that TRUTH
you know that

Wherever you look you see your SELF
According to YOUR beliefs and expectations!

SEVEN PLANES, QUALITIES, RAYS & BODIES

When our Soul decides to experience life as a third-dimensional being, it sends a "copy" of its multidimensional essence on a dimensional journey across the prism of the Rainbow Bridge, then through the fourth dimension and, finally, into the third. There are many planes of existence of our Soul's journey to the physical world, on which it will leave another copy of itself. These copies of our Soul will mature into dimensional bodies that will guide us in our daily third-dimensional life, as well as on our return trip to the ONE.

The ONE

Spiritual

Causal

Higher Mental

Mental

Emotional

Etheric Physical

The planes of existence that our Soul will encounter are vibrations of consciousness, or frequencies of reality, which are inhabited by beings that resonate to the correlate frequency of each plane. The third dimension, our Soul's ultimate destination, is an example of a dimension of existence, and the fourth dimension, through which our Soul/SELF will travel, is another. Each dimension is similar to an octave of planes, and each plane within the dimension is similar to a different note or frequency. All the dimensions are organized with the highest frequency plane closest to the ONE and the lowest frequency plane furthest from the ONE.

The first octave of planes down from the ONE is the fourth dimension, which separated into five frequencies of planes. The first plane of the fourth dimension, the

Spiritual Plane, is closest to the ONE and, hence, has the least polarity and illusions of separation and limitation. The next plane down from the ONE is the Causal Plane, then the Higher Mental Plane, followed by the Mental Plane, and then the Emotional (or Astral) Plane, which has the most polarity and illusions of separation and limitation. The Etheric Plane is next and is actually an interface between the fourth and third dimensions; it's more of an extension of the third dimension than a plane of existence.

Much as different inhabitants of a pond choose to live at certain levels of light, different vibrations of consciousness and/or beings exist within each plane of a dimension. In each case, the highest frequency planes are the least polarized into separation, as they are closest to the ONE in frequency. Thus, there is more unity and little or no illusion of light/dark, love/hate, male/female, and good/bad.

For example, in the Spiritual Plane there is the greatest sense of unity with all life, and the inhabitants have loose, wavering forms that emanate immense light. The Causal Plane, Higher Mental Plane, Mental Plane, and Emotional/Astral Plane have increasing amounts of separation, polarity, and density of form. Once through the Etheric Plane we enter the next octave down from the ONE, which is the third dimension or the Physical Plane. There are different frequencies of existence on the Physical Plane, but for the most part, they have not been named. On the other hand, a hierarchy of needs proposed by Abraham Maslow in 1943 that is now widely used in psychological circles may help to describe these vibrational levels in the physical plane.

The pyramid below represents Maslow's hierarchy of needs, with humanity's survival-based needs (lowest vibration) at the bottom and our aspirations and creative needs (highest vibration) at the top. Maslow states that humanity cannot aspire to what he titles "self-actualization" until the needs below it in the pyramid are fulfilled.

Each level of Maslow's pyramid could easily represent a frequency of existence on the third dimension (physical world), although these frequencies are often intermingled. For example, a self-actualized person may walk side-by-side with a homeless person who has not yet even met his physiological and safety needs. The difference is that the self-actualized person will likely return to a safe, loving, comfortable home of which he is proud, whereas the homeless person will curl up to sleep on a piece of cardboard in an alley or behind a dumpster.

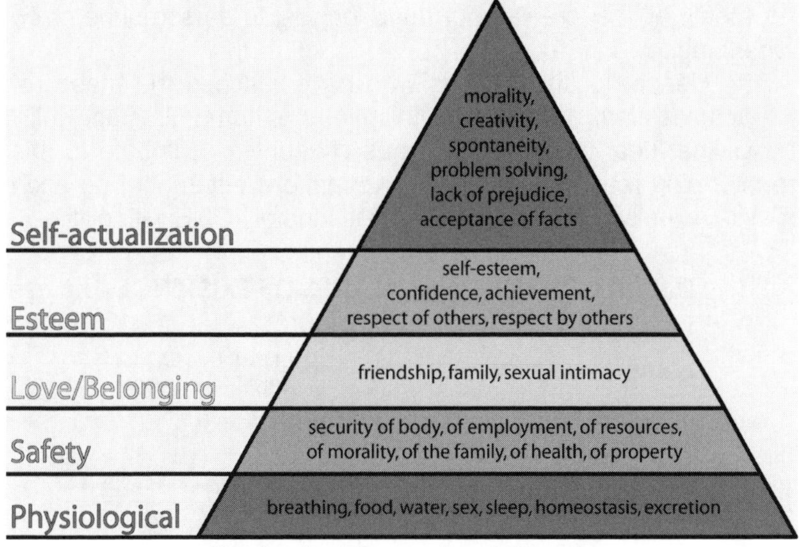

Maslow's Hierarch of Needs

PLANES OF THE FOURTH DIMENSION

As our Soul (our Multidimensional Soul/SELF) travels down the frequency range towards the third dimension, we leave frequencies of expression, or dimensional bodies, on each of the planes of existence in the fourth and finally the third dimension. Including the Etheric Plane and the Physical Plane, there are seven planes of existence, or frequencies of reality, down from the ONE. Each plane of reality has a corresponding ray (which is similar to a thought or expression of consciousness), a quality (which resembles an emotional sense of our self, such as an attribute or trait), a different frequency of our personal human body, and a different frequency of our planetary earth body. Since our Multidimensional SELF resonates to the ONE, it is united with our planetary earth body, as well as with our personal human body.

All of these attributes, expressions of consciousness, and dimensional bodies will be called upon to ground our Divine Ideal into our personal human body and our planetary earth body. Our Divine Ideal is the purpose for which our Multidimensional SELF has chosen to take embodiment in the present time and place.

Just as we have forgotten our Multidimensional SELF, most of us have also forgotten our Divine Ideal. Nevertheless, our ideal is the silent call that creates our deep longing to *be* someone or *do* something.

Hence, for those of us who have reached the "need" of self-actualization, our quest in this life is to remember and fulfill the Divine Ideal that our SELF has chosen to contribute to this transforming reality. Each of us can make a difference, as each of us is actually our Soul/SELF, who is innately ONE with all life.

FOURTH DIMENSIONAL PLANES OF EXISTENCE

PLANE	QUALITY	RAY	HUMAN BODY	EARTH BODY
SPIRITUAL PLANE	POWER	DIVINE WILL	I AM PRESENCE	IONOSPHERE
CAUSAL PLANE	WISDOM	DIVINE FORM	CAUSAL BODY	MESOSPHERE
HIGHER MENTAL PLANE	LOVE	CONSCIOUSNESS	DIVINE CHILD	STRATOSPHERE
MENTAL PLANE	PURITY	CONCEPTION	MENTAL BODY	TROPOSPHERE
EMOTIONAL PLANE	TRUTH	HEALING	EMOTIONAL BODY	BIOSPHERE
ETHERIC PLANE	INVOCATION	UNITY	ETHERIC BODY	HYDROSPHERE
PHYSICAL PLANE	TRANSMUTATION	MANIFESTATION	PHYSICAL BODY	LITHOSPHERE

With our map of the planes in hand, we begin our journey in consciousness down from the ONE and into the third dimension, much as our Soul did when we entered this reality.

SOUL'S FIRST JOURNEY

The ONE lies in-between all polarities in the center point where only unity exists. Our Multidimensional Soul/SELF is of the ONE and hence, is free of the separation into the polarities of the third and fourth dimension. However, as our Soul chooses to experience the third dimension, it must cross the Rainbow Bridge that spans the great void in-between the ONE and the third-dimensional land of polarity.

We take a moment now to imagine ourselves as our Soul/SELF on its first journey into the third dimension. When we cross the Rainbow Bridge, we move thought its prism of light to divide our multidimensional light into a spectrum of the seven frequencies of the fourth and third dimension.

As we move into the Spiritual Plane, we are still fully connected with the ONE of the fifth dimension and beyond. Here, the frequencies of light overlap and blend into a misty white that holds only a potential for color. The beings of this plane are beams of light filled with divine will and power who emanate the familiar calm of the ONE. We take a long moment to leave a copy of the light of our Soul's essence before we continue on our journey.

In the Causal Plane, we experience matrixes of potential form that appear as reflections that will eventually become discernable colors. The beings on this plane are still too mutable to hold any lasting shape, yet they are full of wisdom and the promise of form. We lovingly leave a copy of our essence here, and we find that it fills a matrix with light to become a wavering, transparent form.

In the Higher Mental Plane, we experience the hope of individualizations of consciousness held in vague, changing shapes with the promise of color. We feel a great sense of beginnings here, reminding us to leave a copy of our essence, which fills our wavering form with our consciousness.

In the Mental Plane, we find thought-forms of earthy bodies resonating to varying frequencies that are slow enough to maintain a reflection of colored light. The beings of this plane give us the first hint of life in the third dimension. With a thought, we leave a copy of our consciousness in this plane, which gives our consciousness the ability to think.

As we enter the Emotional/Astral Plane, myriad bright colors greet us like the morning sun on a blooming flower. Forms here are still changeable, yet separate from others and seemingly solid. We feel an instinct to leave an imprint of our personal essence here and realize that this is the first time we *feel* emotions from our self and from the beings around us. It is here that we realize that our essence has remained on the plane above, and also followed us towards the third dimension, gradually taking on more separation, form, and density.

As we continue our journey, we feel this solidity of form and density moving towards us like a wall that gets larger and more foreboding as we advance towards the third dimension.

Fortunately, we see a vortex leading to the Etheric Plane that pulls us into the Physical Plane, which appears to be in great need of our multidimensional light. Will we remember our Soul's light and the bodies of our SELF that we have left as trail markers for our eventual return to the ONE? Before we are able to answer this question, we are pulled into the vortex and deep, deep into the unknown of the physical world.

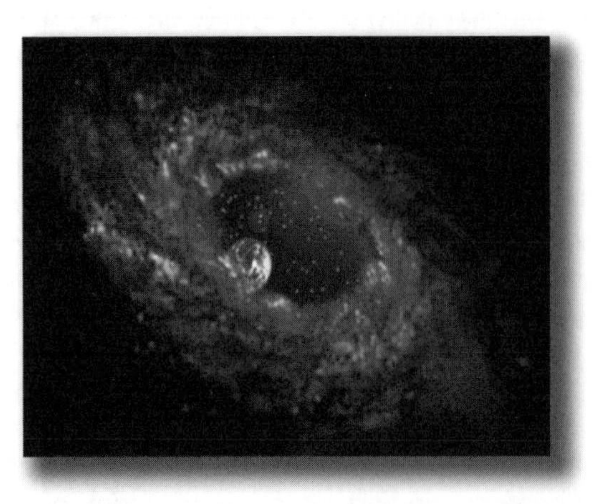

JOURNEY IN CONSCIOUSNESS

Using our great power of imagination, a power many of us lost in childhood, we will now retrace the descent of our Multidimensional SELF down from the ONE and into the fourth- and third-dimensional lands of polarity. Imagine that our Soul/SELF awaits us on the first plane down from the ONE, the Spiritual Plane. Our journey down from the ONE will be traveling in our consciousness. In fact, each of the planes represents a correlate state of consciousness.

We will begin our journey with the first plane and end in the seventh plane, our physical body. As we travel through the fourth dimension, we will align with each of our fourth-dimensional bodies that our Soul has created for us, so that we may bring the awareness of them into our third-dimensional reality. Much like the old stagecoach stations that were located across the wilds of the unknown frontier, our fourth-dimensional bodies are the way-stations through the unknown of our inner worlds.

We *know* that as we descend into our physical body, we also descend into the planetary body of which we are a part. Remembering to activate our imagination, which is our fifth-dimensional thought, we begin our journey towards third-dimensional Earth with a call to the living being, Gaia, to tell her of our "landing."

CONVERSATION WITH GAIA

Dear People of my Planet,

I am Gaia, your Earth Mother. I answer any calls that come to me. I feel your love for me, as I return that love to you. I am glad that you have made the decision to come out from your cave of forgetfulness and into the light of the truth.

Remember, that the "cave" of my inner core will always welcome the return of your consciousness whenever you need me. My representatives of the goddess have often lived in caves and returned to my core between their duties and services in the world. See that cave before you now. And place your small offering in the simple clay bowl at its entrance. What part of yourself do you surrender to me on this day?

Dear Gaia,

Today I surrender my fear. *Please dear Mother, for one day, take this fear into your crystal core and use it as you may. Fear is a powerful force and, once transmuted, can be of great use to the ONE.*

Dear People of my Planet,

I will gladly take your fear because it is offered to me in love. Your surrender, and the love behind that surrender, instantly transmutes your fear into its opposite polarity, love. Hold in your consciousness the fact that you have given your fear away today. Therefore, you have *no* fear. With every fearful feeling or thought, see my clay bowl at the entrance to my cave. Surrender that fear to me again and again as you retrace your original descent from the ONE, through the fourth dimension and back again into your personal and planetary body.

Feel your love for me and mine for you, and the fear that you surrender shall be replaced with *love*.

I am your Earth Mother,
GAIA

THE SEVEN PLANES

Free of fear, and with Gaia's blessing, we begin our interdimensional journey by using the great power of our imagination to find ourselves at the first plane of reality down from the ONE, and hence in the highest frequency of the fourth dimension, known as the Spiritual Plane. Our Multidimensional SELF will leave a copy of its presence, a body, in each of these planes of reality.

But alas, we try and try and are just about ready to give up with this foolish search for our childish imagination when we hear an inner voice. The voice is so quiet that we can hardly hear it, but it feels so calm and loving that we cannot ignore it. Finally, we surrender our frustration and fall into the marvelous, yet unfamiliar, sensation of calm. Slowly, as our frustrations quiet, the voice becomes clear. "I am here," whispers our Soul. "I am here inside your heart. Please remember that your imagination is actually your fifth-dimensional thought. If you become confused or frustrated again, just call me. I am always within."

Calmed by this inner presence, we are ready to trust our imagination and return to our journey to find that we can imagine that we have just stepped off a glimmering Rainbow Bridge and into a plane of pure light and love. From our vantage point of the fourth-dimensional Spiritual Plane, we can look down into the lower frequencies of the fourth dimension and also into the third dimension to see six other realities of existence, which are also six other realities of our SELF.

From the highest to lowest frequency, each plane or vibration of reality decreases in frequency as it simultaneously increases in the illusions of separation and limitation. From our position in the highest vibration of the fourth dimension, we can observe all the levels of reality, along with the rays, qualities and bodies that correlate to the of frequencies of each reality.

While we are still basking in the highest frequency of fourth-dimensional light, (for light and consciousness are synonymous), we can actually *see* each plane as a vibration. In fact, in the higher dimensions, everything and everyone is a vibration, a pattern of resonance. Instead of having a material form here, we have a signature frequency. As we travel down from the highest fourth-dimensional plane toward the third dimension, the resonance of each plane will become lower and lower in frequency until, finally, we rejoin our physical form in the third dimension.

Our descent into the physical world will not be without sacrifice, for here in the fourth dimension we are surrounded by light, peace, joy, and unconditional love. These divine emotions, or qualities, are perfectly balanced. Hence, they always resonate to the center point of unity. Each plane also carries a ray, similar to a divine thought. Once back in the third dimension, our Multidimensional SELF will guide us to combine our divine emotions and thoughts to assist in manifesting our Divine Ideal. As we look at the vibrations of realities, planes of existence that unfold downward, we discern that each plane down from the ONE becomes less balanced and more polarized into separation.

Why would we want to leave this unity and return to a reality in which we are separated from our true SELF and limited in our ability to fulfill our deepest desires and goals?

Here in the Spiritual Plane we are safely standing in peace and love. Do we want to return to the strife and fear of the physical world? Wouldn't it be wonderful if it were so simple that we could just stay here? On the other hand, after we have spent a lifetime of working hard to find the answers, most great truth is found to be quite simple. Therefore, we will return to the third-dimensional land of polarities, for we know we must. There is something that we need to do there, some ONE that we need to be.

From this spiritual vantage point, the fear that stopped us in our physical reality looks like a harmless, gray cloud. In fact, fear is of such a low frequency, we wonder why we didn't just step up our frequency rate so that we would be out of phase with whatever harm threatened us. Perhaps when we return to the third dimension this time, we will remember that we have that ability.

CHOOSING OUR DIVINE IDEAL

With our connection to our Soul, we begin our journey by taking a long look at the first step down from the ONE, the Spiritual Plane. This first plane serves as the threshold of the Rainbow Bridge, which everyone will cross when entering and leaving the ONE. Every idea, plan, and blessing that we will one day manifest in the physical world is initiated in this plane. Hence, the emanation of this ray is divine will.

With divine will basking our consciousness, we consult with our Multidimensional SELF to choose/remember our

Divine Ideal. Our Divine Ideal represents the manner in which we wish to express our Multidimensional SELF in our everyday life, and the service that we wish to create and contribute to our society and planet during this time of great transformation. In the Spiritual Plane, our ideal is a vibrational "seed," which we will carry through all the lower planes so that we may plant it in our physical body and in the body of Gaia. The quality of the Spiritual Plane is power. Therefore, while connected to this reality, we can recognize our *power* and know that *we* are important. The ray of this plane gives us the *divine will* to express our ideal.

THE SPIRITUAL PLANE

We relax a moment into our imagination. If we could do anything or be anyone, what would we choose? The Spiritual Plane represents the un-manifest, masculine energy that can only become manifest when mated with the feminine energy of the Causal Plane. While in this Spiritual Plane, we experience our human will in alignment with our divine will and our human consciousness in alignment with our multidimensional consciousness. Because of this, we allow the *feel*, or the vibration, of our choice to come to us and we accept it into our hearts. We are ready now. We have an idea of what we truly *want* and of our true SELF that wants it. It is merely an idea now, but it will become clearer as we continue our journey.

THE SPIRITUAL PLANE AND THE ANGELIC EVOLUTION

The first plane down from the ONE, the Spiritual Plane, is aligned with the beings of the Angelic Evolution. By supplying a continuous stream of love, these beings serve the function of administering to the spiritual and emotional needs of humanity and of the other members of the third dimension. Similar to rechargeable batteries, Angels absorb into their aura the force of unconditional love from the fount of the ONE. When an Angel becomes totally full, the Angel moves into the lower planes to administer and radiate that love to the members of the physical world. Angels radiate love primarily through their feelings. Once the Angels become empty, they return to the ONE to fill up with love before being sent out once again.

Angels raise their vibration by improving their ability to hold greater amounts of love for longer periods of time without contamination from the adverse, external conditions often generated by humans. As Angels continue to serve, they become fountainheads of love to which many lesser Angels come to replenish themselves. Through the radiation of divine love, Angels remind humans to love themselves so that they can more sincerely love others.

Angels are experts at creating force fields through the use of sacred geometry and symmetric patterns. By joining together and working in unison, they can create more powerful and effective force fields than they could by working alone. Angels also function as inter-dimensional messengers of energies, both up and down the fourth-dimensional planes. In the "up" direction, they gather all the hopes, aspirations, wishes, and prayers of humanity and deliver them to each person's Multidimensional SELF in the ONE. In the "down" direction, they send beneficial, higher-dimensional light (which is actually information) and love (which is their emanation) to persons and places on the physical plane. This is why Angels are often known as the messengers of God.

The highest frequency Angels of the Angelic Kingdom are known as Archangels. An Archangel serves as the fountainhead and guardian for the Angelic Kingdom, as well as the guardian and healer for humanity.

THE FIRST PLANE AND THE IONOSPHERE

Just as the Spiritual Plane serves as the boundary between the fourth and fifth dimension of our aura, our ionosphere serves as the boundary between Earth's atmosphere and the exosphere into outer space. Furthermore, the exosphere communicates with our sun and solar system, much as our I AM Presence communicates with the ONE of the fifth dimension and beyond.

THE SPIRITUAL PLANE AND OUR I AM PRESENCE

Our I AM Presence, also known as our Spiritual Body or our higher human, is the highest vibration of all our fourth-dimensional selves and resonates to the frequency of the threshold of the Rainbow Bridge. When we are ready to expand our consciousness into the ONE, it is our I AM Presence who will guide us. If we can keep our attention focused on our I AM Presence, it can greatly assist us in remembering our true SELF and the Divine Ideal that our SELF has chosen to express in our physical reality. Our I AM Presence and the outermost aura of our planet, the ionosphere, engulf us with their combined glow and guide us to the second plane.

"Wait," it reminds us, "Do not forget your Divine Ideal. And here, take this spark of your Multidimensional SELF and carry it with you back to the Physical Plane. Once there, plant the seed of your Divine Ideal and the spark of your Multidimensional SELF in both your human and planetary bodies."

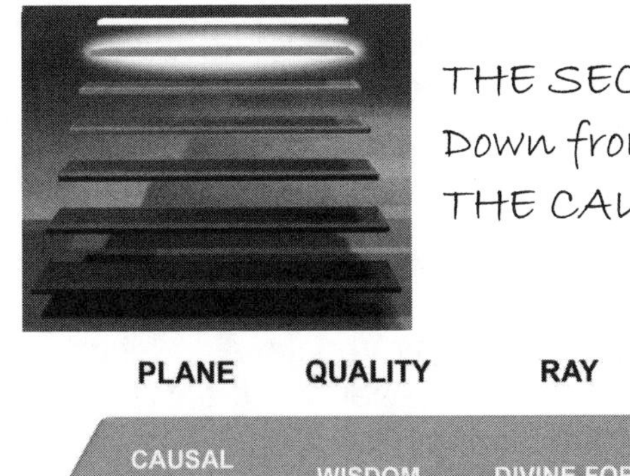

CREATING A THOUGHT-FORM

While in the Spiritual Plane, we acted as our Spiritual Body, the symbolic representative of our Father Sky, to choose our Divine Ideal and to carry it, as well as a spark of our Multidimensional SELF, down into the second plane down from the ONE, the Causal Plane. Here, with the ray of divine form, we will create a thought-form (a potential for form) for both the Divine Ideal and our expression of our Multidimensional SELF in our physical reality. Our Causal Body, the symbolic representative of Mother Earth, has the quality of wisdom to welcome this initiation of creation, so that she may create its prospective form.

THE CAUSAL PLANE AND OUR CAUSAL BODY

Our Causal Body, the body for this plane, accepts the Divine Ideal from our I AM Presence to become our Rainbow Body at the moment of "conception." The beautiful rays of our Rainbow Body are representative of the seven qualities of the ONE. In this manner, the ideal collected in the first plane, the Spiritual Plane, travels down into the second plane, the Causal Plane, to be filled with the quality of wisdom to gestate our Divine Ideal. Thus, as we allow the conception of the essence of divine Father Sky's power to be implanted into the essence of divine Mother Earth's wisdom, the formed ideal, in turn, is passed onward to the third plane, the Higher Mental Plane, to be imbued with consciousness.

Because of this union of ideal and form, the Keepers of Form (the Devic Evolution) are associated with this plane. Elohim, the highest expression of this evolution, are the creator gods and goddesses. The term "Elohim" means "all that God is." Elohim were referred to in the Old Testament more than two thousand five hundred times as the "name of God." In the Kabala, the Jewish book of mysticism, Elohim are referred to as the Divine Mother. The term "Yod Jay Vod Jay," or Jehovah, refers to the Divine Father. Rudolph Steiner, the great German mystic, calls the Elohim the "spirits of form." The great metaphysical book *The Keys of Enoch*, written in 1973 by Dr. J.J. Hurtak, refers to the Elohim as those beings who created the world by the will of YHWH (YHWH being the Jewish name for the Godhead).

CAUSAL PLANE AND THE DEVIC EVOLUTION

The Elohim and Archangels might be thought of as the left and right hands, respectively, of creation. The term "Elohim" is plural, as it refers to many "gods." Just as Angels specialize in emanating love, the Elohim specialize in holding form as they carry out their cosmic service. The Devic Evolution encompasses all the "holders of form" from the highest evolution of Elohim to the lowest evolution of Elementals. The Devic Evolution works from the Mental Plane to translate thoughts into physical forms. They do this by first transforming mental patterns charged with emotion into etheric blueprints and then into physical patterns.

Each being in the Devic Evolution is a specialist in creating a specific form, whether it is an electron, a biological cell, a flower, a tree, a valley, a river, a planet, a solar system, or interstellar space. The Elementals (who are the fourth-dimensional counterpart of the third-dimensional elements of earth, air, fire, and water) serve as the building blocks of form. The Elementals work as one to hold the form of a tree. Just above them in vibration and the evolution, the Devas gather many Elementals together to create a group form, such as a forest.

Finally, the Elohim, who reside in the higher dimension/frequency and are the most evolved, oversee the Devas. Hence, the Elohim may be the guardian for the entire mountain upon which the trees of the forest grow. Our body Deva oversees the many Elementals that join together to create our third-dimensional body, and our Elohim protects us and guides us from the higher dimensions.

Our Causal Body also acts much like a spiritual bank account, as it holds the accumulation of *all* the positively charged energies of our embodiment until we are ready to accept them into our physical world. Our Causal Body varies in size and qualities according to the amount of constructively qualified energy used while both in and out of embodiment.

As we look around the Causal Plane, we find it quite similar to the Spiritual Plane. However, there is an accumulation of the interactions between our feelings and thoughts, which create an emotional charge. This emotional charge is actually a slight feeling of expectation, as if something is about to happen or be born that is not present in the totally balanced and peaceful Spiritual Plane. Like the first plane, there is little form; but on the second plane, the hope of form creates an anticipation and curiosity. We wonder how the form of our Divine Ideal will manifest.

THE SECOND PLANE AND THE MESOSPHERE

The body of Earth's atmosphere that correlates to the Causal Plane is the mesosphere, which serves to protect our earth body much as our Causal Body protects our personal body. The air masses of the mesosphere are relatively mixed together, and the temperature decreases with altitude. Most important, there is a layer of the mesosphere with atmospheric temperatures that reach the lowest average value of around -

90°C, where many meteors burn up while entering the Earth's atmosphere.

The combination of the mesosphere's light collected from the sun and the higher-dimensional light collected by our Causal Body sweeps us down into the third plane.

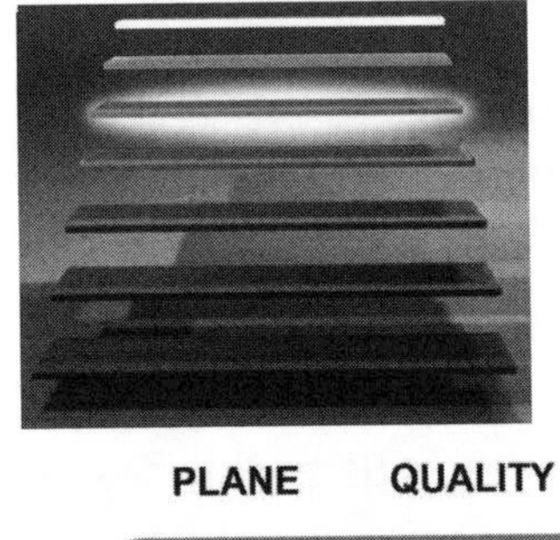

THE THIRD PLANE
Down from the ONE is
THE HIGHER MENTAL
PLANE

PLANE	QUALITY	RAY	HUMAN BODY	EARTH BODY
HIGHER MENTAL PLANE	LOVE	CONSCIOUSNESS	DIVINE CHILD	STRATOSPHERE

INFUSING LOVE AND CONSCIOUSNESS

Because the third plane holds the cohesive quality of love, the Divine Ideal that we chose in the Spiritual Plane and clothed in potential form in the Causal Plane will now imbued with the life-giving ray of consciousness in the Higher Mental Plane. This fourth-dimensional consciousness will serve to give life to our Divine Ideal and the expression of our Soul/SELF in the third dimension. In this manner, the form of the Wise Mother has embraced the will of the Powerful Father to conceive their Child of Love. Except that *we* are the father, the mother, *and* the child.

Just as our divine child is the offspring of the power and divine will of the father/first plane and the wisdom and divine form of the mother/second plane, the Christed consciousness of our divine child empowers its progeny, who are the four remaining fourth-dimensional bodies on the fourth, fifth, sixth, and seventh planes. In other words, the father and mother give birth to a child who, in turn, gives birth to four children.

Our "Christed consciousness" is the purest and most innocent connection that we have to our innate divinity. We are born with this state of consciousness but usually lose it far too quickly. Fortunately, our inner divine child holds our Christed consciousness in our unconscious, ego/self, while our Guardian Angel holds it for us in our superconscious, Soul/SELF, until we reach self actualization and are able to hold this state of consciousness in our third-dimensional life. When we are able to do so, we will become Ascended Masters, as we have gained mastery over our physical self and become ONE with our Multidimensional SELF. As Ascended Masters, we can choose to serve from whatever dimension we desire. Some of us may even decide to remain in the physical dimension.

In the same manner that humans evolve and expand their consciousness to become Ascended Masters, Angels expand and evolve their consciousness to become Archangels, Elementals expand and evolve into Devas, and Devas evolve into Elohim. Like Angels, Elemental Beings begin their evolution small in size and increase their size as they evolve. Humans, on the other hand, maintain the same size as they evolve, although their auras get larger. As our aura expands, so does our influence on others and on the planet.

THE HIGHER MENTAL PLANE AND OUR DIVINE CHILD

Our divine child, the keeper of the human consciousness, is the child of the union of the fourth-dimensional divine masculine, Father Sky, and the divine feminine, Mother Earth. In turn, our divine child gives birth to our fourth-dimensional Mental Body, Emotional Body, Etheric Body and our third-dimensional Physical Body. Our divine child takes responsibility for raising the vibration of these bodies enough to gain mastery of our thoughts, emotions, aura, and physical body, so that we may eventually become Ascended Masters.

We gain mastery of our <u>thoughts</u> by taking responsibility for their power of *conception* and by maintaining the *purity* of thought of our Christed consciousness.

We gain mastery of our <u>emotions</u> by taking responsibility for the *truth* of how we are reacting and responding to life and by using the emotion of unconditional love for the *healing* of others, ourselves, and the planet.

We gain mastery of our <u>Etheric Body</u> by taking responsibility for remaining in *unity* with our Multidimensional

SELF and by using our great power of *invocation* to be the creator of our life.

We gain mastery of our Physical Body by taking responsibility for *all* of our third-dimensional *manifestations* and by using our power of *transmutation* to transform darkness into light and fear into love.

The Human Evolution serves as Keepers of the Mind to uphold the archetype of divine consciousness. The Devic Evolution serves as Keepers of the Form to uphold the archetype of divine form, and the Angelic Evolution serves as Keepers of the Flame to uphold the archetype of divine will.

Humanity has the ability to act as step-down transformers by traveling in our consciousness into the higher dimensions and gradually lowering (or stepping-down) the vibration of divine will, divine form, and divine consciousness into the third dimension. In this manner, we use our power of manifestation to transmute the fear and conflict of Earth into "heaven on Earth."

It is our job, as Keepers of the Mind, to be the protector of the physical plane and to manifest the peace and love of the ONE in the denser planes of form and matter. As creators-in-training, with Earth as our incubator, we are preordained to receive our inspiration from the higher planes, define its form, place it in our consciousness, develop it with our thoughts, energize it with our feelings, invoke it into our physical plane, and manifest it in our daily life.

Just as the Angelic Keepers of the Flame expand into Archangels and Devic Keepers of the Form expand into Elohim, the human Keepers of the Mind expand into Ascended Masters of energy. This ascended being is our Multidimensional SELF.

THE THIRD PLANE AND THE STRATOSPHERE

It is our divine child who holds the responsibility of carrying the ideal we chose to step-down through the remaining four planes and into the physical world. However, free will is greatly emphasized in the physical plane, and we often do not keep our free will in alignment with our divine will. Our sense of responsibility is important as we join our fourth-dimensional aura with Gaia's stratosphere. This plane is Gaia's aura, the stratosphere, is the part of Earth's atmosphere that is under attack due to our being unconscious of the fact that Gaia is a living being who deserves and demands love and respect.

Unfortunately, many in the evolution of humanity have forgotten that we are creators and have instead become destroyers. These humans have lost the connection to their Soul/SELF and have forgotten that we are ONE with Gaia and her planet, Earth. Fortunately, as each of us regains the connection to the Christed consciousness of our Soul/SELF, we will remember to act as a transformer to step-down the magnificence of the ONE into the lower planes of our physical reality. In this manner, we can transmute darkness and fear back into light and love. With our greater consciousness surrounding our human and earthly bodies, we flow into the fourth plane.

THE FOURTH PLANE
Down from the ONE is
THE MENTAL PLANE

PLANE	QUALITY	RAY	HUMAN BODY	EARTH BODY
MENTAL PLANE	PURITY	CONCEPTION	MENTAL BODY	TROPOSPHERE

MAINTAINING THE PURITY

The quality for this plane is purity, and this ray shines the light of conception on our ideal, as well as our true SELF, who we will integrate into our third-dimensional life. It is on the Mental Plane that we can most readily remember what we want to do and who we want to be. The challenge of the fourth plane is to maintain the purity of our Multidimensional SELF and of the ideal that was conceived in the first plane. To face this challenge, we must diligently recognize and release any fearful thoughts that threaten to taint our creations or our consciousness so that our conceptions can come from love.

THE MENTAL PLANE AND OUR MENTAL BODY

The Mental Plane is an octave lower than the Higher Mental Plane, and the body of this plane is our Mental Body. Our Mental Body is the first of our divine child's descendants and represents the fourth-dimensional origin of the thoughts behind all our concepts, opinions, knowledge, and conclusions. Our Mental Body, fashioned from the substance of the Mental Plane, serves as an instrument to create and hold the matrix of form for our Divine Ideal until it becomes manifest in the Physical Plane. Our Mental Body also reminds us that we are a spark of our Multidimensional SELF.

The Devic Evolution, encompassing all the holders of form from the highest-dimensional Elohim to the lowest-dimensional Elementals, helps us to translate thoughts into physical forms. They do this by first transforming mental patterns into etheric blueprints and then into physical forms. The Elementals serving on fourth-dimensional planet Earth have sworn to out-picture the thought-form of our Divine Ideal. In fact, they are under obligation to materialize whatever they pick up from the thoughts and feelings of humanity.

This relationship between humans and the Elementals was intended to facilitate the re-manifestation of heaven on earth, but as humanity's thoughts and feelings fell into fear, the Elemental beings were obligated, against their preference, to out-picture imperfect manifestations. Hence, it is imperative that we use the fourth ray of purity to maintain our original ideal.

Too often, humanity's thoughts and feelings have polluted Gaia's atmosphere and left the Elementals no choice but to out-picture extremes in weather. Thankfully, there are those of us who wish to purify our planet and create peace and harmony. Because of these people, there are also Elemental beings working around the clock in our atmosphere to purify our environment of the accumulation of distorted energies resulting from humanity's negative thoughts and fearful emotions.

For each human Soul who chooses to take a third-dimensional body, there are Elemental beings who volunteer to make that journey with him or her. These Elementals serve to create and maintain a physical body for us. Our individual body Elementals are overseen by the collective consciousness of our body Deva. If we can establish a good rapport with our body Elementals and our body Deva, we can maintain a healthy and vital body. Devas act as the group consciousness of the different Elementals to hold the form of every person, place, or thing on the planet.

THE FOURTH PLANE AND THE TROPOSPHERE

The troposphere of Earth correlates to our fourth plane. As we look around our fourth-dimensional Mental Plane, we see the matrixes and vortexes that our thoughts create. We also see the Elementals busily out-picturing both loving and fearful thoughts. If we were to love the Elementals, perhaps it would be easier for them to out-picture the love and heal the fear. We know that our troposphere would be happy to have some help, as the troposphere is where our weather is created. We have seen our weather as something that is beyond our control, much as we have seen our thoughts and emotions as being beyond our control. However, we are Keepers of the Mind, and since we can choose a Divine Ideal to manifest on Earth, we can also choose the thoughts that we allow to rest in our consciousness.

Once we realize that we have incorporated the divine power of the Spiritual Plane, the divine wisdom of the Causal Plane, and the divine consciousness of the Higher Mental Plane into the thoughts of our Mental Body, we can use our innate power, wisdom, and love to take responsibility for maintaining the purity of our manifestations by disallowing fear to enter our consciousness.

What thoughts do we choose to hold in our consciousness as we step-down our frequency into the fifth plane?

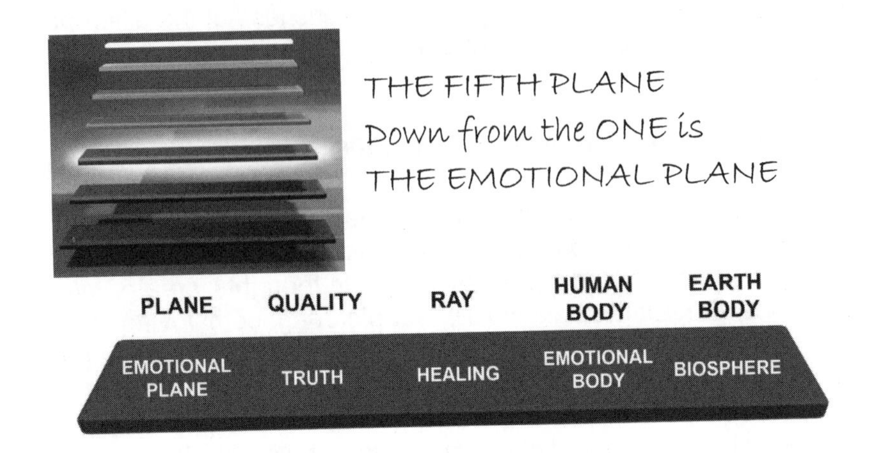

HOLDING THE FORM AND CREATING REALITY

We can choose our thoughts, but we must allow our emotions to express the truth of how we are reacting to our inner and outer world. The conscious knowledge of our emotional responses is important so that we can accept the messages of love and happiness, listen to the warnings of fear, and understand what makes us sad or angry. In this manner, we can honestly know our self and truthfully interact with our world.

Instead of controlling our emotions, we need to listen to their messages, acknowledge and/or act on the information, and then release it. Either way, an emotion is a message, and if we don't release our old messages we become polluted with the waste products of accumulated, past emotions. Just as we must archive or delete old messages in our e-mail or we will not be able to get new messages, we must archive or delete emotions so we don't get so full of the past that we cannot live in the present. It is especially important that we heal and release fear, anger, and sorrow, because they are like viruses that can distort all new, incoming messages.

THE EMOTIONAL PLANE AND OUR EMOTIONAL BODY

The Emotional Plane is also known as the Astral Plane. Our Mental Body creates the matrix for the Divine Ideal, and our Emotional/Astral Body fills that matrix with the life of emotional/creative expression. We then use the power of manifestation of our Physical Body to manifest our etheric in the Physical Plane.

The quality for the fifth plane is truth, and the truth shall set us *free*. Truth is a great force of healing, especially if we can remember that we truly are great, multidimensional beings who have come to create our chosen Divine Ideal. Our thoughts are the paper upon which we leave our mark, but our emotions are the colors that give it life. Hence, it is important that we remember that even if we are unconscious about our emotions, the Elementals are feeling and out-picturing them.

The physical elements are the building blocks for physical existence. For example:

- Oxygen, wind, atmosphere, etc., are formed from the element of *air*.
- Rain, rivers, lakes, etc., are formed from the element of *water*.
- Flowers, trees, rocks, etc., are formed from the element of *earth*.
- Fire, neurons, photons, light, etc., are formed from the element of *fire*.

It is the fourth-dimensional Elementals that hold the fourth-dimensional pattern for every third-dimensional manifestation. The Elementals that are the higher dimensional representatives of the earth elements are:

SYLPHS—AIR

The Sylphs are the Air Elementals. Sylphs are beautiful, wispy fourth-dimensional creatures who fly through the air. Sylphs are also known as faeries. By conscious control of our breath, we can relax into an Alpha or Theta brainwave state in which we can assist the Elementals in purifying our bodies in order to create harmony with our surroundings. Wind can clear the air or be tainted by pollutions, depending on the thoughts and actions of the resident humans. Humanity was meant to be the Guardian of the Earth, but many of us have forgotten that responsibility.

UNDINES—WATER

The Undines are the Water Elementals. Undines can be seen with our psychic vision as fourth-dimensional, translucent creatures in water, waves, currents, or sparkles of light on the water. Mermaids and mermen are also Undines. The water element, which is a large part of our physical body, is related to the emotional body. Negative emotions can damage our health, whereas the emotion of love is a powerful healing force. Seventy percent of our planet is also largely covered with water. Water is a great cleansing agent and one of the many factors in the success of a good harvest. Without clear water, life as we know it could not continue on our planet. If we can clear our fear and focus on love, we will greatly assist the Undines in our body and in our environment.

GNOMES—EARTH

The Gnomes are the Earth Elementals. Elves, Pixies, and Brownies are also Earth Elementals. Gnomes are said to live in caves under the earth and give their service from there. Gnomes work largely with the mineral kingdom, whereas Brownies, Pixies, and Elves serve from the surface to assist the animal kingdom and humanity. It is the earth element that gives our physical bodies substance. If we can learn to truly respect the earth element of our physical forms, then we will learn to respect the earth element of our planet.

SALAMANDERS—FIRE

The Salamanders are the Fire Elementals. Fire can warm a house or burn it down. Fire is pure energy, and it is the intention of the user that determines the activity of this Elemental. The least is known about these Elementals, but we can use our psychic vision to see them dancing in the flames of a fire. Salamanders fuel the core of our planet and assist the neural firing of the human brain and nervous system, and they also represent the metaphysical Three-Fold Flame of our heart. The Three-Fold Flame, also known as our Atma, is the receptor of divine spirit into the matter of our physical form. This flame is often depicted in Catholic pictures of Jesus the Christ.

THE FIFTH PLANE AND THE BIOSPHERE

The fourth-dimensional Emotional/Astral Plane correlates to Gaia's biosphere. The Elementals are gathered together by the Devas to create the forms of Earth's biosphere. These Devas and Elementals out-picture humanity's feelings and emotions to replicate our inner world in our outer, physical environment and our biosphere. Now that we know that our every thought and emotion will be out-pictured in the biosphere of our planet, as well as in our own body, will we choose to allow fear and doubt to linger in our consciousness?

EMOTIONAL PLANE AND ASTRAL BODY

The Emotional/Astral Body's service is to nourish Divine Ideals with the positive feeling of accomplishment and self-love. Thoughts, words, and actions have little efficiency without the sustaining power of the feelings of love, enthusiasm, and other positive emotions. Our thoughts are the matrix, or scaffolding, that surrounds our ideal, but it is the energy of our emotions that fills that matrix in order to give it reality in the third dimension.

Angels assist us in infusing our ideal with the energy of divine love. If we wish to call on an Angel's assistance, we can attract it by using colors, music, flowers, candles, and anything that can evoke a loving emotion. Our Emotional Body is the core of our creativity as well as the night body of our dreams. What kind of planet do we wish to create? First, we must be conscious of the truth that we are, indeed, a part of the great multidimensional being, Earth, as well as a part of our Multidimensional SELF.

The lowest vibration of the Emotional/Astral Plane, and of our Emotional/Astral Body, is the Lower Astral Plane. The collective Lower Astral Plane of Earth, as well as our personal Lower Astral Body (our Dark Side), is the junkyard of all accumulated psychic waste,

The waste material in this dump returns to the sender to form a feedback loop of perpetual problems and dis-ease. It is our responsibility to clear our own psychic junkyard, which will greatly assist Gaia in cleaning hers.

With the power, wisdom, and love of our fourth-dimensional self, we calmly and bravely step-down our resonance through the Lower Astral Plane and into the sixth plane down from the ONE.

THE SIXTH SPHERE
Down from the ONE is
THE ETHERIC PLANE

PLANE	QUALITY	RAY	HUMAN BODY	EARTH BODY
ETHERIC PLANE	INVOCATION	UNITY	ETHERIC BODY	HYDROSPHERE

INVOKING UNITY WITH THE THIRD DIMENSION

Invocation is the divine quality of the sixth plane down from the ONE. This quality gives us the power to invoke (call upon or summon) the ray (consciousness or thoughts) of unity. The Etheric Plane unites our fourth- and fifth-dimensional bodies by serving as an interface between them as well as serving as the vortex through which we can invoke communication with the higher worlds.

THE ETHERIC PLANE AND OUR ETHERIC BODY

Our Etheric Body, also known as our aura, surrounds and extends beyond our entire body, as well as beyond each individual organ within us. In other words, we have an etheric heart, etheric liver, etheric lungs, etc. This Etheric Body resonates at a frequency beyond the perception of our five physical senses and reflects the condition of our physical health, as it is the repository and the transmitter of prana. This prana translates from our Etheric Body to our Physical Body through our chakra system.

Each chakra rules a corresponding organ or organs, a nerve plexus, an endocrine gland, and consequent expressions of consciousness. Because of this, much of the spiritual healing is actually done through our etheric organs and passed on to our physical organs via the flow of prana into the corresponding chakra. The Etheric Body is composed of a very subtle matter and is slightly larger than our physical body, extending beyond it into both our third-dimensional outer and fourth-dimensional inner worlds, thus serving as an intermediary between our inner and outer life.

THE SIXTH PLANE AND THE HYDROSPHERE

The name of our planet, Earth, is a misnomer in that 71 percent of the earth is covered by water and only 29 percent is terra firma. In actuality, our planet should be called Water and not Earth! The abundance of water on Earth is a unique feature that clearly distinguishes our Blue Planet from other planets in our solar system. The range of our planet's surface temperatures and pressures permits water to exist in all three states: solid (ice), liquid (water), and gas (water vapor).

Most of the water is contained in the oceans, and the high heat capacity of this large volume of water (1.35 million cubic kilometers) buffers the Earth's surface from large temperature changes, such as those observed on the moon. Water is the universal solvent and the basis for all life on our planet. Our oceans, which respond to our emotions via the services of the Elementals, play a fundamental and complex role in regulating climate; and climate changes are strongly influenced by the powerful dynamics of the seas.

In the same manner that the Etheric Plane interfaces with the fourth- and third-dimensional bodies, the hydrosphere (which contains all the solid, liquid, and gaseous water of the planet) interfaces between land and water. The hydrosphere functions to maintain the heath of our planet in the same way that our Etheric Body functions to maintain the health of our physical body. It is through our Etheric Body that we are able to download the flow of the light of the fourth dimension to maintain our health and vitality. In the same manner, the waters of the hydrosphere are able to diffuse, and thus cool, the sun's light with clouds, fog, and rain. These forms of water in our atmosphere are vital for a healthy planetary biosphere.

The waters of Earth's hydrosphere unite the land masses, just as our Etheric Body unites our third- and fourth-dimensional bodies. Our chakra system serves as the portal through which our Etheric Body can download the higher-dimensional light into our physical body. Both our physical body and the body of Earth have seven chakras.

Our journey down from the ONE is coming to its conclusion. So, like a loving parent holding on to his or her child's hand, we hold on to our Divine Ideal and our Multidimensional SELF who has chosen it as we cross over into the seventh plane.

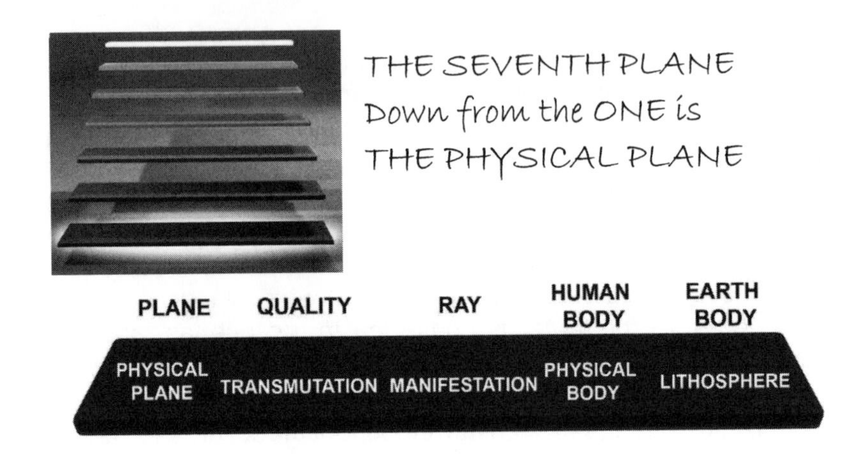

MANIFESTATION IN THE PHYSICAL

As we cross into the seventh plane down from the ONE, we enter our Physical Body, which is the lowest vibration and densest of all our bodies. Just as our higher bodies are made up of the elements of the plane upon which they reside, the physical body is made up of the elements of the Physical Plane and our beloved planet, Earth.

The earth element provides structure and form for our third-dimensional body and represents the physical aspect of our self. The air element provides breath and space within our body and represents the mental aspect of our self. The fire element provides neural synapses (kundalini fire) and represents the spiritual aspect of our self, and the water element provides fluid, liquid, and blood for our body and represents the emotional aspect of our self. All of these elements will be used in the manifestation of our Divine Ideal.

THE PHYSICAL PLANE AND OUR PHYSICAL BODY

On the Physical Plane, our Physical Body overflows with tiny particles of light substances called photons that enter us through our chakras. These particles of light are emitted from our higher bodies and used by our Three-Fold Flame to maintain health and vitality. Our Three-Fold Flame is the representative of the spirit of the father who gives us power, the form of the mother who gives us the ability to gain wisdom, and the love of the divine child who is the progeny of their joining and the truest essence of our being.

The power, wisdom, and love flowing from our Three-Fold Flame are our birthright. No matter what conditions we meet in life, these divine qualities are available to us through the Three-Fold Flame in the core of our Etheric heart. Our Physical Body is our earthly anchor point through which this love can flow into the Physical Plane. As we have now experienced, our Soul sent down a copy of its SELF to create a body on each plane of the fourth dimension, the Etheric Plane, and the third dimension. This replication is similar to the copy and paste function on our computer, for when we copy something and paste it someplace else, it does not diminish the original.

We have now met each of our many bodies, as well as the bodies of the planet of which we are a part. By connecting these bodies we will create a circular stream from the third dimension through the fourth and onto the Rainbow Bridge to the ONE of the fifth dimension and beyond. As we repeatedly make our journey through the fourth dimension and back, this stream will become a river of light. Across this river will flow our inner first plane's qualities of power (power of intention) to follow our divine will so that we use the second plane's wisdom (positive, clear thinking) in creating only divine form, and allow only the third plane's love (balanced emotions) to breath consciousness into our creations.

In this manner, we can maintain the fourth plane's purity of our initial conception and stay centered in the fifth plane's truth to heal ourselves and our planet with our sixth plane's invocation for unity with all life. We will maintain this unity with our innate power of the seventh plane's quality of transmutation so that we may transform our ego/self into our Multidimensional Soul/SELF who will manifest our Divine Ideal on planet Earth.

When we travel again into the fourth dimension, the first fragment of our SELF that we will meet is our Lower Astral Self, our Dark Side. Our Lower Astral Self is the body of the lowest vibration of the fourth-dimensional Emotional Plane. All the fear, sorrow, anger, and pain of our physical life that lies in this fourth-dimensional dump is awaiting our love, healing, and release.

Because of the density of these fearful emotions, they stay at the bottom of the Emotional/Astral Plane like silt and mud at the bottom of a lake. This mud is of our own making. Thus, it is our responsibility to heal our darkness with the light of our Multidimensional Soul/SELF. It is also beneficial to form a relationship with Ascended Masters, Angels, and/or Elohim to assist us in loving and healing our Lower Astral Self, who has become the receptacle for all our emotional pain and fear.

Once our Dark Side is healed, we can create our personal Tunnel of Light through the darkness of the Lower Astral Plane. With this darkness cleared, it will be easier for us to align with our Emotional Body, our Mental Body, the Christ consciousness of our divine child, our Causal Body, and our I AM Presence. With all these bodies in alignment, we can learn to flow with the river of light to travel back to the ONE, as we simultaneously ground the ONE into planet Earth.

Our seventh plane holds the etheric pattern of every aspect of the Divine Ideal that we have lowered through the six preceding planes. Therefore, we are literally bursting with all the good things that have been handed down from one plane to another.

Now we must remember the Divine Ideal that we have carried through all these planes. Remember that we have the *power* and *divine will* to implant our ideal in our Physical Body, the *wisdom* to create its *divine form*, and the *love* to hold it in our *consciousness*. By promising ourselves to remember, we can maintain the *purity* of our ideal's *conception* and *heal* our darkness so that we can live the *truth* of our *unity* with the ONE. Then we can *invoke* the *manifestation* of our Divine Ideal and our Multidimensional SELF in our everyday life.

THE SEVENTH PLANE AND THE LITHOSPHERE

Not only will we remember our ideal, we will ground it deep in the lithosphere, the bedrock, of planet Earth. The lithosphere contains the cold, hard, solid land of the planet's crust, the semi-solid land underneath the crust, and the liquid land near the center of the planet—all the body of Gaia. As we ground, gestate, empower, birth, manifest, master, and expand our personal ideal, we will contribute it to the planetary ideal.

The seventh plane, the Physical Plane, is the contact point between our inner reception of Divine Ideal and its manifestation in our outer world. Through invoking and uniting with our inner life, we align our consciousness with our higher guidance to transmute the lead of our ego/self into the gold of our Soul/SELF. The term "transmutation from lead into gold" is an old alchemical term for transmuting dense matter into a higher vibration.

Transmutation is also a modern-day term meaning the conversion of one object into another. In other words, the object, thought, emotion, or planet is not replaced; instead, it is converted. With the innate abilities of our Multidimensional SELF, we have the power to transmute the ignorance of fear, and the shadow in which it lives, into light and the illumination it provides. This multidimensional power of transmutation is best directed through the use of the Violet Fire.

The Violet Fire is the light of the seventh ray and holds the vibration of the highest octave in our physical, electromagnetic spectrum. Through calling upon the Violet Fire to surround the projections of our third-dimensional imperfections and fears, we can step-up, or transmute, the energy pattern of each thought, emotion, person, place, or thing to raise its vibration to a higher dimensional expression.

We may call upon this fire with the mantra of:

BLAZE, BLAZE, BLAZE
THE VIOLET FIRE
TRANSMUTING ALL SHADOW
LIGHT, LIGHT, LIGHT

The more we use the Violet Fire to raise the frequency of our person—and of places, situations, and things—the more we raise our personal and planetary resonance. We will also contribute that higher vibration to the collective consciousness. It is true that one bad apple spoils the bunch, but it is also true that all great changes begin with ONE person. Fortunately, that change, that transmutation, has already begun.

All the magnificent, multidimensional beings—such as the Angels, Elohim, and Ascended Humans—who have lowered their personal vibration enough to serve on the fourth dimension are working with the Elementals to transmute the suffering and strife of our third dimension into heaven on Earth, which was the first Divine Ideal. We can join them!

CHAPTER EIGHT

A MESSAGE FROM GAIA

Dear People of my Planet,

I am Gaia, your sister, your friend, your partner and your planet. I wish to thank you for including me on your journey into the fourth dimension. I eagerly await the manifestation of the Divine Ideals you have chosen to create on my planet. I know there are those who do not want to move into the higher vibrations, but I can look into their hearts and see their Soul's desire, which they are unable to see.

Still, Earth has always been a free-will planet, and all of my people have the right to create their reality, whether it is from their Soul or from their ego. As the majority of my people choose to partake in our impending process of planetary transmutation, these "sleeping ones" will find that they are more and more alone.

GAIA'S IDEAL

I, Gaia, have also chosen an ideal from the ONE. I have chosen to *be* a planet of peace and *love*. I always felt as though there was a great challenge, a mission I was to fulfill.

That mission was to go out into the wastelands, the outer reaches of a new galaxy, to experience the most extreme, third-dimensional polarity that was possible.

To join me in this endeavor were many of the other members of the ONE. We all looked forward to choosing our own role. I, Gaia, am the expression of the entire ideal, while the other members of the ONE chose to be different expressions of me, the planet.

In this manner, each of "us" is our own interpretation of "being a planet," and I, Gaia, serve as the template. Just as your hands and feet are portions of your human body, each of my elements and inhabitants, including my people, are portions of my planetary body.

Some members of the ONE wanted to experience being first- and second-dimensional life forms. They were the first to send down a portion of their essence into my initial third-dimensional matrix. I say "a portion of their essence," as they, as well as *all* my life forms, exist also in many other planes and dimensions. The ones who desired the experience of being first- and second-dimensional were to become my rocks, water, plants, reptiles, insects, and some animals.

FIRST AND SECOND DIMENSIONALS

The First and Second Dimensionals may seem less evolved to you, but they chose this expression as they knew that they would never lose touch with the planetary consciousness. They've never had the full experience of separation and limitation of third-dimensional individuality, but they've never taken the risk of becoming lost in the polarity of their dark side. Instead, they have remained in their group Soul. Because of this, they've never experienced death.

When they "died," they merely returned to the oneness with which they had never lost contact. Most of my humans have lost their connection with the ONE and with their Multidimensional SELF. Therefore, death feels like leaving. When the connection has not been lost, death feels like going home to visit your family.

There were others, such as yourselves, who chose to be third-dimensional "people." Because you, my third-dimensional inhabitants, wished the experience of individuality, you entered a human body that was prepared for you from the elements of my planet by your body Deva. When you entered this third-dimensional world of polarity, your awareness was limited to the separate package of your personal earth vessel.

You were separated from your planetary consciousness and from your awareness of your Multidimensional SELF. Millennia ago, you, my people, had more of a connection to me, the planet. However, as you have become more individuated by your "civilized" world, most of you have lost that connection.

Each dimension of reality encompasses the lower ones. Therefore, you, my Third Dimensionals, were always aware of the First and Second Dimensionals but lost connection with the Fourth Dimensionals and beyond. Fortunately, many of you are beginning to remember your true SELF. You are doing so because you have learned to expand your consciousness beyond the confines of your separate, third-dimensional earth vessel.

Because of your expanded consciousness, you are remembering to consciously perceive realities that are below, or above, the third dimension. Just as I, Gaia, have many dimensional beings and realities within my planetary body, you are realizing that you have many dimensional beings and realities within your personal body.

ELEMENTALS

Embedded in your earth vessel are all the components of me, the planet, as well as all the components of the ONE who chose to be first-, second- and fourth-dimensional beings. Your first- and second-dimensional selves live in unity with the planet, as these elements of your body and mine are not "evolved" enough to understand the separation of the third dimension. It is from their unity that they commune in oneness with the fourth-dimensional creatures, my Elementals of Earth, Air, Fire, and Water.

Just as some members of the ONE chose to be First and Second Dimensionals, others chose to be Fourth Dimensionals. Unlike the First and Second Dimensionals, the Fourth Dimensionals have some sense of individuality, but they also have a strong unity consciousness that keeps them in constant communication with each other, as well as with all the lower dimensional beings.

The Fourth Dimensionals most directly interfacing with your everyday life are the Elementals. The first- and second-dimensional "elements" of earth, air, fire, and water are given "life" by the spirit/prana of the fourth-dimensional Elementals. The Elementals share their life-giving spirit essence with these elements, just as your Soul shares its spirit essence with your third-dimensional earth vessel.

You, the human expression of the ONE, have Elementals within your physical body, just as my planetary body does. You are the microcosm of me, Gaia. In your carbon-based matter, or your "earth element," you have the Earth Elementals, the Gnomes. In your bodily fluid, your "water element," you have the Water Elementals, the Undines. In the "space" and oxygen within your body, your "air element," you have the Air Elementals, the Sylphs. Finally, in your neural activity, your three-fold flame and the kundalini force, or your "fire element," you have the Fire Elementals, the Salamanders.

Since Elementals are fourth-dimensional beings, they do not abide by the rules of third-dimensional separation. Every experience that any Elemental has is instantly shared with all the Elementals. In fact, all four groups of Elementals, inside and outside your earth vessel, work in concert with each other. Within the *inner* reality of your personal earth vessel, your thoughts and emotions stimulate all the Elementals, who in turn, stimulate all the Elementals in your *outer* reality. In this manner, the Elementals within your physical body and aura live in constant unity with the Elementals in my planetary body and atmosphere.

FIRE ELEMENTALS - SALAMANDERS

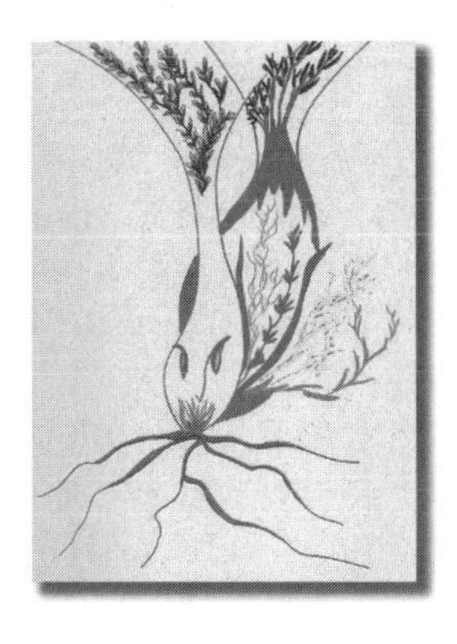

It is through your Elementals that you, my people, impact the planet, the weather, and all the people, plants, and animals that you contact. For example, your thoughts are the end result of the neural activity that your inner Fire Elementals, the Salamanders, initiated and completed. Since your inner Fire Elementals work in concert with all the Fire Elementals of my planet, your individual thoughts become planetary thoughts via the unity in which all the Elementals live. Therefore, your thoughts influence all the Fire Elementals of my planet and all my creatures.

Hence, when your thoughts are clear and kind, your inner Elementals attract other Elementals who are also clear and kind. When you choose positive thinking, you influence your Fire Elementals in a positive manner, which, in turn, positively influence the Fire Elementals of others and of my planet. The photons of the sun, which unify with my Fire Elementals, can more easily integrate into my planet by your passage, and the thoughts of others will be calmed as your inner Elementals share a serene blessing with their inner Elementals.

On the other hand, if your inner thoughts are sad, angry, or fearful, you dispense your own angst and discomfort throughout your environment. You then magnetize others who are suffering, or you create a "bad feeling" in others. Plants won't grow for you, animals will run away or attack, and you will contribute to my weather in a destructive manner. My weather is a response to my occupants, as I am the sum total of *all* my creatures.

EARTH ELEMENTALS - GNOMES

Your thoughts are actually a cooperative event between your Earth Elementals that work with the matter of the neurotransmitters, enzymes, and other chemicals to create the change in polarity that initiates the electrical signal and the Fire Elementals that "fire" the neuron. Hence, your thoughts also have a great influence on the Earth Elementals of your internal and external world. When your thoughts are chaotic, obsessive, and/or confused, your Earth Elementals find it difficult to stabilize themselves. This personal instability then influences the planetary Earth Elementals to perpetuate geological instability.

As you walk my planetary body, Earth, your every step influences its Earth Elementals. The planetary Earth Elementals hold the message that your step has sent and relay it to the next person or animal that walks in your footsteps.

Have you ever wondered why it is so glorious to walk in the wilderness, on a deserted beach, or in virgin snow? It is because it is psychically quiet, and your Elementals are not resonating to others. Hence, it is easier for them to resonate to your SELF.

This experience is also the origin of the saying, "Walk in the footsteps of the Masters." The Masters are beings, human and non-human, who have gained a mastery over their thoughts and feelings, and hence have gained a mastery of their inner elements and Elementals. These Masters consciously work with their personal and planetary Elementals, as well as the inner elements of others, to convey the deep, inner peace of living in constant communication with their Multidimensional SELF.

AIR ELEMENTALS – SYLPHS

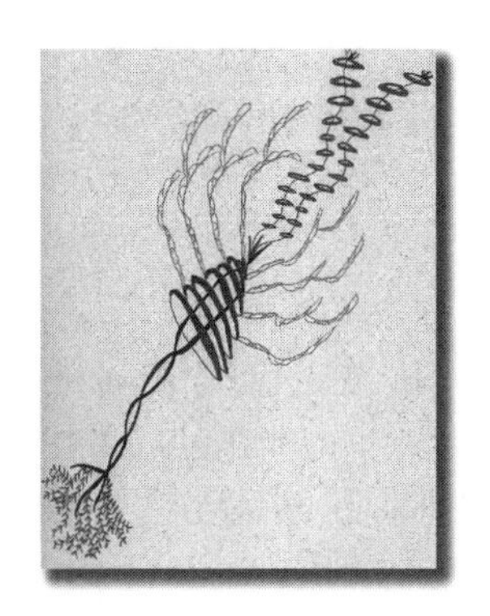

The Air Elementals assist the flow of life-giving oxygen, which gives you consciousness. The first thing that happens when you suffer from oxygen deprivation is that your thinking becomes increasingly confused until you become unconscious. Hence, an adequate flow of oxygen throughout your system is vital for clear thinking, a reason why the element of air is also associated with your thoughts. The Air Elementals, the Sylphs, assist you in breathing.

The Air Elementals also blend your thoughts with the thoughts of others through the unity consciousness that all Elementals share. With every inhalation you are receiving the thoughts of others, and with every exhalation you are distributing your thoughts throughout your world via your Air Elementals. Your thoughts then feed into the collective consciousness and the planetary consciousness to influence your daily experiences, as well as the experiences of others.

Allow me to take a moment to differentiate collective and planetary consciousness for you. Collective consciousness is the combined consciousness of all my humans, whereas planetary consciousness is the combined consciousness of all my *inhabitants* in *all* my dimensions. Hence, planetary consciousness is more expansive than humanity's collective consciousness.

The Sylphs live in your aura and constantly contribute to my aura, the atmosphere, and the quality of my planet's atmosphere. When you have cloudy thoughts, you relay that message to the atmosphere. On the other hand, when you have clear thinking, you contribute to a clear day. You are all aware of how my weather is changing. This is because we, our planet, are now transmuting. Therefore, reality is more mutable and more easily influenced by the thoughts and feelings of my inhabitants.

Please do not be frightened by this statement, for it also offers great hope. As each of you, the Keepers of the Mind, gain mastery of your own inner elements, your inner Elementals will assist you in holding that resonance of mastery. The Elementals also serve to contribute that resonance of mastery to the inner Elementals of others and to the Elementals of my planet. In this manner, the Elementals serve to raise the vibration of "their person," while they also raise the vibration of my planet and all my inhabitants. In this manner, we are all transmuting into my planetary ideal of being a planet of peace and love.

The mastery you gain over the physical elements of your earth vessel allows you to move into an active partnership with your inner Elementals, as well as the Elementals of my planet. You have the innate power to call upon your inner Elementals to assist you with your personal health and transformation, as well as the health and transformation of my planet. Do you realize now what a truly powerful being you are?

WATER ELEMENTALS – UNDINES

Water has been associated with emotions just as air has been associated with thoughts. Your Water Elementals, the Undines, rule your bodily fluid, blood, and the circulation of your blood, which is the domain of your heart. If your heart does not function, you die. Hence, if your heart is not functioning correctly, you experience the emotion of fear—fear of death.

Conversely, the emotion of love is also associated with your heart. This is likely because your heart is also the home of your Soul/SELF from whence unconditional love can be felt.

Your emotions are the basis of your consciousness for they represent your ability to *feel* or be aware of your Self. When you were first born, your "self" was your Soul/SELF. Then, as a process of growing up, you became more and more aware of your physical body and your ego who ruled it. Eventually, your "self" became your ego/self. Fortunately, as you expanded your consciousness, you could *feel*, or be aware of, your inner guides, Elohim, Angels, and other members of your inner world. Eventually, as you continued on your path, you began to be conscious of your Soul/SELF.

Your cerebral spinal fluid is also a water element and hence is under the domain of your Water Elementals, the Undines. Cerebral spinal fluid flows between your brain and your skull, through the ventricles of your brain, and up and down your spine between the nerves and the spinal cord to cushion your nerves and facilitate your primary neural synapses.

THE MYSTICAL MARRIAGE

As you awaken, your kundalini (known as the Lady Shakti in the Eastern world), sweeps up from your root chakra and into each chakra to join her divine complement, (known as Lord Shiva in the Eastern world), in your crown chakra. This mystical marriage of your inner male and female not only initiates the process wherein you are freed of the polarities of the third dimension, but it also greatly amplifies the frequency rate of your cerebral spinal fluid and potential voltage of your entire nervous system.

When goddess Kundalini rises up to your brow, or the sixth chakra, she leaves her seed of transformation in the third and fourth ventricle of your brain. Lord Shiva, who has been awaiting his divine mate in the crown, or the seventh chakra, then extends his energy into your third and fourth ventricle to fertilize the "eggs" which his mate has left for him. Their coupling opens your third eye, initiates the gestational period of your total transformation, and activates the octave leap in the voltage of your cerebral spinal fluid.

This jolt of higher frequency travels throughout your entire brain and down your spinal cord via your cerebral spinal fluid. Your cerebral spinal fluid, now charged with a higher vibration, basks every nerve ending in your brain and spinal cord. Your spinal cord then shares the shift in frequency with the nerves that leave your spinal column to innervate your entire body. As the vibratory rate of your physical body rises, so does your ability for greater expansion of your consciousness. As the anchor is raised, the ship can begin its journey.

You, my people, have begun your journey and are lovingly assisting others to begin theirs. I wish to thank you for delaying your total transformation until the moment of the *now* in which my entire planet and all my inhabitants shall out-picture my ideal of peace and love. In preparation for that moment, I wish to lead you in communing with your fellow members of the ONE, the fourth-dimensional Elementals who, in turn, will share your message with your first- and second-dimensional elements to heal and transform your current earth vessel. Your Elementals will then, also, communicate with the Elementals of my planet and all my inhabitants.

COMMUNING WITH THE ELEMENTALS

Communing with your inner Elementals is an important step towards becoming the master of energy that is your birthright. As you work in conscious partnership with the Elementals of your human body, you shall also be working in conscious partnership with the Elementals of my planetary body. We shall begin the process with your inner Fire Elementals.

SALAMANDERS

Take a long, slow, deep breath and *feel* the Salamanders, the Fire Elementals, moving like little jolts of lightning throughout your body. Experience the flash of each synapse within your system as you see the Salamanders busily at work. Feel your inner fire. Call upon your Salamanders to update your electrical circuitry to accept and integrate the higher frequencies that are entering your vessel.

Now, remember a time when you were out of control with your inner fire. In your mind's eye, re-visit this situation by closing your eyes and calling upon your inner Fire Elementals to calm your excitation and ease your struggle. They may be quite surprised that you even know of their great contribution to your life. Nonetheless, they quickly respond to your request.

Thank them now for their service, and through them, thank all the Fire Elementals of my planet. Determine that you will continue to seek to regain your birthright of being a master of energy, so that you can spread that Mastery to *all* through your inner Elementals.

GNOMES

Now, inhale deeply the essence of the Fire Elementals and slowly exhale into their partners, the Earth Elementals or Gnomes. Imagine these Gnomes doing construction and reconstruction of your physical body.

Scan your body for any areas of pain or discomfort, and consciously call the Gnomes to assist you in healing this area. They, too, may be surprised at first to realize that you know of them, but they then rush to follow your request.

Thank your inner Earth Elementals for all that they do for you, and through them, thank all the Earth Elementals of my planet. As you cooperate with your inner Earth Elementals to create greater personal stability, you are also contributing to greater planetary stability.

SYLPHS

Breathe now into the space within your body, the places in-between that appear empty yet are full of potential. Call upon your inner Air Elementals, the Sylphs, to cleanse these spaces as well as all the oxygen in your body. With your body clear, feel how your clarity of mind increases.

Thank your Air Elementals for all that they have done for you, and through them, thank all the Sylphs of my planet. With your every exhalation, be conscious of the thoughts that you are sending out before you. Also, with every inhalation be aware of the thoughts of others. You are not alone, except in your third-dimensional illusions.

Feel how the Air Elementals spread unity of thought throughout my entire planet. Determine to be aware of the thoughts that you contribute to the collective consciousness, as you thank your inner Sylphs for their great service to you and to the planet.

UNDINES

Take a moment now to emotionally connect with your inner Water Elementals, the Undines. Fell these Undines as they beat with your heart and flow with your blood. Feel how they cooperate with the Air Elementals, the Sylphs, to carry life-giving oxygen throughout your system. Experience the flow of your Water Elementals. They neither work nor toil. They simply *are*.

Call upon your Undines to teach you the art of living in the flow, as you thank them for their contribution to your well being. As you feel the flow inside of you, you spread the steady sense of calm awareness to your outer world through the unity of all Elementals.

Sense how your inner Undines facilitate the flow of communication and cooperation between your inner Elementals, who then unite your inner elements of earth, air, fire, and water, within the "society" of your physical earth vessel. *You* are the captain of this vessel, and *you* have the power and the responsibility of that position. Your inner alliance, or discord, will now be projected out into your outer world via the unity consciousness of all Elementals. Be aware of what you are projecting, for others surely will be!

GAINING MASTERY

You can only gain mastery over that of which you are consciously aware. With attention and recognition, your Elementals can function in greater harmony with you and with each other. Once you have achieved conscious, multidimensional teamwork within yourself, you initiate that spirit of cooperation with your outer world by your mere presence. The sun will shine above your head, the waters will calm with your passage, the earth will bloom with each footfall, and the skies will shine above you.

Yes, dear people of my planet, that is the grandeur that you expressed when you first walked my body, and the grandeur you will regain at the time of the fulfillment of our Divine Ideals. We shall *create* that moment *together*, person, planet, and, of course, the Keepers of the Flame (the Angels), and the Keepers of Form (the Elohim).

Arise my Ones, our new *day* has begun.

Gaia

A MULTIDIMENSIONAL MEDITATION

THE JOURNEY

To begin your journey, sit comfortably on the floor, a chair, or a couch. Relax your body. Allow it to sink deeper and deeper into your couch. Lie back against the cushions and feel their support. As you feel yourself sinking deeper and deeper into your own body, calm your emotions and ease your mind. Know that you are totally supported in all that you endeavor.

Listen attentively now. Listen carefully. Hear you Soul's call. It wants to enter your physical form now. It wants you to know its glory and feel its grace. Your Soul wants to enter into a partnership with you. It wants to experience your third-dimensional world while it awakens your multidimensional consciousness.

Feel your Soul like a warm blanket that is light, yet warm and comforting. Wrap this blanket around you. Cover yourself from the tip of your head to the tips of your toes. Now you can see nothing—except your Self. Now you can hear nothing—except your Self. You are completely enshrouded in your Self.

As you sink more and more deeply into your couch, feel this blanket of your Soul as it sinks more and more deeply into your physical form. Feel this blanket of your Soul upon your skin. Yes, there it is, a very subtle sensation of soft gossamer warmth upon your flesh. It is invisible to others and visible to you only through your imagination. It is so smooth and light, like your own personal cloud, a cloud of protection and comfort.

Now begin to allow this cloud to melt into your physical form at the same time that it also retains its shape as a cloud. This may be difficult for you to imagine, but it is a simple task for your Soul. Many difficult tasks will become simple as you allow your Soul to completely integrate with your physical form. This integration is beginning at the top of your head. Your Soul is entering the top of your head, through your crown chakra, your soft spot when you were an infant. You are becoming an infant again—an infant to your enlightened self.

Your Soul is expanding down through your head, past your face, and down into your neck. The world around you looks different now, as if you are looking through a filter of love and comfort. Your hearing is also altered. Everything and everyone sounds far away, except for your Self, the self that you have always found so difficult to hear. Your mind feels empty. There is nothing here to analyze or understand. All simply *is*.

Experience how this cloud blanket is wrapped tightly around your shoulders and across your heart. Your arms and hands are tucked in tightly, securely, and safely. This cloud of your Soul sinks into the tops of your shoulders and the back of your neck. All the burdens of your life are lifted from you as you surrender them to your Soul. Remember, you are forming a partnership. You can do the work and your Soul can carry the burden. The burden, which has always been so heavy for you, is infinitesimal for your Soul.

As you feel the warmth and protection of your Soul entering your heart, you realize that now you can love all that you do. The love of your Soul entering your heart expands your ability to love—love what you do, love who you are with, and love who you are. Yes, most important of all, your Soul teaches you how to love yourself. Wave after wave of euphoric love enters you and simultaneously emanates from you. Your breath calms and slows as the warmth of your Soul enters your lungs. With each slow deep breath, you allow its essence into your lungs, into your blood stream, and into your heart. Your heart then sends this Soul-filled blood through your entire system.

This cloud, this blanket of your Soul, extends down across your back, past the small of your back, and around your stomach. The weight of your life is lifted and the nurturing that you seek is fulfilled. Tightly wrap this blanket across your buttocks, around your hips, and across your lower torso. Your arms and legs relax with its touch and your feet and hands welcome the calm, loving presence of the warmth of your Soul. All the stress and strain, all the fear and pain, all the confusion and doubt that you have felt throughout your life is absorbed into your Soul. Your Soul then breathes it all free, cleansed and purified.

Your third-dimensional form is completely cloaked by your Soul. But your Soul wants more, it wants to merge with your first- and second-dimensional self as well. Deeply into your biological matter your Soul travels, into your flesh, into your muscles, your tendons, your adipose tissue, and into your bones and bone marrow. The earth vessel that has housed your life-spark glows with the radiance of Soul.

You feel like you have just been to a spa and you have been massaged with luxuriant oils. Your body hums with health and vitality. Your organs relax deeply as they feel the warm caress of your Soul and release all toxins so that they can be transmuted into light. With the entrance of your Soul into your second-dimensional body, you can fully appreciate the human vessel that has housed your consciousness.

Now your Soul extends its essence into your first-dimensional self. Down into your very cellular structure, into every atom and molecule, your Soul travels. It penetrates deep into your DNA, where it alters your genetic code so that your physical form can maintain the habitation of your multidimensional essence. For a brief moment of the Nowness, you are in oneness with all of life. You are a clear bright crystal, the foundation for all life, of all manifestation. From this perspective, you are a molecule of Earth, a speck of the collective consciousness of Lady Gaia. Within that same moment, you are the core, the point of consciousness that is your Self.

Then, in a flash, your unconscious opens itself up to you. You go back in time. All the memories that you have healed welcome you and thank you for acknowledging them and healing their pain. Old beliefs and patterns come to your awareness as you see how they have been replaced.

You see your child now who rushes to you to thank you for your recognition and for your love. Your child guides you through the tunnel of light that you have created in the Lower Astral Plane and into the Astral/Emotional Plane of the fourth dimension. Your youngest child and your ageless Soul now accompany you as you travel from the first dimension, the beginnings and endings of all, into the fourth dimension.

In the Astral Plane you feel as though you are dreaming. Objects and locations shift and waver before you. Every thought and feeling finds an image or experience for its expression. You walk, jump, float, or fly according to your wish. Here you see all your loved ones whom you thought you had lost. No, they are not gone; they are here, or on the higher dimensions. Here, if you wish, you can relive your favorite experiences, or get the opportunities that you could never achieve on the third dimension. In fact, all that you wish for can become manifest. But beware, for your fears can manifest just as easily.

Yes, it is much like the third dimension, but your manifestations are more immediate and much more vivid. The colors here are so bright that they hurt your vision until you have adjusted to them, like coming from a dark cave into the brightness of day. If you desire, these colors will lead you back into the land of Faerie, the land where your inner child shall always exist and where your imagination is your greatest treasure. You could stay here for lifetimes, in fact you have. But your journey is continuing.

As you move into the Mental Plane, the images are not so intense. You experience your environment through a misty lens and you experience your mind as pure thought. You are awed by the power of your thought. It is tangible, breathing, and alive. Conscious awareness of your Self is your greatest asset. Here you realize the machine that is your mind and you understand how your mind is truly a computer.

Each of your communications and interactions are like the Internet. *You* are your Word Wide Web. But, here you do not need an external machine to access the Web. You are the machine. You are the computer. Here, you compute the reality which you wish to manifest and experience.

As you move into the Causal Plane, the environment becomes more abstract. This plane is like the software that augments the operation of the hardware of the Mental Plane. This is where the finer abstractions of cause and effect sort themselves out, where mind and imagination merge into your personal computer program.

But who is the programmer?

"It is I," calls your I AM Presence from the Spiritual Plane. "Your programmer may be your unconscious, or your ego. However, if you allow *me* into your consciousness, I shall connect you with the heart of your Soul. All you need do is to unite with *my* essence."

You relax into the shinning being whose essence is yours, yet much, much more. For a long moment there is only light. Then, you hear a still, small voice which seems far away, yet also deep within.

"I AM you Soul. You can hear me because you have listened. Together we shall be your programmers. But first, you must bring into your conscious mind all that you have experienced."

"But, how can I do that?" you ask.

"You must return now to your physical body and take all that you have learned from your multidimensional journey and share it with your conscious mind. When you have fully grounded my essence in your conscious, physical form, you may return to me, and I shall take you across the Rainbow Bridge and into the fifth dimension."

In a flash, you are back upon your couch.

"Wow, what a dream," you say as you rub your eyes and stretch your arms. "But what was that last thing that my Soul said?"

SECTION THREE

If we are going to *heal* the planet,
we must also *heal* ourselves.

CHAPTER NINE

THE ILLUSION OF SEPARATION

When we stood at the threshold of the ONE there was *no* separation, because we could perceive the sub-atomic particles of light that comprised the larger particle of light who was our SELF. Now, back in our mundane life, we vaguely remember our Divine Ideal. The only memory we can retain is the feeling of a vague possibility that maybe we can actually fulfill our deepest desire. Unfortunately, the oneness of the higher worlds, and the joining of our many bodies, seems like an abstract concept in the face of "real" problems: the bills have to be paid, we have to work, our car needs repair, the kids are sick, we lost our big ball game, etc. Besides, what can we do? We are only one person. What can just one person do to make a difference anyway?

Perhaps, if we could take a moment of reflection, we could remember when we were not "just one," but we were ONE—ONE with our Divine Ideal and ONE with our Multidimensional SELF. When we chose our Divine Ideal, it had no form. In fact, it was not separate from us, as there was no separation at that frequency of reality. Instead, it was, and still is, the highest frequency of light we could perceive, the purest power we could embrace, the clearest wisdom we could understand, and the greatest love we could contain.

MOMENTS OF REFLECTION

We have stepped-down the frequency of our Divine Ideal and kept alive the spark of our Multidimensional SELF through all of the planes of the fourth dimension. Our challenge has been to keep our attention on our ideal and remember our true SELF as we go about our mundane life, as well as in our moments of quiet reflection. In fact, our greater challenge has been to create those moments of quiet reflection and to honor them as we honor going to work or taking care of others. We need to consistently take time for our SELF and *know* that others in our life will benefit from this as much as we will.

If we can also take some time to enjoy Gaia's beautiful Earth, a walk in the park, gardening, playing in the yard with the kids, going camping, even looking at the trees or into the sky, we can remind ourselves that *we* are part of a greater whole. *We* are part of a planet, and whatever we do for or against ourselves, we do for or against the planet. Taking a moment to reflect on our true, personal being, as well as on the planetary being upon whom we live, assists everyone and everything. Yes, each ONE of us is truly important!

PLANTING OUR IDEAL

Now that we have stepped-down the frequency of our SELF and our Divine Ideal, it is time to plant them in our body and in the planet. We will do this through our chakra system, beginning with the first chakra. Once planted and integrated into our first chakra, the high frequency of the spark of our SELF and our Divine Ideal will awaken a great transformation in our consciousness and in our bodies. It is important that we fully ground this higher frequency, or we can cause harm to our physical body. Only two prongs are required to ground an iron, but if we plug in a stove, a third grounding prong is very important.

In order to fully ground our Divine Ideal, it needs to be in alignment with Gaia's Divine Ideal to make Earth a planet of peace and love. If our Divine Ideal is not in alignment with Gaia's, it will be like a sunflower that is planted in the shade. It may take root, but it will never fully bloom. Of course, we can all think of many personal ideals that have fully bloomed and prospered that were not in alignment with peace and love.

However, these were not ideals taken from the ONE. These ideals were based on selfish, personal gain with little or no concern for others or for the planet. Many of the originators of these ideals have gained great material wealth. However, they will not gain enlightenment, nor will they help Earth. In the past, as well as the present, the shortsighted vision of these people has inflicted grievous wounds on the body of Gaia, our planet. These wounds are so severe that Gaia's ability to provide a safe home for us is vastly diminished.

GAIA AS A "THING"

In the previous 200 years the population was smaller and the technology primitive enough that we could behave in a selfish manner. After all, Gaia had become a thing over which we had Manifest Destiny. Therefore, forests could be destroyed (there were more). Game could be killed (there was more). The land could be ripped apart in search of minerals (there was more). The water could be polluted and diverted from its natural course (there was more). The oceans, rivers and lakes could be over-fished (there was more). And the sky could be polluted (there was more).

However, now things are changing. According to estimates published by the United States Census Bureau, the Earth's population reached 6.5 billion by February 25, 2006. By 2050, the population on planet Earth is projected to be 9.1 billion (as mentioned in Al Gore's *An Inconvenient Truth*). With this population, not only is there not *more*, but for many, there is not *enough*! The days of our shortsighted, selfish search for personal wealth and power have come to an end.

In a classroom of 20, a teacher can handle one or two difficult children. However, in a classroom of 40, these one or two are more difficult because there are 38 or 39 more to care for. Much like an overworked teacher, Gaia is on survival mode, constantly trying to repair the damage done by the few. Earth is a magnificent self-repairing unit. However, she can only receive so much damage to her body and to her systems of self-recovery before she is unable to repair the damage that her children have done to her.

Gaia is trying to get the attention of her naughty children. However, people don't usually listen to "things" (except some people who own the "thing" in question or need something from it). At the smallest sound of distress, the automobile goes into the shop, the tech support person is called for the computer, the plumbing is fixed and the roof is repaired—unless the owner is overwhelmed or under-financed.

OVERWHELMED AND UNDER-FINANCED

Gaia is now overwhelmed and totally under-financed. Her body is drained of her precious blood/oil. What would we do without our blood and other bodily fluids? Her land has been used to explode bombs and store toxic waste materials. What if we ate poison or swallowed explosives? Gaia's vast forests, which created huge ecosystems to replenish the land and provide homes and food for entire food chains, have been mercilessly extinguished. Clear cutting has destroyed entire regions for generations.

When the forest is stripped, mud and sledge flows into the water as land is purged of precious topsoil that takes decades to recreate. Rivers are rerouted into concrete runways, and waters and skies are polluted. Thanks to Al Gore's wonderful movie, *An Inconvenient Truth*, released in 2006, more and more of us are aware of the Green House Effect that is the result of our unchecked pollution. Also, according to a research team led by James Hansen of NASA's Goddard Institute for Space Studies in New York, Earth has been warming at a rate of 0.36 degree Fahrenheit per decade for the past thirty years.

How can Gaia keep up with these selfish, destructive children who defile their own home for a bit of personal wealth and power? Fortunately, more and more of Gaia's people are awakening to the truth of the world crisis which humankind has created. More of us now realize that if we are not part of the solution, we are part of the problem. In fact, we are not only *part* of the problem, to a large extent, humanity *is* the problem.

We, the people of the planet, have not kept our personal ideals in alignment with Gaia's planetary ideal of peace and love. We would have to search deeply into history and, even then, we would find few societies in which peace and love were the primary objective. Great avatars have been born to remind us of this truth. But as soon as they die, and others carry their word, the message becomes distorted and manipulated beyond recognition. It is up to those of us who are willing to recognize Earth as a living being with whom, and on whom, we live to repair the damage that has been done.

THE ILLUSION OF SEPARATION

The question is, how could we have so damaged the very being that allows us the experience of physical life? The answer is that we have forgotten that we are all ONE. The concept of separation from others, the planet, and our

Multidimensional SELF is the primary illusion of our "modern," third-dimensional reality.

Our Multidimensional SELF can perceive the sub-atomic particles that connect all life, but our ego/self, the current captain of our earth vessel (or physical body), is able to consciously perceive only a very small segment of the third-dimensional, electromagnetic spectrum.

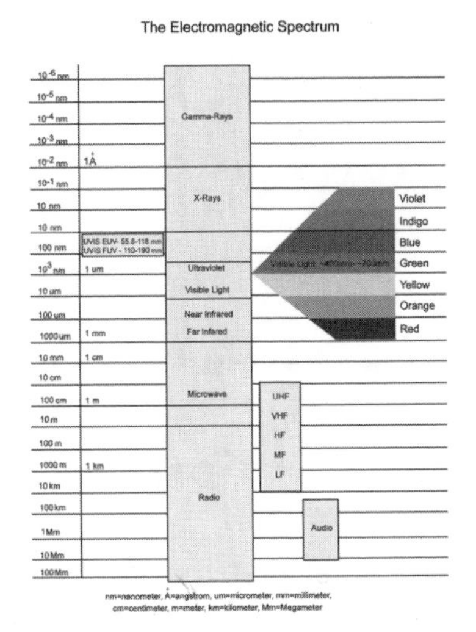

When we decided to take a third-dimensional earth vessel, we left the oneness of the fifth dimension and beyond and journeyed down the river of the fourth dimension, experiencing more and more separation and limitation as we moved through the various planes of the fourth dimension and into the third dimension.

When we were first born, we still remembered our true SELF, but as we "matured" we accepted the beliefs of our parents and role models. Unfortunately, these beliefs seldom included the fact that we are a multidimensional being who has the innate ability to merge and commune with all life on every dimension. Therefore, we shut down 95 percent of our brain and more than 90 percent of our DNA so that we could fit in. Those of us who did not shut down our vast potential were considered either geniuses or insane. In either case, we certainly did not fit in.

As we awaken to the plight of our planet, which is our plight as well, we realize that fitting in is not as important as surviving. We might think, how can I make a difference? When the "I" is ego/self, we may not be able to make a difference. However, when the "I" is our Multidimensional Soul/SELF, we are ONE—not "just one." With the power of the ONE, we become a beacon of light and an example to all. The process of personal and planetary transformation begins as we plant the spark of our Multidimensional SELF, and our Divine Ideal, into our physical body and into the heart and Soul of Gaia, planet Earth.

THE RIVER OF UNITY
FLOWING INTO SEPARATION

I am eager to take a third-dimensional body now. Actually, I am quite excited. I know that the third dimension, which is based on free will and separation, will be wonderful. I am told that I will forget who I am now, but I am sure that won't happen to me. How could I forget myself? It can't be that difficult down there. In fact, I think it will be great fun.

As I come to the threshold into the lower worlds, I feel the oneness of the fifth dimension around me. I understand that the separation from the ONE will happen gradually, so that I will have a chance to get used to the feeling of individuality as I flow down the fourth-dimensional River into Separation. I wonder what it will be like to be only one form with one gender that never changes. I guess I will find out soon enough.

SPIRITUAL PLANE

I am ready! I boldly step across the threshold of the Rainbow Bridge into the Spiritual Plane. Surprisingly, as I travel the bridge, I feel a sense of trepidation that I did not expect. However, once I step off the bridge, I am so distracted by the blazing white light of this plane that I forget all my apprehension. This white light contains all possible colors, but the polarity filter here is not extreme enough for the light to separate into colors. I sense the consciousness of the many sparks of light around me, as my sparkling light connects and merges with theirs. The Divine Ideal that I shall manifest in this upcoming life lovingly surrounds me as a formless potential.

Because there is no separation here, it takes no time to travel across space. When I desire a new experience, I just hold that concept in my consciousness and the potential for that encounter is revealed. I can easily see all the lower dimensions, just as I am told I will be able to see the first and second dimensions from my third-dimensional earth vessel. I move on now, as I am excited to continue my journey. Hmmm, "excited," a unique experience and quite different from peace and joy. I guess in a very discrete way the separation is beginning. Yes, this feeling is lowering my resonance.

CAUSAL PLANE

I am now in the Causal Plane. My, this is a unique experience, as well. There is a sense of brewing here, like a pregnancy or a concept gestating within the nothingness of a vast potential. The frequency has dropped one more octave. Hence, there is more separation. The sparks of light that I felt in the Spiritual Plane are now "pregnant" with potential, as they waver through a rainbow of possible colors. I watch as they swirl and spin in an attempt to decide on a form that best expresses their Divine Ideal. Oh, I also have a lovely Rainbow Body, but it has no real form. I, too, am a light show of potential.

As I flow through this plane, I feel certain vibrations that are an invitation to higher or lower planes. It is not too late. I can still turn back and return to the ONE. I must admit, I am a bit tempted, except that there is an urge to continue down this River of Light. There is something I must *do* and someone I must *be*. However, there is no time, so I feel no urgency to decide; there is simply an inner desire to change. As I allow this desire to build, I experience my essence dropping in frequency to the resonance of the Higher Mental Plane.

HIGHER MENTAL PLANE

Look, there I am. I mean, here I am. I am a bit confused. I am still my spark of light, but there is a form, my form. Actually, it is a potential of form, which I can breathe my consciousness into with the force of my love. I think that if I do that, there will be no turning back, and I will indeed be on my way to the land of polarities. I wonder how it will be to have good and bad, dark and light, fear and love. Yes, I am told, I will also be male or female. On the other hand, I hear that things are rapidly changing down there, and men and women are more alike than they have been in millennia.

Time is still a vague concept, so I can't say how long it took for me to decide to breathe my consciousness into my form, but *I did it.* I have a form, and I am now on my way to being human. I can perceive other loose, changing, light forms, which carry the potentials for individual consciousness. Like me, they are not yet polarized into male or female, and thank heavens, into good or bad. There is still only a thought of separation and a potential for limitation. Happily, I am still in constant contact with the consciousness of my Multidimensional SELF, as I allow my vibration to drop one more octave.

MENTAL PLANE

Wow, look at all the form. It is still in matrix form, the skeleton of form without any mass or density, but is very beautiful. Everywhere I look I see thought-forms awaiting the appropriate emotion to pull them down one octave closer to physical manifestation. I hope the emotions are loving, as I am going to enter that world now. Even from here, I can feel the fear in the third dimension. Oh, I must ignore that feeling, as when I give it my attention I start to forget my SELF. I keep getting distracted by all the thought-forms who are pulling at me to take them on. *No*! I have my own Divine Ideal inside of my matrix form and I can't lose sight of it.

Yes, I do remember now that I am to make my form on Gaia. Gaia is a beautiful consciousness whose planet is called Earth. I search with my mind to find her. Oh, yes, there she is, and she is not very happy. Things are not going too well down there. Maybe this won't be as much fun as I thought it would be. *No*! That was fear that created that thought. *I am* a multidimensional being, and *I am* going to Gaia's Earth to make a difference! As long as I keep my ideal in alignment with Gaia's, I shall be able to remember my SELF. I am going to Earth to help Gaia create a planet of peace and *love*.

Deep inside my consciousness, I hear Gaia reminding me that I must enter the center current of the flow of the River into Separation so that I don't get lost in the emotions of the Astral Plane. As I create my physical body in earnest now, I must stay centered so that I can gradually step-down my higher vibrations while maintaining a connection to my Multidimensional SELF. I'm afraid I understand now how the physical world can be so difficult. There is that fear again. I call upon the *love* of my SELF to safely guide me down the center of the river as I flow into the Emotional Plane.

EMOTIONAL PLANE

There are many, many forms here, with colors so bright I find I must adjust my spectrum of perception so as to not harm my new form. Yes, now I can understand why humans shut down so much of their potential. The stimuli here are overwhelming. "Here," yes, now there is time, space, and polarity. There are many beings of many differing forms flying, walking, swimming, and teleporting from one place to another in an instant. The shapes and genders of the forms constantly shift and change as they all play with the colors of emotion filling their thought-forms. Like me, they have also been pulled into this plane.

Actually, it is quite enjoyable here, as the addition of emotion adds a dimension to my experience that is new and exciting. I can barely remember my life in the ONE, but I will take a moment right now to remind myself. Yes, I remember now. I remember that there, too, I could take on forms, be a spark or light, or even pure consciousness with a mere focusing of my essence.

As my Multidimensional SELF, I traveled in my essence to many different dimensions, planets, and worlds, taking on the appropriate form for that reality. In fact, that is what I am doing now. I have allowed my essence to take a body in the third dimension, and I have placed copies of my SELF on each of the planes in the fourth dimension. Meanwhile, my SELF in the fifth dimension and beyond remains fully intact as it overviews my process. Yes, I feel me there, as well as here. But wait, what is that horrible darkness?

LOWER ASTRAL PLANE

I constantly calibrate and recalibrate my consciousness to remain in the center of the flow as I travel through the rapids of the Lower Astral Plane. This is, indeed, the junkyard for the third dimension. Don't the Third Dimensionals realize that their every fear, anger, cruelty, and selfish emotion hovers in this plane like sludge at the bottom of a polluted pool? These low-frequency fears and angers linger at this, the lowest octave of the fourth dimension, just waiting to return to their source on Earth. However, they return not to punish, but to be healed.

Time here is forever, as hope is lost and fear abounds. But wait, I see some tunnels of light opening through the darkness. As I look through the tunnels, I can see the beautiful, grounded light beings who have remembered their SELF. It is these awakened ones who are creating the light tunnels. With surprise and hope, I watch as more and more Third Dimensionals awaken to their true SELF and open yet another tunnel. I feel Gaia's great gratitude for this service. She has allowed herself to be diminished in order that her people can learn. Now, she welcomes those who are willing to assist her, as she, too, is returning to her true SELF.

THE PHYSICAL PLANE

Wait, what is happening to me? I feel a great density engulf me. I can see nothing now. All is black, I look for my SELF, but I feel only a pressure against my body. I feel a body around me, but it is so little. I see another tunnel, which is far too small for me to go through. No! I am going through it. Nonetheless, somehow is seems to open as I move through it. Oh! The light, the light is so harsh and bright. What could it be?

I hear a cry, a newborn's cry. It is me, I mean, my body! I have been born. I am watching my new body from above, while I am also inside of it. I don't know how long it will be before I totally forget my SELF. Already, my tiny brain is limiting my ability to remain in connection with the ONE. I am here now. I am in the third dimension.

Quickly, as my final fourth-dimensional act, I *promise* Gaia and my SELF that I *will* remember who *I am* and I, too, will create *many* tunnels of *light*! As I feel my essence being pulled into my third-dimensional body I vow:

"I *will* remember that *I am* a multidimensional being
who has come to Earth to create a planet of *peace and love*.

I *will* remember that *I am* a multidimensional being …

I *will* remember…

I will…

CHAPTER TEN

ENTERING OUR EARTH VESSEL

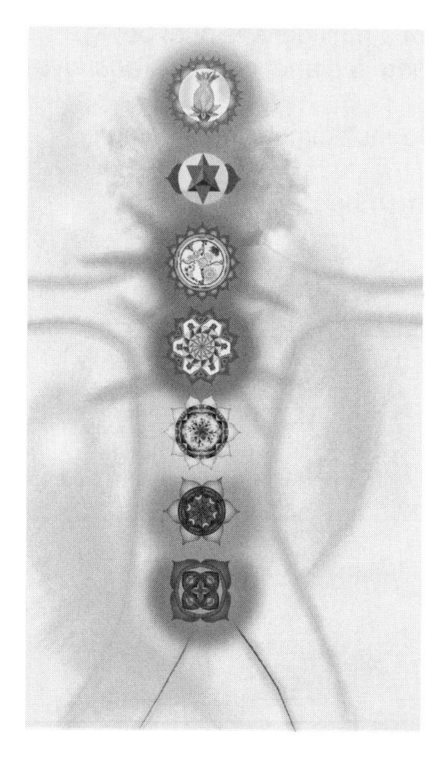

Violet Light—Seventh Chakra

Indigo Light—Sixth Chakra

Blue Light—Fifth Chakra

Green Light—Fourth Chakra

Yellow Light—Third Chakra

Orange Light—Second Chakra

Red Light—First Chakra

When our Multidimensional SELF came from the ONE of the fifth dimension and beyond, we traveled through the fourth dimension, creating copies of our true essence in each of the planes of the fourth dimension. All of our fourth-dimensional bodies flow to the center current of the River of Light, which is also known as the River from Unity into Separation or the River into Unity as it flows back into the ONE. All our fourth-dimensional bodies are connected to our SELF and to the planet like a string of pearls. As with a necklace, each pearl is unique and connected by a string—in this case, the string is the center current of the fourth-dimensional river.

In order to remember our vow to awaken to our SELF and fulfill our Divine Ideal, we must stay in alignment with our Multidimensional SELF in the ONE and with our multidimensional *planet* in the third dimension. This union is created by aligning our fourth-dimensional bodies of:

This center current also flows into the third dimension, so that we can maintain our alignment by flowing through life in this current. When our river becomes blocked, the higher-dimensional flow cannot enter our earth vessel. Then our resonance drops and the forgetfulness of the third dimension overtakes us. Because of this, it is important to stay centered. A top that is perfectly centered spins faster and faster for as long as it stays balanced. However, once it falls off center the top begins to wobble and spins slower and slower until, finally, it falls. The path to walk is narrow, indeed. Fortunately, we walk it *together*!

Each one of us is meant to be vessels for the flow of the higher-dimensional River of Light. When our consciousness is centered on our Multidimensional SELF, and we are living within the center current, we can maintain an alignment with all of our fourth-dimensional bodies and our river flows swiftly. On the other hand, when our consciousness wavers from our SELF, and from the center current, we can easily become lost in the rapids and lose our way. Because of this, we must constantly and diligently confront our <u>unconscious</u> Dark Side, <u>consciously</u> heal and balance our physical reality, and allow our <u>superconscious</u> Multidimensional SELF to become the captain of our daily life.

THE ETHERIC BODY

Our ideal was chosen when we began the journey through the fourth-dimensional Spiritual Plane. With the focus of our conscious intention, we used our consciousness to carry our ideal, as well as the spark of our SELF that chose it, through all the planes of the fourth dimension and into the third. To manifest this ideal in the physical plane, it must be planted into our physical body and the planet upon which our ideal will come to life. Our Etheric Body is the vehicle through which the stream of higher-dimensional prana flows into our physical form. This body acts as the interface between our fourth- and our third-dimensional bodies and serves as the transfer point at which our ideal and spark of SELF will transition from the fourth dimension into the third via the flow of prana.

To clairvoyant vision, the Etheric Body, also known as the Etheric Double, is a faintly luminous violet-gray mist that interpenetrates and slightly extends beyond the physical body about 1/4 of an inch. The Etheric Body is not separate from the Physical Body, nor does it have a separate consciousness, and serves solely to receive the vital forces that emanate from our third-dimensional sun and our Multidimensional SELF. Once these forces are received, they are distributed to the Physical Body via the chakra system. Every solid, liquid, and gaseous particle of our body is surrounded with an etheric envelope. Like the Physical Body, the Etheric Body ages, decays, and dies.

PRANA

Prana is a Sanskrit word that means "to breathe." According to occult science, the sun releases three forces. One is electricity, the second is prana, and the third is kundalini, or Serpent Fire. The uses of electricity are well known to our Western world, but only those who are familiar with the esoteric philosophies and Eastern medicine are aware of prana and kundalini.

Prana, which emanates from and is directly related to the sun, enters the physical atoms that float in the Earth's atmosphere. On sunny days there is more prana in the atmosphere, but on cloudy days, and at night, there is less. Prana forms into vitality globules that cause physical atoms to glow when it enters them.

The combination of balanced feelings and clear thinking causes a chemical reaction in the body that allows it to assimilate more prana (see *The Chakras*, by C.W. Leadbeater). Prana, often known as a "subtle energy," is the force of vitality and the life breath of all earthly organisms. Prana is also known esoterically as a cohesive force in the universe that bonds light to matter. In this context, electromagnetism is seen as a manifestation of prana.

Prana flows into the Etheric Body, which interfaces with our third- and fourth-dimensional bodies, allowing them to align and merge. Once in the Etheric Body, the prana flows into our chakras and runs along the nerves of the physical body via our meridians. In Chinese Medicine, meridians are invisible channels through which qi (or chi), another term for prana, flows. Each meridian is related to and named after an organ or function. The main meridians are: the lung, large intestines, spleen, stomach, small intestine, heart, liver, gall bladder, kidney, urinary bladder, pericardium, and San Jiao (or Triple Heater).

THE CHAKRAS

Chakras are small vortexes that rest on the surface of the Etheric Double. We each have seven personal chakras and seven planetary chakras, which will later be covered in great depth. Chakras are like wheels with varying numbers of spokes. Prana rushes into the center of each chakra from a right angle, which sets up a secondary force once it enters the center of the chakra. This secondary force sweeps around the chakra with its characteristic wavelength, creating an undulation that catches the spokes and causes the chakra to spin. The characteristic wavelength is the frequency of light that resonates to each particular chakra.

Our Earth vessels are huge, step-down transformers that download light from the higher dimensions into our bodies. The highest frequency of light enters our seventh chakra at the crown of our head and the lowest frequency enters the first chakra at the base of our spine, with the other five chakras accepting the frequencies in between. Once the light enters each area of our body, its frequency is lowered chakra by chakra until it is a frequency that can be grounded in and absorbed by Gaia's earth. Gaia, in turn, shares her earth energy with us. In this manner, spirit and matter can continually commune through our personal earth vessels.

Humanity was meant to hold physical form in the third dimension and be protectors of the Earth. It is within the divine plan that we are to re-manifest the ONE into the denser planes of form and matter. This manifestation begins with the acceptance of the highest frequency of light into our highest chakra, at the top of our head, which is gradually lowered in frequency until it can be grounded in dear Gaia. In this manner, each chakra represents the location of a step-down transformer. Also, each chakra gives our body seven different opportunities to accept, integrate, and ground the multidimensional light of prana.

ELECTROMAGNETIC WAVES

All living things are tied to Earth's natural magnetic field and to the energy it gets from our sun. Earth's magnetic field permeates and contributes to all life on the planet by generating the atmosphere. Our physical bodies also have a magnetic frequency, and our bio-field patterns react to any change in our Earth's magnetic field. In fact, all matter on Earth assists in creating this field and also becomes charged with Earth's magnetic resonance. Electromagnetic waves are formed when a vibrating electric field of light couples with a magnetic field.

Prana comes to us within the electromagnetic light waves, which are capable of traveling through a vacuum of space from sun to Earth. Electromagnetic waves have an enormous range of frequencies, known as the electromagnetic spectrum, which is broken into specific vibrations. The longer wavelength/lower frequency regions are located on the far left of the spectrum and the shorter wavelength/higher frequency regions are on the far right. The very narrow region, marked "visible," within the spectrum, is the light visible to the human eye.

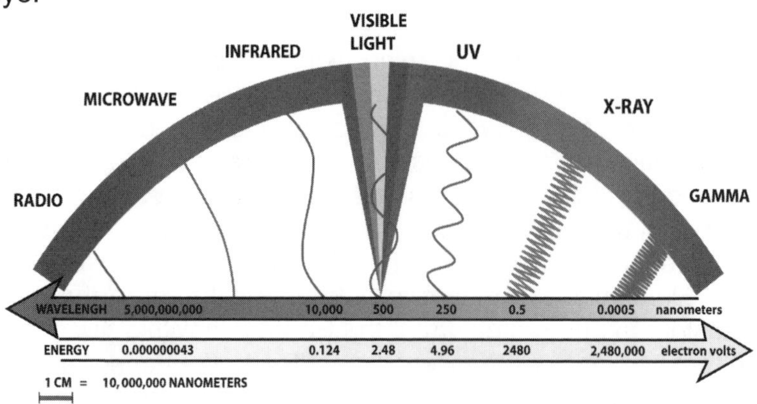

Though electromagnetic waves exist in a vast range of wavelengths, normally when we use the term "light," we are referring to the light that stimulates the retina of our eyes. In this sense, we are referring to a very narrow spectrum of visible light. When all the wavelengths of the visible light spectrum strike our eye at the same time, we perceive the light as white. Thus, visible light is sometimes referred to as white light.

Technically speaking, white is not a color at all, but the combination of all the colors of the visible light spectrum. Black is not actually a color either, as black is merely the absence of the wavelengths of the visible light spectrum. Hence, when we are in a room with no lights and everything around us appears black, it means that there are no wavelengths of visible light striking our eye.

Electromagnetic waves are "transverse waves," which means that they travel out from the source in a radial fashion, as in light radiating out from the sun, a flashlight, or a candle. This type of light is referred to as "un-polarized light." Such light waves are created by an electric charge that vibrates in a variety of directions, thus creating an electromagnetic wave that vibrates in a variety of directions.

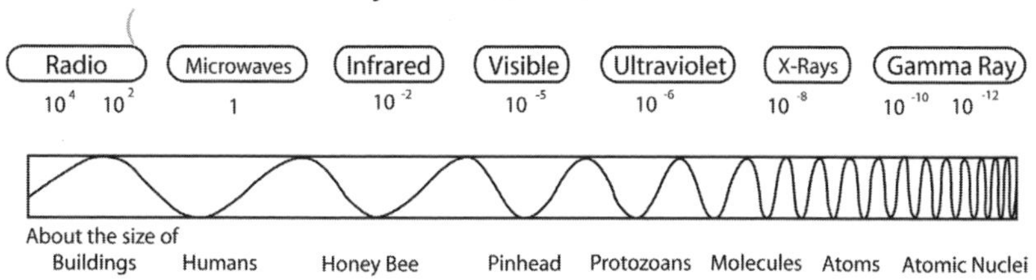

From longest wavelength to shortest, the electromagnetic spectrum includes: radio waves, microwaves, infrared, optical, ultraviolet, x-rays, and gamma rays. The wavelength of an electromagnetic wave is the distance between one wave crest to the next. Waves in the electromagnetic spectrum vary in size from low frequency (very long radio waves that are the size of buildings) to high frequency (very short gamma rays that are smaller than the nucleus of an atom).

POLARIZED LIGHT

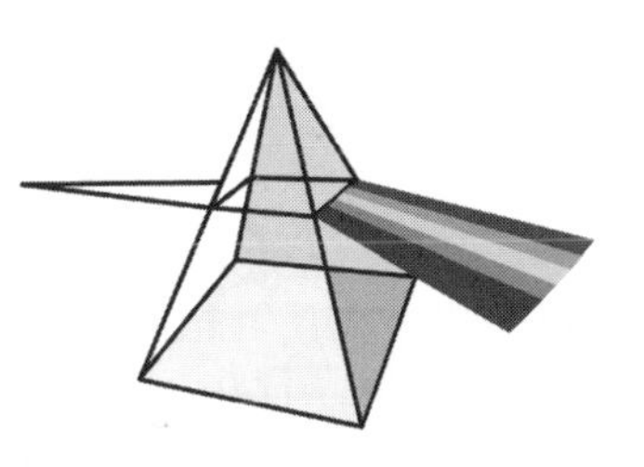

The polarization of light into colors is largely based on how the light waves interact with matter. Polarized light waves are light waves in which the vibrations occur in a single plane. One of the ways to polarize light is to direct it through a prism, such as the prism between the ONE and the fourth dimension. After light moves through a prism, each individual wavelength within the spectrum of visible light wavelengths is representative of a particular frequency.

When light of that particular wavelength strikes the retina of our eye, we perceive the sensation of that specific color. Each color is characteristic of a distinct wavelength, and different wavelengths of light waves will bend varying amounts as they pass through a prism, dispersing visible light into the colors of red, orange, yellow, green, blue, indigo, and violet. The red wavelengths of light are the longest wavelengths and lowest frequency, and the violet wavelengths of light are the shortest wavelengths and highest frequency.

CHAKRAS AND COLORS

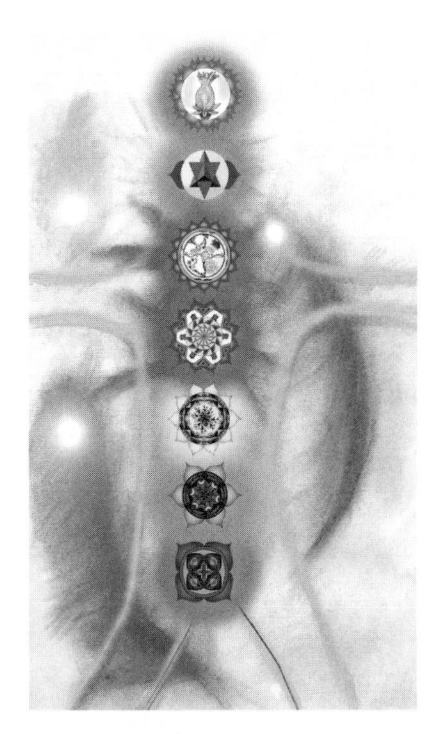

Multidimensional SELF

I AM Presence

Causal Body

Divine Child/Guardian Angel

Mental Body

Emotional Body

Etheric/Physical Body

The color red is the lowest frequency, then orange, yellow, green, blue, and indigo, with the highest frequency being violet. The longest wavelength, lower frequency *red*, is the characteristic wavelength that resonates to and is received by the first chakra. *Orange* is the wavelength for the second chakra, *yellow* for the third chakra, *green* for the fourth chakra, *blue* for the fifth chakra, *indigo* for the sixth chakra, and the shortest wavelength, higher frequency *violet* is the wavelength for the seventh chakra.

As the River of Light of the ONE flows across the Rainbow Bridge into the fourth dimension to become the River from Unity into Separation, the highest frequency *violet light*, fresh from the ONE, flows into our seventh or crown chakra. The other chakras serve as "tributaries," which collect the lower frequencies of light and contribute them to the river as it flows down our spine and into Mother Earth.

The sixth or brow chakra receives the river's *indigo light* from the fourth-dimensional Spiritual Plane. The fifth or throat chakra receives *blue light* from the fourth-dimensional Causal Plane. The fourth or heart chakra receives *green light* from the fourth-dimensional Higher Mental Plane. The third or solar plexus chakra receives *yellow light* from the fourth-dimensional Mental Plane. The second or navel chakra receives *orange light* from the fourth-dimensional Emotional Plane, and the first or root chakra receives *red light* from the fourth-dimensional Etheric Plane as it bounces up from the Earth.

CHAKRA ALIGNMENTS

CHAKRA	DIMENSION	SUB-PLANE	ATMOSPHERE	QUALITY
7th Chakra Crown	5D	The ONE	Exosphere	KNOWING
6th Chakra Brow	4D	Spiritual	Ionosphere	Power
5th Chakra Throat	4D	Causal	Mesosphere	Wisdom
4th Chakra Heart	4D	Higher Mental	Stratosphere	Love
3rd Chakra Solar	4D	Mental	Troposphere	Thoughts
2nd Chakra Navel	4D	Emotional	Biosphere	Emotions
1st Chakra Base of spine	4D	Etheric Physical	Hydrosphere Lithosphere	Foundations

Gaia is also receiving the flow from the River of Light as it travels from the exosphere into the ionosphere, mesosphere, stratosphere, troposphere, biosphere and into her hydrosphere and lithosphere. Just as we share our grounded higher light with Gaia, she shares her grounded higher light with us. However, in the same way that the pollutants in her atmospheric body diminish the great flow from the ONE into the planetary body, so do the pollutants within our consciousness diminish the great flow from the ONE into our personal body.

Gaia is meant to assist us in accepting the light just as we are meant to assist her in grounding the light. Unfortunately, our ignorance, domination, foolishness, fear, confusion, erratic emotions, and lack of a spiritual foundation pollute and block the flow of our personal river, which in turn pollutes and blocks the flow of our planetary river. In order to gain and maintain the alignment with our Multidimensional SELF so that we may create the reality in which we are living our Divine Ideal, we must renew our contract with Gaia to work as a team of people and planet to clear our collective chakras, clean our collective atmosphere, and heal our collective personal and planetary bodies.

Once each chakra is clear, it can accept and assimilate more light, which will allow it to spin faster, so that it can accept and assimilate even more light, which will make it spin faster to accept and assimilate even more light, and so on, and so on... Willingness and conscious intention to balance and clear our chakras, through deep introspection and intimate observation of our behaviors and actions, initiates and facilitates our process of aligning our Multidimensional SELF with our multidimensional *planet*. As we align each chakra, from our foundation up, we can plant our Divine Ideal into our personal and planetary chakras.

REALITY AS A PERSPECTIVE

There are as many versions of reality as there are different perspectives of life. The reality we experience is actually the version of reality upon which we choose to place our focus. Hence, reality is a perspective. For example, let us imagine that it is a beautiful day at the beach and we are walking along the pier. We had a good week at work, our family life is working well, and we feel creatively fulfilled.

Because we feel clear and balanced, we perceive reality as a glorious day on the pier and all is well in the world. We choose to look up into the clear, blue sky to see the puffy, white clouds slowly moving above us. We can focus on the laughter of children, the smell the delicious food in a nearby restaurant, and the happy people who are also enjoying a relaxing day.

On the other hand, let us imagine instead that we are a homeless person who has fallen down on the ground from destitution and despair. In this case, because we are unclear and out of balance, we can manage to look only at the littered sidewalk for signs of possible food and the nearby trash can, which our empty bottle of cheap wine has rolled against.

In this state of consciousness, or unconsciousness, we can hear only our own inner torment and feel only the gurgling sensation of our empty stomach and the dark red lower-astral mist that seems to lie on the sidewalk. Could these two people be living in the same city? Yes. In fact, they could be standing next to each other, yet invisible in each other's reality.

THE TOWER

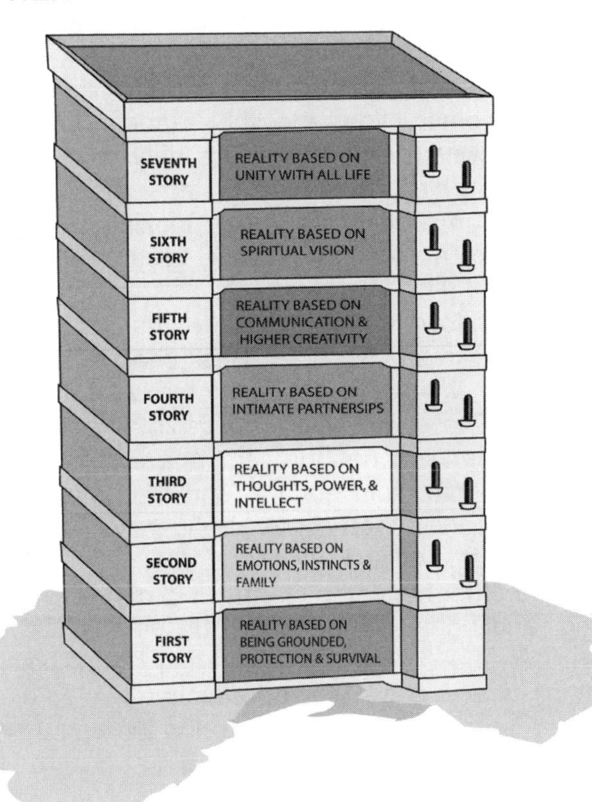

Imagine reality as a seven-story tower with windows around each of the stories. Each of the seven floors of the tower represents a different frequency, and so a different color, as well as a different perspective of reality. The windows of each story are covered with a filter specific to that frequency, with the windows at the top and the bottom of the tower representing the two extremes of the electromagnetic spectrum. For example, the top or seventh story of the tower has violet filters; the sixth story has indigo filters; the fifth story has blue filters; the fourth has green filters; the third has yellow filters; the second, orange filters; and the first or ground floor has red filters.

As we look into the tower, each window filters in a different frequency of light to create a corresponding perception of reality. Each of these realities is based on the belief system corresponding to that octave of light. Because these filters allow a different octave of perception from outside the tower looking in, there would appear to be many different realities. However, inside the tower, there is actually only ONE reality, seen through many different viewpoints.

Some of these windows have a clean filter, so the light enters without obstruction and the window offers a clear perspective. However, other filters are dirty or damaged from too much fear, which blurs and distorts the light. Looking through these damaged filters is like looking through a dirty windshield, which makes reality dark, dreary, and difficult to understand.

Each window in this tower represents the spinning wheels of the chakras in our body. Each chakra has a resonant center frequency, which is reflected by the color that is specific to that chakra. The energy field of love is attracting, unifying, and balancing. Hence, when the perspective of life is based on love, the chakra can spin quickly, and the color reflects the purest expression of that center frequency. Therefore, the vision through that window is clear and true.

On the other hand, the energy field of fear is dispersing, separating, and unbalancing. When the perspective of life is filled with fear, the chakra is unclear and out of balance, the chakra spins slowly, and the color reflects a tainted expression of the center frequency. Hence, the vision through that window is unclear and distorted. For example, a first chakra filled with love is a bright, clear ruby red; whereas a first chakra filled with fear is a dull, brownish red, tainted with dark slashes.

	LOWEST RESONANCE	CENTERED RESONANCE	HIGHEST RESONANCE
Seventh Chakra	gray violet	violet	violet/magenta
Sixth Chakra	muddy blue	indigo	indigo/violet
Fifth Chakra	gray blue	sky blue	blue/indigo
Fourth Chakra	dull green	forest green	green/blue
Third Chakra	dusty yellow	lemon yellow	yellow/green
Second Chakra	dirty orange	clear orange	orange/yellow
First Chakra	brownish red	ruby red	red/orange

*Magenta is an octave above red and the next octave above colors, frequencies and chakras

When a chakra is balanced, it can accept the clearest color of light specific that that chakra, which allows the chakra to spin faster, allowing it to accept more light and spin faster still. In this manner, each chakra can spin fast enough to push the energy up into the next, higher chakra. For example, when the red, first chakra is clear and balanced, it can spin fast enough to push the energy from the red spectrum into the orange spectrum of the second chakra. In this manner, the kundalini, which is an escalating force, is able to move up the spine.

Each chakra has a highest and a lowest resonance, with the purest expression of that chakra being in the middle of the spectrum. The low frequency of the spectrum is the area of the chakra where fear and toxins hide. The high frequency of the chakra is where the energy is pushed up into the chakra above it. It is the center frequency that is responsible for recalibrating the chakra to accept higher and higher frequencies of light. The integration of these higher frequencies of light further increases the spin of the chakra, and projects the kundalini energy up the spine.

KUNDALINI AND THE DIVINE MOTHER

The word "kundalini" is derived from a Sanskrit word "Kundal," meaning coiled up. It is the primordial dormant energy, also known as the sleeping serpent, present in three-and-a-half coils at the base of the spine in a triangular bone called the sacrum. Whereas our personal kundalini rests at the base of our spine, the planetary kundalini rests in the core of Mother Earth.

Kundalini is the force that calls us to expand our consciousness, to remember our Divine Ideal and to connect with our Multidimensional SELF. For us to accept this call, the great mass of kundalini energy locked in the first or root chakra must be released to travel up to the crown chakra at the top of our head.

The first, root chakra, the lowest frequency wavelength, interfaces with the most matter and represents our connection to the feminine goddess energy that is manifest in the body of planet Earth. The seventh, crown chakra, the highest frequency wavelength, interfaces with the least matter and the most light and represents the masculine God energy that exists as pure potential in the non-physical dimensions.

The kundalini force emanates from our Father Sun and is implanted into our Mother Earth, as well as our first chakra. With the awakening of the sleeping kundalini in our first, root chakra, the goddess Shakti begins her journey up our spine to be united with her divine mate, Lord Shiva, in our crown chakra. As Shakti begins her journey, she sweeps us up in her tremendous passion to reunite in the mystical marriage of separation into unity.

THE MYSTICAL MARRIAGE

This mystical marriage symbolizes the combining of the male and female energies within our bodies, which awakens us to our multidimensional consciousness and frees us of third-dimensional illusions of separation and limitation. In preparation for this marriage of our inner feminine and inner masculine energies, the polarities of separation and limitation will be gradually blended into the unity consciousness of the ONE, chakra by chakra.

In the Western world, kundalini is symbolized by the medical symbol of the caduceus, the rod with two snakes coiled around it in spirals. At the top are two wings, which are images of Mercury or Hermes, the messengers of the Gods. The caduceus is the symbol for healing, health, and transformation.

The center rod of the caduceus symbolizes the spinal cord. In yoga philosophy, the center cord is called the sushumna and represents the grounding, neutral cord of the three parts of the rising kundalini. The left cord is the ida, which represents the feminine side. It is negative/female charged, ends in the left nostril, and has characteristics of coolness related to the moon. The right side is called the pingala, which represents the positive/masculine charge, which ends in the right nostril and has characteristics of heat related to the sun. The ida and the pingala represent the masculine and feminine energies which we all carry, regardless of our gender.

According to the Indian guru Muktananda, in his book *Play of Consciousness*, kundalini has two aspects. One aspect is often perceived as the outer, cosmic energy of spiritual life force, which comes to us through the sun. We would not be able to live without this energy, for it truly is our life force. The second aspect of kundalini is our innate birthright, resting within our first chakra at the base of our spine, coiled around our sacrum. This energy usually becomes dormant early in our lives, as the kundalini power could greatly distract us from the business of third-dimensional living.

If it is our choice, the implantation of our Multidimensional SELF and our Divine Ideal into our first chakra can slowly awaken our sleeping serpent from her long slumber. In this manner, the goddess Kundalini, or Shakti, can begin her long journey up our spine to merge with Lord Shiva, the god Kundalini, and return us to the unity consciousness of our Multidimensional SELF.

RETURN TO UNITY

When our inner kundalini awakens, it turns our awareness inward to the ONE and offers us an opportunity to uncover who we are, where we come from, and what our true purpose is. In order for the latent kundalini energy to rise up the spinal cord without physical incident, our male and female energies need to be balanced and our chakras clear. The awakening of our sleeping serpent releases a dramatic, transformational force that rises up from the base of the spine via the sushumna. The sushumna is the center current, which will serve to balance the polarities of our male and female channels. With the balancing of these polarities, the illusion of separation will slowly be replaced by the truth of unity.

Once kundalini has entered a chakra, the spin will greatly accelerate, creating a centrifugal force that spins off the lower frequency memories, emotions, thoughts, and physical limitations, thus allowing the higher frequency of love and peace to enter. Without the density of the third-dimensional concepts of separation and limitation, the chakra will spin even faster, spinning off more toxins and allowing kundalini to rise further up the spine.

In this manner, the low frequencies of our body are released to make way for the force of kundalini, which will begin the transformation of our physical earth vessel into our true, Multidimensional SELF. Unfortunately, this can be a difficult process, as we are remodeling our house while we still live in it. Since this transformation can be uncomfortable and confusing, it is important that we stay balanced and centered so that the flow of kundalini can rise up the center path of the shusumna.

In his book, *Kundalini: The Evolutionary Energy in Man*, Gopi Krishna talks about the great discomfort of kundalini rising in an unbalanced manner. Lee Sannella, M.D., documents the many physical symptoms that arise from the rising kundalini in his book, *Kundalini: Psychosis or Transcendence?* Just as we must live in the center current of the flow to keep our Multidimensional SELF and multidimensional planet in alignment, we must also keep our consciousness balanced and centered to direct the upward flow of kundalini through the center channel.

LIVING IN-BETWEEN

To live in the center current means to be centered in-between the extremes of polarities. For example, if we can live in-between the polarities of good and bad, we will not risk being so good that we become judgmental, or so bad that we live for the reaction of others rather than for our self. If we are so loving that we can forget to also love ourselves, we can become doormats for others to step on. On the other hand, we can also become so fearful that we are frozen by our own terror. We also want to live in-between our ego and Soul, so that we can remain grounded in daily life, while we seek to constantly allow guidance form our true SELF. As a final example, if we can live in-between being too feminine or too masculine, we can find the inner androgynous nature of our Multidimensional SELF.

We may try to be too this or that to seek a reward or to gain attention. However, when we are calm within our SELF, another's assessment of us is nonessential to our self esteem. When we try to be right, we must make another person wrong, but if we can just be honest with our self, we give others the freedom to just be honest, as well. When we love another we can become too enmeshed, and if we fear another, we push him away. On the other hand, compassion, detached by nature, embraces the acceptance of unconditional love.

One of the most confusing polarities to live in-between is the polarity of ego/self and Soul/SELF. It is difficult to conceive how to live in-between our self and our SELF. However, our Multidimensional SELF encompasses our most primitive Dark Side and wounded child with the same unconditional love and acceptance as it embraces our highest character and divine child. Our Multidimensional SELF can easily see through the third-dimensional illusions of separation and is free of all false beliefs in limitation.

As the polarities of self and SELF merge into ONE, we become masters of both our outward, proton, masculine energy and our inward, electron, feminine energy. In this manner, we can more easily find the center current that connects our Multidimensional Soul/SELF with our Multidimensional Planet/SELF.

During this special time of planetary challenge, more and more of us will answer kundalini's call and consciously or unconsciously awaken our inner sleeping serpent. Dreams of snakes interacting with us or moving up our body are often an indication that we have activated our kundalini force. Furthermore, with the clearing of our chakras, our polarities of light/dark shall also be merged into ONE as well as love/fear, right/wrong, good/bad, and ego/Soul. Perhaps, most important of all, the polarity of people and planet will be merged, as people and planet become ONE.

Like any journey, kundalini's journey begins with a single step. That step is our determination to consciously break through the barriers of our unconscious mind so that we can consciously unlock our superconscious wisdom, power, and love that has been trapped behind the veil of our forgetfulness. As the kundalini energy rises up our center channel, it is important that we keep our consciousness in alignment with our Multidimensional SELF and with our Divine Ideal. In this manner, we will be able to see the light at the end of the tunnel, as well as maintain communication with our SELF.

TO MY SELF

No need to lie nor to pretend
The beginning has become the end

The end of all that lies between
So far away and what is seen

Hold me tight within your mind
'Till you and I are of ONE kind

The blending of the future's NOW
Will lead the way and show me how

I lean my heart against your door
And release my pain 'till there's no more

Please take me now into the life
That's free from work and daily strife

I give you all my darkest traits
Release my fears, redeem my hates

I ease my fist to take your hand
And walk into your peaceful land

As your door opens, so does my heart
And at this ending, new life does start

CHAPTER ELEVEN

INTRODUCTION TO THE CHAKRAS

Each chakra serves as a portal of experience and communication with different dimensions to align with our Multidimensional SELF. The first or root chakra is our grounding point to our finite planet, whereas the seventh or crown chakra is our grounding point to our infinite SELF. Our fourth or heart chakra serves as the meeting ground of these two polarities of infinite and finite. The second (navel) chakra is the lower octave of the fifth (throat) chakra, just as the third (solar plexus) chakra is the lower octave of the sixth (brow) chakra.

7th Crown Chakra
Infinite SELF

6th Brow Chakra
Infinite Power

5th Throat Chakra
Infinite Creativity

4th Heart Chakra
Meeting of Polarities

3rd Solar Plexus Chakra
Finite Power

2nd Navel Chakra
Finite Creativity

1st Root Chakra
Finite PLANET

CHAKRAS AND CONSCIOUSNESS

Chakras, which rule certain areas of our body, can also be divined into three levels of consciousness. Chakras of our unconsciousness rule the lower body and area of our life to which we are normally unconscious, such as grounding with the planet, digestion, and elimination.

- The first chakra rules the skeleton, legs, knees, and feet.
- The second chakra rules the genitals, abdomen, and lower back.
- The third chakra rules the liver, gall bladder, stomach, spleen, and pancreas.

Chakras of our consciousness rule the middle part of our body and areas of our life of which we are generally conscious, such as relationships, health, and communication.

- The fourth chakra rules the heart, lungs, immune system, arms, and hands.
- The fifth chakra rules the throat, mouth, speech, and hearing.

Chakras of our superconscious rule the upper part of our body and areas of our life that are larger in the realm of the superconscious, such as higher ideals and expanded consciousness.

- The sixth chakra rules the vision, face, head, sleep, and dreams.
- The seventh chakra rules the brain and nervous system.

The chakras represent not only a particular part of our body, but also a part of our consciousness. Consciousness is the experience of "be-ing," which represents everything that is possible for us to experience. These senses, perceptions, and possible states of awareness can be divided into seven categories that are associated with each of the seven chakras.

- The first chakra is survival, vitality, and grounding to physical life.
- The second chakra is emotions, nurturing, and shelter.
- The third chakra is thoughts and power systems.
- The fourth chakra is love, health, and relationships.

- The fifth chakra is communication and higher creativity.
- The sixth chakra is inspiration, imagination, and spiritual power.
- The seventh chakra is unity with multidimensional consciousness.

Tensions that are felt in our consciousness are also felt in our body via the chakra system. Conversely, tensions that are felt in our body are felt in our consciousness.

- A first-chakra problem would express through our:
    - consciousness as difficulties with our daily survival, vital energy, or dedication to physical life.
    - body as problems with our skeleton, legs, knees, or feet.
- A second-chakra problem would express through our:
    - consciousness as difficulties with our emotions, ability to give or receive nurturing, or our home.
    - body as problems with our reproductive organs, intestines, or lower back.
- A third-chakra problem would express through our:
    - consciousness as difficulties with thinking and power struggles with others or within our self.
    - body as problems with our liver, gall bladder, stomach, spleen, or pancreas
- A fourth-chakra problem would express through our:
    - consciousness as difficulties giving or expressing love in our relationships and our over-all health.
    - body as problems with our heart, lungs, immune system, arms, or hands.
- A fifth-chakra problem would express through our:
    - consciousness as difficulties with communication and creativity.

  - body as problems with our throat, mouth, speech, or hearing.
- A sixth-chakra problem would express through our:
  - consciousness as difficulties with inspiration, imagination, and spiritual power.
  - body as nightmares or problems with our vision, face, head, or sleep.
- A seventh-chakra problem would express through our:
  - consciousness as difficulties with mind expansion.
  - body as problems with our brain or nervous system.

SYMPTOMS OF TRANSFORMATION

As kundalini carries the spark of our Soul/SELF and the seed of our divine idea up into each of our chakras, their higher frequency will create a faster spin in each chakra. This increased spin will initiate a centrifugal force that separates the denser, fear-based physical and psychic toxins from our true love-based SELF. These toxins, the elements of experience in a third-dimensional polarity-based reality, will then be released from our bodies in many different ways. The release of these physical and psychic toxins is the cause of our "symptoms of transformation."

These "symptoms" are often thought of as illness but in reality are wellness. They are the process of our purging the thoughts, emotions, and behaviors that have driven us for our entire life. It is wonderful that we can adapt to conditions that are far less than loving and healthy, but magnificent that we can realize when it is safe to release these adaptations. We have taken in the toxins because they were what we were exposed to, heard, saw, felt, and ate. We were wise to take in these toxins, as this created physic and physical antibodies so that we could survive in a reality filled with fear.

However, as we take in the great unconditional love of our Multidimensional SELF, a frequency net is created to filter out the resonance of fear. We can still perceive the fear that is abundant in our external world, but our Soul/SELF is able to reject fear's entrance into our great vessel of light, our physical body. It is the rejection of fear that allows us to release our old physical, mental, and emotional defense mechanisms. We can release these past adaptations to fear because we will no longer need to "join them" if we can't "beat them." We cannot beat fear, for it is an element of the third-dimensional illusions of separation and limitation. However, with the integration of our Multidimensional Soul/SELF we can see through illusion to *know* the truth.

The truth is that we are ONE with the planet and *all* her inhabitants. The truth is that Earth is alive and we are a member of Gaia's consciousness. The more we embrace these truths, the more of the higher light of our SELF we can accept into our earth vessel, *and* the more symptoms of transformation we will experience as we release the toxins of fear. This release of fear will cause different physical, emotional, mental, and behavioral symptoms in each chakra. As the lies of fear confront the truth of our Soul's unconditional love, our symptoms of transformation will swing between moments of sickness, pain, and inner darkness and flashes of joy, love, and illumination.

Physical symptoms of transformation will often be perceived as illness, pain and/or injury, as well as moments of vibrant health beyond which we have never experienced. Emotional symptoms will likely be perceived as floating anxiety, depression, and emotional extremes of anger and sorrow as well as of intuition, greater instincts, empathy, and joy. Mental symptoms will create confusion, distraction, poor initiative, as well as clarity to the point of insight, intuition, illumination, and immense expansion of consciousness. Through this expansion of consciousness we begin to regain our innate psychic abilities of clairvoyance, clairaudience, clairsentience, and psychogenesis. Our behaviors will run the spectrum of regression into fear-based reactions to rising above situations and managing it in a calm and loving fashion.

Our ego/self and Soul/SELF are jockeying for position, and we may feel like we are two people in one body. In fact, we are *all* people in one planetary body, but only our Soul can understand that concept. While the ego/self is in charge, our creations are subject to fear and limitation, as we are separated from the flow of the ONE. On the other hand, as we surrender to our Soul/SELF, ego is the mud at the bottom of the pond that we can observe as we float on the calm surface of the water. From this perspective we can create the reality we choose to live. We will create each moment of our life by perceiving, loving, healing, and releasing the old ego-created life, so that we may surrender all control of our physical life to our Soul.

It is through surrendering to the higher frequency flow of the ONE of our SELF that we create our new life. Our ego/self has worked hard to get us to this point of our personal evolvement, for which we are deeply grateful. However, as our Soul enters our earth vessel, our ego will be reassigned to ground our earth vessel and manage our mundane life, so that we—Soul/SELF—can create the reality for which we have taken embodiment. Within the consciousness of our Soul, we have access and full use of our expanded perceptions to assist us in our creativity. In this manner, we become our Divine Ideal with every thought, emotion, intention, and action. As we remodel our house in which we still live, we will experience our symptoms, knowing that we are in a process of great transformation. These symptoms of transformation may include:

- Feeling spaced out and ungrounded. This feeling is due to our consciousness expanding into frequencies that were formerly beyond our conscious recognition. We feel spaced out because we are not yet sufficiently grounded to receive a clear signal. We are also spaced out because our scope of awareness is so much broader than it used to be that we have difficulty fine tuning our perceptions to *just* the third-dimensional world.

- Sensing that time is moving more rapidly. When we first consciously experience the higher-dimensional light, time appears to pass very quickly because our vibratory rate is so much faster than those around us. However, when we become more accustomed to the "no time" of the *now*, we feel a need to slow down. When we feel at home with our higher consciousness, we live beyond the confines of third-dimensional time. Hence, we feel no need to rush, as we *know* that all will occur at the perfect moment.

- Suffering from headaches, even migraines, and abdominal pain. Acid reflux syndrome is a common condition for one in the process of transformation. Our biochemistry has to adapt to a new vibration, and our organs of digestion are compromised.

- Experiencing cold or flu symptoms. We may have fuzzy vision, and our eyes may appear to be weaker, with neck pain or a headache at the back of the head.

- Experiencing further cleansing symptoms such as dizziness, diarrhea, joint pains, nausea, disorientation, disturbed sleeping patterns, or exhaustion. These symptoms are all signs that our body is trying to adapt to the new vibration.

- Experiencing an increase in joy and playfulness and an added sense of adventure. Our fear is gradually diminishing, as we feel the protection of our higher vibrations. We become more disconnected from the dramas of daily life, and this freedom allows us more time to be creative.

- Experiencing an increase in our physic abilities of telepathy, empathy, clairvoyance, clairaudience, clairsentience, etc. We may have dreams about or a sudden recall of early childhood events that have affected our lives more than we formerly knew. Our sense of purpose will also become stronger, as we feel that we must do something of importance with our growing awareness.

- Having increasingly vivid dreams as the veils between dimensions blur. We may even wake up with an inner voice giving us an interpretation of our dream or a special message. We will find that some dreams will haunt us until we take the time to determine their meaning. These experiences occur as the veil between the third and fourth dimensions are thinning and we are able to hear the silent voice of our SELF.

- Experiencing feeling more and more connected, although we may not be sure yet to what or to whom. We know only that many of the things, people, places, and activities that we once enjoyed no longer hold much of an attraction. We also care more about who we are *being* than what we are *doing*. We are increasingly obsessed with finding our purpose and remaining true to our SELF.

IN STEP WITH GAIA

We have been out of step with Gaia for too long and have not thought of her as a being. Humanity has been so polarized to its ego/self that we have not been able to realize that our behaviors, thoughts, and emotions have a huge impact, not only on other people but on our planet as well. Our Piscean Age search for individual consciousness has separated us from the planetary being that is our home, and our selfish, short-sighted choices and actions have caused great damage to our Mother Earth.

This damage is now evident to us all through the immense changes in our weather. In September 2006 a study led by James Hansen of NASA's Goddard Institute for Space Studies was released confirming that the world's temperature is reaching a level that has not been seen in thousands of years. The report states:

> "There has been a rapid warming trend over the past 30 years, and the Earth is now reaching and passing through the warmest levels in the current interglacial period, which has lasted nearly 12,000 years. 'This evidence implies that we are getting close to dangerous levels of human-made pollution,' said Hansen. In recent decades, human-made greenhouse gases have become the largest climate change factor.
>
> "Global warming is already beginning to have noticeable effects in nature. Plants and animals can survive only within certain climatic zones, so with the warming of recent decades many of them are beginning to migrate poleward. A study that appeared in *Nature Magazine* in 2003 found that 1700 plant, animal and insect species moved poleward at an average rate of 6 kilometers (about 4 miles) per decade in the last half of the 20th century. 'Rapid movement of climatic zones is going to be another stress on wildlife,' according to Hansen. 'It adds to the stress of habitat loss due to human developments. If we do not slow down the rate of global warming, many species are likely to

> become extinct. In effect we are pushing them off the planet.'"

Almost a decade earlier, in 1997, Dr. Alexsey N. Dmitriev, a Russian expert on global ecology and fast-processing Earth events published *Planetophysical State of the Earth and Life*. In this report, he stated that the overall volcanic activity increased by 500 percent from 1875 to 1975, while the earthquake activity has increased by 400 percent since 1973. Dr. Dmitriev says that by comparing the years 1963 to 1993, the overall number of natural disasters such as hurricanes, typhoons, mud slides, and tidal waves has increased by 410 percent.

According to the latest climate model calculations from the German High Performance Computing Centre for Climate and Earth System Research (as reported in *Science Daily* on October 2, 2005), scientists at the Max Planck Institute for Meteorology in Hamburg state that over the next century the climate will change more quickly than it has any time in recent history. The global temperature could rise by up to four degrees by the end of the century.

This rise in temperature could cause the average sea level to rise by as many as 30 centimeters. Under certain conditions, the arctic sea ice could completely melt. In Europe, summers will be drier and warmer, affecting agriculture. The winters will become warmer and wetter. Another consequence of the heated atmosphere will be extreme events like heavy precipitation with floods.

Meanwhile, former Vice President of the United States, Al Gore, has been traveling around the world spreading the message that we must take responsibility for our actions. In Gore's book, *An Inconvenient Truth*, a testament to his love of our planet, he writes:

> "Many people still assume—mistakenly—that the Earth is so big that we humans cannot possibly have any major impact on the way our planet's ecological system operates. That assertion may have been true at one time, but it's not the case anymore. We have grown so numerous and our technologies have become so powerful that we are now capable of having a significant influence

> on many parts of the Earth's environment. The most vulnerable part of the Earth's ecological system is the atmosphere. It's vulnerable because it is so thin."

The pollution in the third-dimensional atmosphere is so extreme that it is difficult for the fourth-dimensional Elementals to clear the atmosphere. To make matters worse, many humans are allowing fear, anger, and sorrow to linger in their consciousness, which obliges their body Elementals to out-picture a reality filled with fear. On the other hand, if we can focus on love and peace, we can create a high-frequency love-energy wave that attracts, bonds, and unifies our personal body Elementals with Gaia and all her inhabitants. By choosing love and releasing fear, all humanity can work as ONE to heal the planet.

Gore reports that from 1 AD to 2006, the planet's population has increased from 250 million to 6.5 billion. It is projected that that by 2050, the population on planet Earth will be 9.1 billion. The damage that we humans have done to our planet is as extensive as the damage we have done to other humans. It is essential that we each awaken to our Multidimensional SELF, for our limited third-dimensional consciousness separates us from the truth of our planetary crisis and our innate ability to halt it. The miracle is that as we reunite with our true SELF, we automatically realize that our SELF encompasses Gaia, our planet, and *all* her inhabitants, human and non-human.

A WHALE'S TALE

Dear humans,

We, the whales, have come to speak with you, as we wish to work in partnership with you to protect and heal our planet, Gaia. Since you primarily live on the land, you are meant to serve as Keepers of the Land, while we cetaceans, who live only in the water, are meant to serve as Keepers of the Water. As you know, our weather is influenced not only by the factors of pollution and the resulting Greenhouse Effect, but also by the thoughts and emotions that are held in your consciousness.

The fourth-dimensional Elementals of your body are obliged to out-picture your thoughts and emotions. Your thoughts are out-pictured as a thought-form, the matrix for a possible reality. Then your out-pictured emotions adhere to that thought-form to create a fourth-dimensional form and/or a reality. Once your thoughts and emotions are sent out into Gaia's environment, the fourth-dimensional planetary Elementals work to out-picture that reality in the third-dimensional world.

If your thoughts are of unity and peace, you will create a high-frequency, loving reality which can be lowered into the third dimension by the grounding force of your loving emotions. However, if your thoughts are of conflict and war, you create a very low-frequency thought-form which will be lowered into the third dimension by the emotions of fear and anger. Often your thoughts and emotions are in conflict, in that your thoughts want to have peace and unity, but your emotions are ruled by fear and anger. In this case, the matrix of love and peace is of too high a vibration for the low-frequency fear and anger to adhere to the matrix, and the thought-form remains only fourth-dimensional.

In the same manner that pollutants cloud the atmosphere, negative thoughts and fearful emotions cloud your consciousness. Each individual cloudy consciousness contributes fear to the collective consciousness. When the population of the planet was small, greenhouse gases were not a problem. However, with our greatly increased population, there are more cars, more factories, and more pollutants. In the same manner, there are more people and there is more fear to cloud the collective consciousness.

We, the cetaceans, also have fear and anger. Day by day we see our ocean world dying more and more. We know that you are seeing your landed area suffering the same fate. Our dear planet Gaia is going through the narrows now, which means that she is finding the place in-between the polarities of the third dimension, in-between the good and evil, in-between love and fear, and in-between the reality that she has been and the reality that she is becoming.

We the whales, who are the guardians of Earth's water, and you the humans, who are the guardians of the land, have also begun our journey of in-between. This is partially why in-between the land and water has suffered such damage. The scientific reasons for the weather extremes are, of course, also correct. However, the scientists are only speaking from the third-dimensional perspective. We are asking you to take a moment to look at this process from a multidimensional perspective.

While trying not to sound arrogant, we must say that our fear is not as strong, nor as toxic, as the fear of humanity. We believe that this is largely because we *know* that we can trust our own. Like every other member of this planet, we have endured humanity's many torments and violations of rights. But for the most part, we have always felt safe with our own species. We believe that it is this lack of safety with your own kind that has created the great fears and angers of humanity.

We will not tell you that the times ahead will be easy, although there are many ways to make them easier.

One of these ways is to find co-operation with the species of our dear Mother Gaia's land and water. All the kingdoms—Earth, mineral, plant, animal, and even the Kingdom of Faerie in the fourth dimension—are on the verge of great transformation. Hence, it is vital that we all work in unity and mutual respect to assist each other in this process. Humanity, in its great journey from tribal, group consciousness to the extreme of today's individual consciousness, has done great damage to itself and to the other kingdoms. We plead now not just for ourselves, but also for the rest of the inhabitants of Earth that you humans find a way to rise above your fear and conflict to live in love.

In this very moment, the conflict between the polarities of good/evil, love/fear, life/death, and land/water rages on. We implore you, dear Guardians of the Land, to find the balance, the center point, the place in-between these polarities. It is from this center point that you ride the wave of unconditional love into the detached compassion of your Multidimensional SELF. In this manner, you can calm your emotions of fear, anger, and sorrow, which combined with your destructive thoughts and accusations, will create greater and greater weather extremes. Once your emotions are calmed and you have returned to your natural state of love and compassion, your thoughts can be constructive and positive.

Remember, dear humans, *you* are the weather. *You* are the reality that you have created. We, the whales, mourn the loss of humans who have died, as well as the land that has been wounded, due to the many clashes between land and sea. Do you morn the loss of our pure waters and our many water inhabitants who have died as well? Can we learn to cooperate, land and water, thoughts and emotions, humans and animals? The animal and plant kingdoms are transforming, just as are many humans. The domination of humanity must now transform into the cooperation of humanity with all the other species of Gaia's body. Of course, humanity must also learn to cooperate with humanity.

We, the cetaceans, well know the difference between the humans who have sought to murder us and the humans who have sought to protect us. What we are saying now is that you also need our protection. We are highly evolved beings, just as you are. In fact, we have been on this planet millennia longer than humanity. For the good of all, including the good of the planet, we ask that you join forces with us. If we, the most evolved beings on Earth, could work together, imagine how much easier we could transform our planet from a reality of fear and war to a planet of peace and love.

This inter-species cooperation, however, must begin with the cooperation of your thoughts and emotions. We understand how difficult it must be for many of you humans to have compassion for the members of your species who still live by greed, selfishness, and power over others. We, too, have suffered greatly at their hands. The experiment of third-dimensional humanity has been a victory, as well as a mistake. The higher SELVES of both our species look upon this adventure of life on the third dimension with mixed reviews. Much was learned, yet much was lost.

It is time now for all of us to find the center point in-between learning and losing to discover the neutral point of detached compassion. Detached compassion is neutral because in it, you are not attached to any given outcome. Instead, you realize that everyone must learn and grow in his or her own manner. When you are detached from the fear and anger of your ego/self, you will be able to access the unconditional love and detached compassion of your Multidimensional Soul/SELF.

To make this shift in you consciousness, you must monitor your thoughts and release all judgment and negativity. Constantly listen to the inner voice of your Soul/SELF to regain and maintain the mental state of detached compassion. Continuously be aware of your emotions so that you can release fear, anger, and sorrow to find the center point of love.

Gaia and *all* of her inhabitants are going through the narrows in an effort to find the in-between, the center path. You, dear humans, are like mountain climbers climbing between two huge rocks. In order to ascend, you must reach up to find a strong point to which you can attach your safety cord. This point of strength is not only above, it is also in-between the extremes of polarities, as well as in-between the reality that we are leaving and the reality that we are becoming.

Not all humans have awakened to their responsibility as Guardians of the Land, and not all cetaceans have awakened to their responsibility as Guardians of the Water. Because of this, it is up to those of us who have awakened to carry the responsibility for all of our species. The few have always led the many, but the many must be willing to follow. What is important in this instance is that the leading must be with love and the following must be of free will.

Where we are going can only be traveled with unconditional love and detached compassion, as well as the unity of purpose attained only by expanding our individual consciousness to planetary consciousness. We who are awakened must embrace the responsibility that accompanies our power within to be the safe point to which others can attach their safety cord. In this manner, we can set a shining example for others.

Dear humans, imagine what a celebration it will be when we, the Guardians of the Water, join in cooperation and unconditional love with you, the Guardians of the Land. In this joining, we can more easily find and travel the center path into our new Earth of peace and love. We, the cetaceans, the Guardians of the Water, wish to join you in this celebration.

The Whales

MESSAGE FROM SOUL/SELF

We, all the aspects of your Multidimensional Soul/SELF, wish to remind you that we are always with you. And since you are about to implant a spark of our multidimensional essence, along with our Divine Ideal, into your physical body, we will soon be *in* you!

Take a moment as you go about your busy day to feel our great presence as the guiding force that leads you into the center current, which is the place in-between. Once in that current you can relax into the *flow* and enjoy the *show*. Learn to enjoy this show, for everything in your show is *you*.

You are the stage, the set, the director, the writer, and all the actors. Simultaneously, you are the planet, the earth, the air, the fire, and the water. You are also all the dimensions of reality: the atoms, the DNA, the sub-atomic world, the insects, the plants, the birds, the mammals, and the humans.

You are all of this for *you* are a window, a window into reality. The show you see through your window is interactive, and whether or not you are conscious of it, each time you have a thought or an emotion, it is instantly projected through your window and into your show. Hence, your window is the stage upon which you create the play about your reality. *You* create the set, you direct the play, you write the script and you act *all* the parts.

If you don't like the set—CHANGE IT.
If you don't like the direction—CHANGE IT.
If you don't like the script—CHANGE IT.
If you don't like the acting—CHANGE IT.

How do you make all these changes?
Basically, you change *you*.
And how do you do that?

You become *me*, Your Multidimensional SELF
Remember,
that which is impossible for your ego
is simple for your Soul!

As, chakra by chakra, you integrate *me* into your physical body, you will find it increasingly natural to surrender to my inner guidance and direction. In order to integrate my great multidimensional essence into your/our grounded form, you will need to recalibrate your chakras, so that they can accept my higher frequency light. Listen for my call and remember me always for

I am your SELF.

RECALIBRATING THE CHAKRAS

Before our physical earth vessel can accept the higher frequency of even a spark of our Multidimensional SELF and the thought-form of our Divine Ideal, our chakras will need to be recalibrated. This adjustment will be facilitated by our rising kundalini. The recalibration of our chakras will allow us to slowly and safely integrate our Multidimensional Soul/SELF into our third-dimensional body and manifest our Divine Ideal on the physical plane.

As the force of kundalini rises up into each chakra, it will initiate a centrifugal force that will greatly increase each chakra's rotation. In this manner, each chakra will spin off the effluvia of our third-dimensional history. This process will clear our physical body of low-frequency toxins, infections, habits, and behaviors that are specific to each chakra.

Once a chakra is re-calibrated by the higher light of kundalini, it can more easily accept the spark of our fifth-dimensional Soul/SELF and Divine Ideal. Furthermore, the illusion of polarities of the third dimension will gradually blur into the oneness, expanding our consciousness from that of our ego/self to that of our Soul/SELF. Hence, our perceptions will expand from individual consciousness to group consciousness to collective consciousness to planetary consciousness to galactic consciousness.

However, our consciousness does not rise; it expands into the higher and lower dimensions. The higher we go into infinite spirit, the deeper we go into finite matter, even down to a sub-atomic level. Through expanding our consciousness, we greatly enhance our power of creativity, awaken our extra-sensory abilities, and merge with our planet. We will address the chakras in three different categories: the unconscious, the conscious, and the superconscious.

CHAKRAS OF OUR UNCONSCIOUS MIND

The unconscious represents our past history, thoughts, emotions, and behaviors that arise from our hidden, unconscious mind. In this category are the first or root chakra, the second or navel chakra, and the third or solar plexus chakra. These three chakras serve to align us with and connect us to our multidimensional planet Earth.

As kundalini rises into the chakras of our unconscious reality, memories, behaviors, innate extrasensory abilities, and dark secrets will be revealed. As we balance, clear, and heal each of these chakras, our unconscious mind will become an easily accessible library, rather than the forgotten vault archived in our lowest storage basement. This important information will assist us in healing our past and releasing any areas of life in which we are still a dependent victim.

As polarities blend in these chakras, we will release our unconscious creations and expand our consciousness from individual consciousness to collective consciousness. As we connect with the collective consciousness of others who are awakening, we will find the support to ground our multidimensional Soul/SELF into the ego/self of our physical body. With our SELF grounded in our personal and planetary body, we can plant our Divine Ideal and allow it to gestate in preparation for manifestation.

CHAKRAS OF OUR CONSCIOUS MIND

Our conscious mind represents our present reality and the thoughts, emotions, and behaviors that create and maintain that reality. In this category are the fourth or heart chakra and the fifth or throat chakra. As kundalini rises into these chakras, we can accept and express love in an open and creative manner. The inner confidence derived from this love will expand our independence to dependability. In this manner we will consciously create our reality in partnership with others and the planet to expand our collective consciousness to planetary consciousness. As polarities blend in these chakras, our expanded love and creativity will allow us to create form for our Divine Ideal, as well as expand our latent, extrasensory abilities.

CHAKRAS OF OUR SUPERCONSCIOUS SELF

Our superconscious mind represents our Multidimensional Soul/SELF, who is beyond limitation and separation. In this category are the sixth or brow chakra and the seventh or crown chakra. These two chakras serve to align, connect, download, and become ONE with our Multidimensional Soul/SELF, so that our Soul can become the captain of our Earth vessel.

As kundalini rises into these chakras, the sixth and seventh chakras will merge to open our third eye. With our third eye opened, we more readily become the masters of energy, which is our birthright. As polarities blend in these chakras, we will move from being dependable to being compassionate, and our awareness will expand from planetary consciousness to galactic consciousness. The universe will be much smaller then, as our consciousness will no longer be separated from it.

GREETINGS FROM GAIA

RECALIBRATING THE CHAKRAS

Dear Guardians of my Land,

I wish to thank the dear whales for their loving message to you, my Guardians of the Land. I am joyously looking forward to the emergence of planetary consciousness, in which all the inhabitants of my Earth commune with each other and with me. Planetary consciousness is vital for the fulfillment of my Divine Ideal to make Earth a planet of peace and love, as it is the sum total of our planetary thoughts, emotions, and intentions which create our planetary reality.

When you recalibrate your chakras to accept your Multidimensional SELF and your Divine Ideal, your consciousness will gradually become multidimensional, and you will be able to perceive reality through many different perspectives within the same moment of the *now*. At that time, consciousness will no longer just mean awareness. Consciousness will also mean reality. In other words, you will choose your reality by placing your consciousness, or your focus of intention, on a specific point of view.

CHOOSING REALITY

Take a moment now to look around your external world. How many thousands of realities could you perceive if you changed your point of view? For example, take a moment to imagine that you are viewing reality from the lower-dimensional perspective of a rock. Now imagine perceiving reality through the consciousness of an insect and the plant upon which it sits. What about a bird, a cat, a lion, a whale? How do you imagine that they perceive reality?

Now look at reality through the many different viewpoints of humanity. See life from the viewpoint of a beggar, a millionaire, a laborer, a genius, a schizophrenic, and a guru. Use your imagination to see life through the vantage point of the fourth dimension and beyond. For example, imagine reality from the perspective of a Faerie, an Elemental, a Deva, an Ascended Master, an Angel, and an Elohim.

As you recalibrate your chakras, you will release the limitation of living reality. Instead, you will be choosing reality. The entire multidimensional universe is yours. All you need do is *choose* your point of perception. The question is not how many realities there are, as there are more than you can count. Reality is not a static or absolute. Reality is a viewpoint, a perception, as seen through the eyes of the beholder.

Hence, the question is, which reality do you wish to behold? And which reality do you wish to *be*? Fortunately, as a multidimensional being you will no longer need to limit yourself to just one reality.

EXPANDING YOUR SENSE OF SELF

As you recalibrate your chakras, your sense of self will greatly expand. You will no longer be just your ego/self; you will also be your Multidimensional Soul/SELF and your Divine Ideal, which is the *doing* of your *being*. The question will no longer be, what is reality? Instead, it will be, how many realities can you experience at once without becoming overwhelmed?

To avoid feeling overwhelmed, relax in meditation, fun, and/or creativity to release the singular focus of Beta brainwaves and move into the expanded focus of Alpha brainwaves. Also begin to train your thinking to focus on unity with all life and to train your emotions to focus on the feeling of love.

The recalibration of your chakras and the rising kundalini will allow your Soul/SELF to become the captain of your earth vessel. Your ego/self will then be re-assigned as the Director of Mundane Life. As your Soul ushers in multidimensional consciousness, your ego will keep you operational in your everyday life. To ease this transition, remember to stay in connection with your inner SELF. Take long, slow, deep breaths to clear your mind so that you can feel the inner love of your Soul/SELF.

While you are undergoing the process of changing operating systems from ego/self to Soul/SELF, you will likely experience some disruptions in your daily life. It may feel as though you are being barred from stepping forward into your new reality. In fact, this may be true, as your ego may be waging its final battle to maintain its attachment to the third-dimensional structure of limitation and separation. Although your Soul encourages you to look just beyond the veils of illusion, your ego declines, as it feels safer within the habitual blankets of illusion and denial.

Because of this inner conflict, simple things that once seemed easy may cause you problems. Your Soul says, "Relax, I can handle this in a new, more efficient manner," while your ego simultaneously says, "Do it the way you always have, as you know that works. Besides, it is much easier to stay the same than it is to change." It is in these moments of confusion that you stand at the crossroads of familiarity or change. However, before you make your decision, remember that what is difficult for your ego is simple for your Soul. Over time, you will make your decisions, and it is these choices that will direct your process of transformation. Most of all, know that *you* are *always* in control. The question is, which *you* is in control?

To assist you in choosing Soul:
BELIEVE in unity,
KNOW love, and
RELEASE judgment.

In this manner, you will be allowing your Soul/SELF to correct the situation that appears to be outside of you. The truth is, *you* are creating the outer battle by projecting your inner confusion into your external reality. *Let go* of these battles, both inner and outer, and surrender to Soul. From the perspective of your new captain, your solutions will be revealed and the problem will be solved. While your ego is lost in the dense forest of life, your Soul has the viewpoint of a control tower on the highest mountain peak.

The higher dimensions are aware of the lower dimensions, but the lower dimensions can only imagine the higher dimensions. Just as you can clearly see a rock, but the rock does not see you, your Soul can see you, even if you cannot see it. It is this connection to your Soul/SELF that will carry you through your transition. Once you have fully integrated the higher dimensional light into your earth vessel, you will be able to perceive reality through the eyes of your Soul. Then, reality will not be something that happens to you. Instead, reality will be something that you are constantly creating.

You are now ready to begin the recalibration and integration of your chakras, beginning with your root chakra. I will return soon, as I have never left. How could I? *I am* the Planet
Gaia

SECTION FOUR

When we look into the *face* of SELF
we see all that stands in the way
of *being* SELF.

CHAPTER TWELVE

UNCONSCIOUS CREATION
Re-Creating the Past Until it is Healed

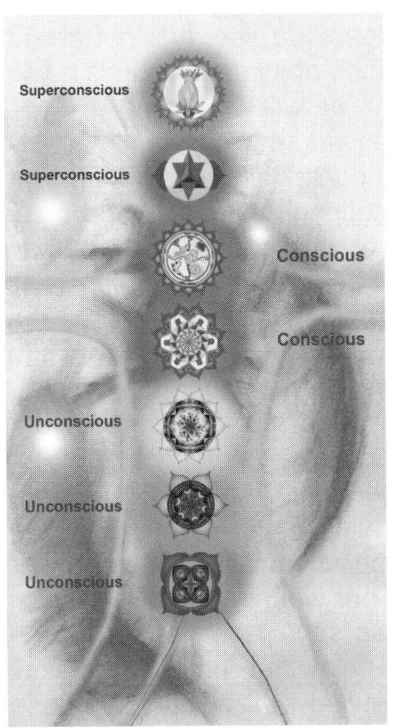

The first three chakras at the base of the spine, the navel, and the solar plexus rule areas of our life that are often under the direction of our unconscious mind.

Furthermore, these three chakras represent our first, second, and fourth dimensional bodies, of which we are usually unconscious. Hence, these chakras are known as the chakras of the unconscious.

As we allow the spark of our Multidimensional SELF and the seed of our Divine Ideal to enter into these first three chakras, the low-frequency portion of our history is spun-off to reveal the many unconscious obstacles obstructing our forward motion. Although this may be an uncomfortable experience at times, it does allow us the ability to heal, balance, and release these archived memories, emotions, and thoughts so that they no longer act as the inner saboteur who constantly thwarts our progress.

Like dirty dishes in the sink, these obstacles have waited for us to wash them so that we can have a clean plate upon which to create our life. Fortunately, the clearing, balancing, and healing of these chakras reveals many hidden talents and abilities that have been lost in the process of growing up in a third-dimensional, polarized reality where fear abounds and love is far too often conditional. These latent abilities are the tools we will use to create our new life.

THE WOUNDED EGO

Our wounded ego is the part of us that has created these obstacles that constantly thwart our efforts to reveal our true SELF. Our wounded ego restricts us, not as a punishment, but as a protection. This protection is created by the wounded part of us who cannot take the risk of further injury from others. Our wounded ego sees what it expects to see. It is not aware that it is actually projecting out images of its past wounds again and again in the hopes that this time we will get it right.

However, we must be kind toward this part of us, for it is our thoughts and emotions that are continuing the problem. Our old issues have such a strong <u>emotional</u> charge around them that they are accompanied by the hopeless <u>thinking</u> that "I can never change this part of me." Therefore, our <u>intention</u> is to "just put up with it." "Will you ever get this right?" says the wounded ego, as it unknowingly projects the "problem" out into our external world *again*. In this manner, the pattern continues.

If we can heal the inner wound that first created our protective behavior, we can rise above the perspective of our wounded ego and into the higher perspective of our Soul/SELF. Then, when the old issue arises again, we can consciously <u>feel</u> the emotional charge and send the unconditional love of our Soul/SELF to heal this memory of our wounded ego/self. From the perspective of our Soul we can say, "Here is that *lesson* (not the problem) again. However, I am patient with my grounding point (ego/self), for I *know* how difficult life can be in the third dimension."

Our <u>thoughts</u> can then be ones of comfort, love, and patience, which is exactly what our wounded ego needs. With these thoughts and emotions, we can more easily correct our <u>intention</u> to: "I am ready to release this problem." In this way, we see our problems as lessons that we have enough control over that we can, actually, release them. As soon as a problem is seen as a lesson, it becomes a teacher rather than an enemy.

The secret is that once our internal wounded ego is healed by the unconditional love, acceptance, and forgiveness of our integrated Soul/SELF, the external dramas greatly diminish. It is through the integrating of our Multidimensional Soul/SELF into our chakras that the voice of our SELF becomes louder than the voice of our wounded ego, and we can hear our Soul's voice reminding us: "I AM the teacher who will assist you with your lessons."

CREATING REALITY

Our wounded ego is especially active in the chakras of our unconscious: chakras one, two, and three. Each of these three will express our wounded ego in a different manner and create reality according to a different vision. Whether we know it or not, we are constantly creating our reality by the perceptions to which we choose to attend, the thoughts we allow to live in our consciousness and the emotions we permit to settle into our bodies. Unfortunately, while we are unconscious, we are not aware that we are choosing, allowing, and permitting. The first three chakras of our unconscious are the unconscious creators of our reality, in which our repressed past dictates our present.

Life is a pass/fail system, in which we repeat the same issues, or classes, over and over until we get them right, passing that class. In other words, in order to create a new present, we need to heal our past. Because of this, until the first three chakras are recalibrated to accept the higher light of our Multidimensional Soul/SELF and Divine Ideal, our unconscious, wounded ego is the creator of our reality. Actually, our wounded ego is our re-creator, as our ability to choose a new experience is thwarted until we are able to successfully heal and release our past.

For example, we may have had a domineering parent who diminished our personal power and constantly told us that we were not good enough. Because we were children, we were unable to disagree with our parents and even began to believe them. The re-do, in which we do the same thing over and over again until we get it right, returns again in adulthood. We might, for instance, unconsciously choose a boss or a spouse who is very critical and constantly tells us we are not good enough.

We might judge ourselves and say, "Wasn't it enough to grow up with that treatment? Why would I want to continue it into my adulthood?" The answer is that as children we were unable to confront our parents. Therefore, as adults we have re-enacted the same scenario so that, *this time* we can stand up for ourselves and regain the innate power that was lost in our childhood.

Each of the first three chakras represents how our unconscious mind has been creating our life. As our SELF and our Divine Ideal enter these chakras, a true healing can commence to free us from false beliefs and limitations. In this manner, our Multidimensional Soul/SELF can release old patterns so that we can perceive, create and *be* our Divine Ideal.

A MESSAGE ABOUT LOVE

Our reality is based on the resonance, vibration, and frequencies of light, which create a matrix. This matrix is then given form when it is filled with the corresponding resonance of sound. Light is consistent with our thoughts and sound is consistent with our emotions. Some creations begin with a thought, which awaits an emotion to fill it. On the other hand, some creations begin with an emotion, which seeks a matrix to give it form.

Since the signature frequency of love is multidimensional and embraces the ONE, the emotion of love creates an energy field which expands and unifies. On the other hand, the third- and lower fourth-dimensional emotion of fear repels and creates an energy field that constricts and separates. Love's lowest resonance is conditional love, which means that the emotion is incased in a matrix of fearful thought such as, "If I let my loved one go free, I will lose him or her." Only the lowest resonance of love, tainted and polluted with fear, will choose to unite with such a matrix.

However, since the third dimension is so filled with fear, too often the only love that can be given or received is this hybrid of fear/love, conditional love. Conditional love is limited to the physical plane and the Lower Astral Plane of the fourth dimension. There is also some conditional love in the Realm of Faerie, the next keynote of vibration up from the Lower Astral Plane. Since everything in Faerie can easily morph in and out of form, the fear/love that can be a lifelong trap in the physical world is more easily escaped in the Realm of Faerie.

In the ONE, love is not conditional or unconditional, as the concept of condition is unknown. Condition is not a part of that reality. In our polarized, third-dimensional world, though, love and fear are opposite polarities of the spectrum of unconditional love. While love projects the feeling that it is safe to unite and share, fear projects the feeling that there is danger, and we should run, hide, or prepare for battle. There is a great destructive power in conditional love, as the recipient of this energy field is constantly challenged to move towards love but, simultaneously, away from fear. As we have all experienced, conditional love creates a sticky web which can be very difficult to escape.

It is a sorry truth that the precious jewel of unconditional love is rare in the third dimension. Fortunately, as we integrate the higher light into our chakras, the memories and scar tissue of fear/love are spun-off by the rising force of kundalini. With the spin-off of these low-frequency emotions, our chakras can amplify their spin enough to accept the high-frequency emotion of unconditional love.

As we integrate our Multidimensional Soul/SELF into each chakra, we begin to feel unconditional love through the enhanced perceptions of our true SELF. Furthermore, the integration of our Divine Ideal into each chakra expands our avenue of expression for unconditional love and enhances our power of creativity and multidimensional communication.

ALIGNING OUR BODIES

When we clear, balance, and heal each chakra, we align them with each other, as well as with our fourth-dimensional bodies. This alignment can be likened to pearls on a string. Each chakra/fourth-dimensional body is a pearl and the center current of the fourth-dimensional River of Light is the string. The chakra/fourth-dimensional pearls, strung together with the current, permit a greater flow of unconditional love from the ONE to enter our physical body. When we choose to unite our pearls with Gaia's fourth-dimensional bodies, this enhanced flow of unconditional love enters our planetary body, as well.

This constant personal and planetary connection with the ONE encourages us to expect, perceive, and accept the unconditional love that continuously radiates from the higher octaves of the auras of all of Gaia's people, creatures, and places. All we need do to receive this gift is to calibrate our perceptual filter to filter in these high-frequency stimuli. Once accepted, we can integrate the unconditional love into all our bodily systems, as well as share it with our world by grounding it into the planet.

With the inflow of multidimensional stimuli, the third-dimensional illusions of separation begin to blur into a world which is connected by lower dimensional sub-atomic particles and higher dimensional waves of light. Once our multidimensional vision is activated, we no longer feel alone and isolated. With this ever-present feeling of unity, we feel safe enough to fully release fear and focus our conscious intention on love. In this manner, our thoughts can generate pure matrixes which we can fill with unconditional emotions to create a reality based on creativity, peace, and love.

The fourth-dimensional River of Light travels at the exact center point between the polarities of every third-dimensional spectrum. This center current, the fulcrum point, is the place of neutral charge where neither the negative emotional charge of conditional nor the positive emotional charge of unconditional exists. Within this current, there is no polarity and no imbalance. The positive/negative charge of extreme emotion is a consequence of third-dimensional polarities. When we live our lives in the flow of the center current, we fuse the opposite polarities into ONE, and the third-dimensional charge is neutralized. It is then that our consciousness can easily glide along the center current to keep the alignment between our multidimensional Earth and our Multidimensional SELF.

As we choose to connect our balanced and aligned personal fourth-dimensional bodies with Gaia's fourth-dimensional spheres, we pull Earth into the fulcrum point, as well. In this manner, each of us serves as a portal through which the multidimensional stimuli of the ONE can enter the planet. As we accept, integrate, and circulate the higher light through our personal body, we also accept, integrate, and circulate the higher light through our planetary body. Each of us then becomes a great highway of light to balance, heal, and enlighten all life.

THE HIGHWAY

I'm sending out my longing
To be what I can be
And opening up my heart's light
To see what I can see

I'm trying to become
That for which I long
To purify my heart and mind
And fill them full with song

My Soul feels far away
But its Light lives in me still
To lay its mark upon the earth
Would give me such a thrill

I know this Light inside me
Can extend up to my Soul
And communicate with Spirit
To help me with my goal

But, I fear that in my trying
The "work" will stop the flow
Instead, I wish to walk the path
I'm sure my Soul will show

I've decided to release now
The effort and the strife
And believe the light of Spirit
Will guide me through my life

As I create a highway
To my Soul and back to me
My Light can shine upon the earth
To set all Spirits free

CHAPTER THIRTEEN

GROUNDING OUR NEW REALITY

THE FIRST CHAKRA

We open our highway by grounding the spark of our Multidimensional SELF and the seed of our Divine Ideal into our first, or root, chakra. Our Divine Ideal is the perspective, form, and function of the reality we promised to create before we entered this lifetime. We ground our SELF and ideal with our focused, conscious intention, which has the ability to open the floodgates of prana, to direct our fourth-dimensional River of Light to flow into the base of our spinal cord at our root chakra. This flood of multidimensional light will likely awaken the sleeping serpent of our kundalini force, which will assist the light in carrying our SELF and ideal up our spine.

Once the amplified light has entered our first chakra and our kundalini has been awakened, the increased rotation of the chakra will spin off the old darkness in preparation for more light. We will then need to recalibrate each chakra so that it can accept and integrate the higher light, which will alter the area of our body and consciousness which that chakra rules. The process of releasing darkness, recalibration, and integration will be consistent with every chakra from the first to the seventh.

The lesson of the first chakra is to live fully in our bodies and send our roots deep into Gaia, as we allow her to share her vast wisdom and love with us. This sharing initiates the partnership between person and planet that was intended before we were born. It may sound unusual to say "live fully in our bodies," but we often place our consciousness outside of our body, as well as outside of our planet.

We often get so pulled into what we are doing that we forget to stay centered in who we are being. The root chakra reminds us to ground our energy in the Earth and to align our consciousness with our third-dimensional planet, our fourth-dimensional bodies and our Multidimensional SELF, which always resonates to the fifth dimension and beyond.

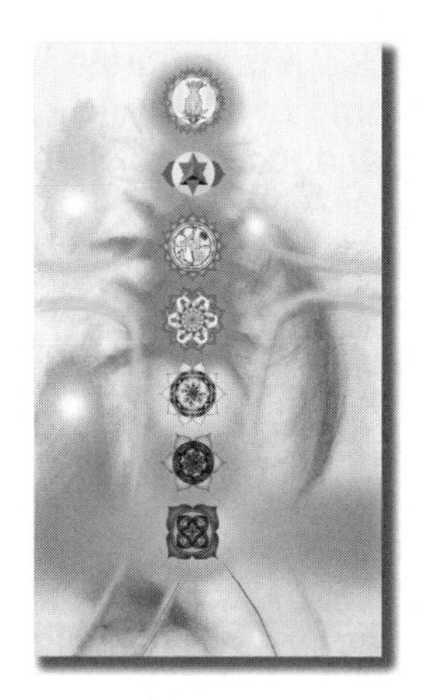

LOCATION: The first chakra is located at the base of the spine.

PETALS: This chakra rules the lowest vibration of our body and has the slowest wavelength. It has four spokes or petals. Four is the number of the square and foundations. The square is related to being honest or giving a "square deal," to the four energies of earth—earth, air, fire, and water—and to the four directions. Four walls, four legs, or four wheels represent a strong foundation.

NOTE and MANTRA: The note for this chakra is C and the mantra is "lam" or "e" as in red. Chanting these mantras in the key of D while focusing our attention on this area of our body can enable us to more consciously access the first chakra.

COLOR: The color for this chakra is red, which is the lowest frequency of a human's visible light spectrum. Red is the color of anger and/or vitality.

RULES: The first chakra rules our *physical* energies. Also known as the root chakra, it governs our vigor, heredity, survival, security, passion, money, job, and home. This chakra aids us in our everyday survival.

SENSE: The sense of smell is related to this chakra. Our sense of smell is our most primitive sense and is the first sense that awakens upon our physical birth. The receptors for smell are located at the base of our brain and feed directly into our limbic system, which is the area of memory and emotion. Therefore, aromas can immediately access emotional memories stored in our unconscious.

ASTROLOGICAL SIGN: The astrological sign associated with the root chakra is Taurus. The symbol for Taurus is the bull. Like our root chakra, the bull is a symbol of masculine power and fertility. The bull roots in the earth with his front hooves and lowers his nostrils toward the ground to warn any who would threaten his herd. Many cows are in the herd, but only the strongest bull will be able to preserve the genetic integrity of the group.

The first chakra is actually the basis of both our masculine and feminine energy. It represents our masculine will and male sexual organs as well as the feminine energy of the goddess Kundalini. Therefore, a man can learn to integrate his feminine power and a woman can learn to integrate her masculine power through the clearing and opening of this chakra.

ELEMENT: Earth is the element associated with the first chakra and the mineral kingdom is the top of that hierarchy. Crystals have been prized by humankind for eons and have also been used in esoteric healing. Since this chakra rules our first-dimensional self that is unable to reflect upon itself, perceptions from our root chakra are usually unconscious. This first-dimensional portion of us can only be aware of a hive or species consciousness.

Even though the first chakra has many masculine qualities, it is also the seat of the goddess Kundalini and is, therefore, often associated with our relationship with our mothers and with Mother Earth. Our relationships with our mother set up our attitude toward home, security, and money. If we are cut off from our roots, we feel cut off from the earth as well.

CONSCIOUSNESS: The first chakra rules our survival consciousness and represents our deepest unconscious and most primitive self. This chakra represents the reptilian portion of our brain, which is our brainstem, our center for life support. The brainstem and the area immediately above it are called the reptilian brain because all creatures from reptiles to humans possess this area. For reptiles, this area is their entire brain, but for humans it is the base, or stem, of their brain.

PERSONAL TIMELINE: The first chakra represents birth to two years of age. This is the time before we have completed our process of individuation and still perceive ourselves as a part of our parents. This chakra represents our struggle to come to terms with our physical life and physical body. Our multidimensional spirit is new to the limitations and separation of our new third-dimensional reality, and we are struggling to learn how to control our physical earth vessel. Fortunately, we naturally travel into the higher dimensions at this age and can return home whenever we are desperately in need of comfort and understanding.

SOCIAL TIMELINE: Anthropologically, the first chakra represents the time when humankind was cave dwellers. At that time in our civilization, we lived from day to day. To assist in our struggle for survival, we worshiped animals and other aspects of our physical environment.

ENDOCRINE GLAND: Each chakra feeds prana into a different endocrine gland. Just as we have seven chakras, we have seven endocrine glands. Both the chakras and the endocrine glands are located along the spinal cord. The endocrine glands manufacture hormones and supply them to the bloodstream. These glands are called "ductless" because there is not a duct to any specific part of the body. Instead, hormones are released into the bloodstream where they are carried by the blood to every organ and tissue to exert their influence on all functions of the physical body.

Each gland is internally related to the other glands and also works closely with the nervous and circulatory system. In order for the organs of the body to work efficiently, the blood must contain certain chemicals. Many of these chemicals are secreted by the endocrine glands, and this secretion is vital for the health of the entire system. Our bodies can become diseased if there are too many or too few hormones.

The endocrine gland for the first chakra is the two adrenal glands, located one on top of each of the two kidneys. The adrenal glands are the body's call to battle. When adrenaline is released into the system, our perceptions become clearer, we have added vigor, and we feel more courageous.

The release of adrenaline activates the fight or flight syndrome, which prepares us to either fight or take flight and is vital for the survival of every species. For this reason, the first chakra is the survival chakra. Release of adrenaline and activation of fight or flight can be brought on by either real or imagined danger. Therefore, our emotions can activate a release of adrenaline when we feel extreme fear or even chronic anxiety.

NERVE PLEXUS: The first chakra is located near the sacral plexus. The sacral plexus is the nerve center that rules the skeleton, legs, feet, elimination system, male reproductive organs, and the prostate. If there is a problem with the leg or foot on the right, masculine, side of the body it can indicate issues of trust in one's will. If there is a problem with the leg or foot on the left, feminine, side then it can indicate issues with trust of one's emotional life.

CLEAR: When the first chakra is clear we feel secure, grounded, and stable. We can use good common sense to balance our finances as well as our everyday responsibilities and still initiate new activities and interest. Our eliminatory system functions well, neural activity in our legs and feet is healthy, and our ability to initiate sexual encounters is comfortable and natural. Our root chakra is the home of the sleeping serpent, our kundalini. When this chakra is clear and balanced the goddess Kundalini, or Shakti, can awaken and begin her gradual rise towards reunion with Lord Shiva.

UNCLEAR: When the first chakra is unclear, we feel insecure and fearful. We can also become absent-minded because we are ungrounded. We may also have a difficult time with our finances and day-to-day necessities. Whatever security we derive from material things can become threatened. We may also have problems with our home, which is our base of operations in physical life. We can become self-indulgent and self-centered and suffer from depression and grief. We may suffer from hemorrhoids, constipation, sciatica, or prostate problems.

All of the above emotional, behavioral, and physical health issues have to do with the ability to let go. We cannot let go of our sadness, let go of material sources of comfort when finances require, or even let go of the waste material of our bodies. If we cannot release what is holding us back, we cannot move forward. Difficulties with our sciatic nerve and problems with our legs and feet indicate this dynamic. Prostate problems can arise from frustrated sexual or creative drives.

EARTH'S CHAKRA: Just as the first chakra represents our physical body, the Earth's first chakra represents Gaia's physical body. The planetary first chakra is located at Mt. Sinai in the Middle East. Lady Gaia is allowing her kundalini to rise to meet her divine mate. It is *time* now that we hear her call. Hence, this area of the planet is the center of great unrest.

DIMENSIONS: The first chakra rules our first- and second-dimensional selves. Our first-dimensional self represents the genetic coding, cells, and minerals of our bodies. It also represents our most primitive animal self, which is represented by the fight or flight response that serves to assure the survival of the species. The root chakra also rules the male sex glands and the testosterone that they secrete. This testosterone drives the males in our society, and the male polarity of our psyche, to perpetuate and protect humanity.

BECOMING ONE

We stand at the end
To see the beginning
And dream of an Earth
Where ALL life is winning

No one is hungry
And no one is poor
No one is greedy
And no one wants more

We dream of an Earth
Where the land and the sea
Become ONE with people,
Like you and like me

On this Earth we are ONE
With the rocks and the trees
And commune with all nature
Through the land and the breeze

We open our senses
To dear Mother Earth
Who offers a platform
Where we can know birth

This birth gives us form,
A world filled with mystery
And offers a theater
Where we create history

But history is ending
The future is NOW
We know we're a planet
But don't know quite how

Something inside us
Remembers a deal
We made long ago
Before we were "real"

We didn't have form as
We soared through the sky
But wanted a body
And didn't know why

An urge deep inside us
Called from our Being
For a "place" that had "time"
For hearing and seeing

A place we could learn
A time we could grow
And share our true Spirit
With "others" we'd know

The concept of "others"
Was new to our "ONE"
We'd not known a planet
Or even a sun

Together with Gaia,
The heart of us all,
We entered a form
And began our great fall

We fell from the heavens
And landed right here
To remember our love
And learn about fear

We've learned all we need
And feel quite complete,
Our memories are gathered,
Some bitter, some sweet

Together we journey
Deep—deep inside
Where only the TRUTH lives
With no place to hide

We know that this journey
That starts will NOT end
And that is the message
That we will all send

Awaken, dear Spirits,
Adventure is here
We can ALL live in Love
And release ALL our Fear

If we open our hearts
And let the TRUTH in
That's all we need do
So it can begin

And what will begin
We are not quite sure
But FEEL it is Loving
And KNOW it is Pure

For with our hearts open
Our “feeling” and “knowing”
Projects the reality
Our Being is showing

“Our” Beings are many
For together we stand
The people, the creatures,
The sea and the land

For NOW, we remember,
We chose to come here
To call in our Soul/SELF
Who resides beyond fear

This true SELF we ground
Into the Great Mother
To return to the ONE
Where there is NO “other”

Then people and planet
Will all Become ONE
As TOGETHER our Light
Will outshine the Sun

BECOMING ONE WITH SELF

Our process of becoming ONE begins as we integrate our Multidimensional SELF and its Divine Ideal into our earth vessel, one chakra at a time. Our chakras are the portals through which the fourth-dimensional River of Light enters our etheric, and then our physical, body. We have aligned our Multidimensional SELF and its Divine Ideal with each of our fourth-dimensional personal and planetary bodies, as well as with planet Earth. Our Multidimensional SELF and Divine Ideal are now in our Etheric Body, awaiting entry into our third-dimensional reality. This entry point is our first, or root, chakra.

As our multidimensional light floods into our physical earth vessel, the flame of kundalini has ignited to begin the process of transformation of our physical earth vessel. In order for our Multidimensional SELF to be grounded in our earth vessel, the resonance of the body will need to expand so that it can tolerate the extremely high and low frequencies of our Multidimensional Soul/SELF. The root chakra is vital for our process, as we must become, and remain, fully grounded. In this manner, the *spirit* of the River of Light can enter the *matter* of our physical form so that we may fully live *in* our body.

It may sound unusual to say "fully live *in* our body," but many times we (including our essence and our consciousness) are *not* grounded in our bodies. This lack of grounding is usually because of fear. Fear forces our attention away from the process of living from our SELF and places it instead upon the real or imagined enemy. As we become accustomed to recognizing the many faces of fear, we can release it and choose love.

Our first chakra serves to create our reality from the hidden depths of our unconscious mind. Therefore, when we desperately want one thing and get another, our unconscious intention is what has won the struggle for manifestation. The unconsciousness of our root chakra chooses to calibrate its attention on what is necessary for us to survive, what we have the energy to do, and what we are willing to fight for.

Hence, we may wish to create a certain reality that the first chakra may know is not best for our survival. In this case, we may find that we don't have the energy to fulfill that creation, nor are we willing to fight for it. Our conscious self may become disappointed and disillusioned that we are unsuccessful in our creation, when actually we have created the very reality that our unconscious has chosen. Our unconscious root chakra is dedicated to creating strong foundations for our future creations, but all creations are based on the premise that they are what is best for our survival.

Our root chakra represents our most primitive self, as well as our personal evolution from being dependent on others for survival to living independently with a strong individual consciousness. Our primitive self functions largely from Alpha brainwaves and is instinctively connected to the land at all times. In order to learn independence in our modern world, the Beta brainwaves of left-brain, logical, analytical thinking must be activated. Unfortunately, as we activate our Beta brainwaves, we often forget the innate instincts of our Alpha brainwave consciousness. As our consciousness expands, however, our innate, latent, expanded perceptions return.

FIRST CHAKRA MEDITATION

To prepare for the first chakra meditation, you may want to find a comfortable place to sit, either on the ground or with your feet on the ground, as this first chakra's main focus is grounding.

The first chakra's element is earth, so you may wish to find a crystal or a rock to use as a focal point for this meditation. The sense of smell is ruled by the first chakra, so you may wish to light incense or scented candles and/or focus on environmental aromas.

To begin the meditation, align your third-dimensional body with your fourth-dimensional bodies, as well as with the bodies of Gaia:

Align the base of your spine—*first chakra*—with your
Etheric Body and Gaia's hydrosphere
and your physical body and Gaia's lithosphere.

Align your navel—*second chakra*—with your
Emotional Body and Gaia's biosphere.

Align your solar plexus—*third chakra*—with your
Mental Body and Gaia's troposphere.

Align your heart—*fourth chakra*—with your
Guardian Angel/divine child and Gaia's stratosphere.

Align your throat—*fifth chakra*—with your
Causal Body and Gaia's mesosphere.

Align your brow—*sixth chakra*—with your
I AM Presence and Gaia's ionosphere.

Align your crown—*seventh chakra*—with your
Multidimensional SELF and Gaia's exosphere.

Breathe the color *red* into the base of your spine . . . .
Visualize yourself in your favorite place in nature . . . .

<u>Now you can begin to ground your personal body into Gaia.</u>
Feel the loving energy of the Earth as it enters the base of your spine. In turn, send your love down, deep into the Earth. Feel your energetic "tail" from the base of your spine connecting with the Earth and your energetic "roots" entering the earth from the bottoms of your feet.

Follow your roots down into the core of Mother Earth's lithosphere, or land, and into the Mineral Kingdom. Experience yourself as the matrix within the crystal of the planet. All around you are consistent, repetitive geometric patterns, which lead you deeper and deeper into the Earth. Deep inside Earth's core now, you see and feel Gaia's crystal heart, pulsing the heartbeat of the planet.

Your increased instincts feel the planet around you. When you know that *you* are in the heart of Earth, repeat three times:

I am fully grounded and connected with the Earth.

Gradually, you begin to rise to the surface. On your way, you enter deep, underground caves and commune with and become a bat hanging from the ceiling. Then you become a drop of water flowing through the underground caves. You follow this flow of Earth's hydrosphere, or water, to the surface and become a brook, a stream, a river.

Now, you are a fish, a tadpole, a frog, and you jump onto the shore to become the insect that the frog is pursuing, then the plant that the insect is feeding on. As these "primitive" beings, your reality is one in which all you *do* is eat, mate, procreate, survive, and die. Your consciousness is very small, yet simultaneously connected with the body of the entire planet. You sense when it is about to rain, when the wind will blow, or when the sun is rising and setting. You don't ponder these events, they just *are*. You do not think, you do not feel, you simply *are*.

Imagine your human self now sitting on the earth, beside a tree or on a rock. Welcome the essence of Gaia into the base of your spine, as you feel inside your human earth vessel *all* the dimensions of life that you have just experienced. As you do so, allow Gaia to assist in the recalibration of your root chakra. Experience the sensation of being the first- and second-dimensional aspects of your physical body.

You are your individual cells and the atoms within each cell. Your first-dimensional perspective allows you little consciousness of the external reality, yet it also ushers you into the quantum reality of the sub-atomic particles that connect all life. You are a wormhole, a vortex, into all that can be imagined. Your consciousness now expands into the second dimension.

You are the organs of your body, independent in your casings, yet dependent on the entire body for life. You are your genitals, your kidneys, your pancreas, your heart, your brain. Your first-dimensional self connects all these organs through the hormones of your endocrine system, your blood, and the molecules of oxygen that your blood carries. You are your body, without thought or emotion. You are the physical form that holds your essence. You are every organ, every bone, every cell, and every atom. You are the chemical factory of your DNA.

Take a long moment to breathe your conscious awareness and personal Essence into *every* portion of your body. Your first chakra activates adrenaline for survival, fight or flight, and testosterone for your masculine power source. Feel your inner warrior who is activated with these hormones. *Feel* your inner warrior within your root chakra as you emanate your power of initiation and responsibility for protection of your self, your intimate others, your home, your land, and your planet.

Breathe this power and responsibility down from the base of your spine, through your thighs, past your knees, down your calves, into your ankles, through your feet, and deep into the Earth to ground your inner warrior into your everyday life. Your inner warrior gives you the courage to pursue what you want and protect your right to a happy life.

If you have physical symptoms with your right hip, leg, knee, ankle, or foot, your inner warrior is held back because you fear your own *will*. If you have problems with your left hip, leg, knee, ankle, or foot, your inner warrior is held back because you fear your *instincts and emotions*. Use the courage of your inner warrior to confront these fears, and *do it anyway*!

Your first chakra also rules many of your eliminatory organs. Breathe into your root chakra again. Feel your inner warrior. What do you need to release so that you can move forward? Call upon your inner warrior to find the *courage* to release it *now*!!

Say this <u>mantra</u> three times:

I call upon my inner warrior to release ________ so that
I may have the *courage* to ___________.

Because I AM a warrior, I AM brave enough
to initiate the total transformation of my earth vessel!

Feel a shift in your root chakra, an opening, a release of tension like turning on a faucet or flicking on a light switch; the circuit that was once closed is now opened. The *spark* of your Multidimensional SELF and the *seed* of your Divine Ideal flow through this opening; you are connected to your SELF, your ideal, *and* you are connected to the planet.

Welcome your Soul/SELF as the new captain of your earth vessel.

Feel your body as a vessel in which *you* live.
Remember how you took many years developing a strong ego.
See your ego step aside to hand the reigns over to your Soul—*you*!
You are your Soul who has *now* become captain of your earth vessel.
Ego is your first assistant.

Within the area of your body and consciousness that are ruled by the root chakra, you are ONE with your Soul now and ONE with your SELF! In fact, you are ONE with everyone, for as you recalibrate your first chakra, the strong polarities of "I am" begin to blur into the unity of "we are."

Your ego and Soul are blending into ONE, as the spark of your Multidimensional SELF expands into a flame and the seed of your Divine Ideal grows into your manifest purpose.

Do not worry how your ideal or your SELF will look or feel. Instead, be constant in your recognition of them, for with the force of your conscious intention, *you* will integrate your ideal and your SELF into your daily life to create the *new reality*, which your inner warrior will protect!

AWAITING SPRING

Love is like the seasons.

When first it is awakened, it is spring and new blossoms appear with the hope of a blooming flower.

Then the heat of passion guides you into summer.

After a long, hot summer, autumn begins.

The world cools down in preparation for the winter, where life closes its doors for a while to allow the old to be released, so that the new can be reborn in the spring.

When spring returns, the trees are a bit taller, the flowers that were strong enough to hide their seeds from the winter's chill, bloom more heartily, and the lovers' roots have moved deeper into the earth to create a strong foundation.

Love is not all spring, though; nor is it always summer.

Autumn allows the lovers to release old habits and behaviors, so that the relationship can continue through the long, cold winter.

The cycles of life are everywhere, and a tree is not much different from a person. We are all lovers, of something or someone.

We each move through our personal seasons, which teach us to live in the moment.

Spring is time for planting new beginnings, some of which will bloom as quickly as a flower and others which may take as long as a tree to gain full splendor.

Love, either for another, for ourselves or for what we are creating, is that which plants the seeds and nurtures them into seedlings. Love creates the first blossom or the growth of each new limb.

Without love, birth cannot be carried through each season and creation remains a concept, an idea, a hope.

To plant our seed we must first love it, love it unconditionally, for only our patience knows if it will survive and flourish through the seasons or if it is a harbinger for new plants that can only sprout from that which has appeared to die.

Once we plant our seed, it is the spark of our true SELF that will tend it. It is our SELF that will allow that which is temporary to pass away, so that which is permanent can arise from the death of the old.

All we can do is plant our seed, water it with our tears, and allow the sun of our joy to feed it.

Our emotions are the land in which we plant our seed. Hence, we must choose the proper emotions, much as we would choose the proper soil.

Our thoughts are the weather that either support or injure our delicate creation. Therefore, we must guard our thoughts, just as we guard an infant.

To plant our ideal into the earth, we must plant our SELF into our body, for planting precedes gestation and birth. In between this alpha and omega is the vast land of *patience*.

Only patience will survive the heat of summer, the pruning winds of autumn and the long, cold winter. Patience reminds us that we have planted a seed, as well as where it has been planted.

Patience carries us through our hard work, disappointment, fear, and self doubt.
"A tree takes longer to bloom than a flower," patience reminds us when disillusionment knocks on our door.

"Spring *always* follows winter," patience reminds us when it is taking too long.

Patience is the voice of our SELF, the one who is ONE with all life, all creation. Listen to the voice of patience to hear the words of the ONE.

As the seed silently puts down roots into the soil, and the two first sprouts lay invisibly just below the surface, awaiting the warm sun of spring, our SELF quietly moves into our vessel.

The roots of our new SELF gradually integrate into each area of our life as it travels up the current of light towards our heart and mind. As the seed's sprouts first break ground, our greater potential begins to reveal itself in small, yet significant ways.

Can we remember our ideal that was brought down to Earth, as well as the SELF who has chosen it? Can we always hold the memory of our journey even though fear threatens to pollute the soil in which our seed has been planted? Can we remember to always guard against negative thinking? *No*, we cannot.

The autumn's winds must blow off the weakened and dying leaves, which will nourish the tree during the long winter. We must go within our SELF, again and again, to release a lifetime of fear and self-doubt.

"Spring always comes," the voice of patience reminds us. "That which is over must be released, so that which is beginning can be born."

We are still human; but, fortunately, we are also divine. A new love affair has begun between our ego and our Soul. At first it appears that our ego will dominate, but our Soul lives beyond time, so it is infinitely patient, and lives beyond fear, so it is unconditionally loving.

Most importantly, our Soul now lives within our physical body, quietly awaiting spring.

GAINING MASTERY

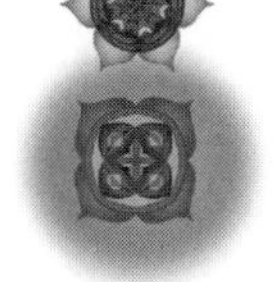

Once we have fully integrated our Soul/SELF into our earth vessel, our Multidimensional SELF will tune and retune each chakra like a musician tunes a guitar. Different "songs" of life will put certain chakras out of alignment, create a purging of old toxins, or open a chakra for an amazing burst of creative expression. This calibration allows a continuous flow of the fourth-dimensional River of Light into our earth vessel, which initiates a great transmutation of our physical body, behavior, and reality.

The Etheric Body flows into the first, root chakra of the physical body and into the hydrosphere of our planetary body to permit a free and balanced stream of prana into Gaia. The Etheric Body, interwoven with the physical body, passes along the greater current of the fourth-dimensional River of Light and begins to create unity between the Elementals of the personal body. Then the personal Elementals share this cooperation and unity with the planetary Elementals, thereby assisting in the harmonious flow of water over, under, around, and through the land.

The root chakra rules the third-dimensional element of earth, and hence, our fourth-dimensional Earth Elementals. As our Multidimensional SELF fully captains this chakra, we will have direct communication with our personal Elementals, and through them, with all the Earth Elementals of the planet. Via this connection, we can more easily gain mastery of the physical/Earth energy. It was the divine intention that humanity serve as masters of energy. It is through the process of integrating our Soul/SELF into our physical form that will commence that process of mastery.

This mastery begins by releasing fear and choosing love. If we fill our consciousness with fear, our personal Elementals must out-picture constriction, separation, and limitation. Fear also separates us from our connection to the earth and our innate, perceptual instincts. On the other hand, if we fill our consciousness with love, our inner Earth Elementals can out-picture expansion, unity, and re-birth. Our love allows us to merge our consciousness with the land to activate our instincts, as our inner warrior gladly takes on the responsibility of protecting the area of land that we call home.

COMMUNING WITH THE EARTH ELEMENTALS

With our Multidimensional SELF grounded in our root chakra, we are able to share the higher frequencies of the fourth-dimensional River of Light with our personal Elementals. We share our greater SELF with them by taking a moment to raise our consciousness into Alpha or Theta brainwaves so that we can deeply focus within. We can then allow our imagination to sweep through our bodies and commune with our form. As we recognize the great service of life that our earth vessel has allowed us, we pass that gratitude on to the fourth-dimensional Elementals who constantly serve to integrate prana into every atom of our body.

We can then send love and peace into each portion of our physical body, blessing the Elementals as we bless our physical vessel of light. As we do so, we not only give our Earth Elementals peace and love, which they can use as building blocks for a healthy and vital body, but with every step, we allow our Elementals to out-picture love and peace to the earth upon which we walk.

Furthermore, our inner warrior, who feels the same sense of duty for our planetary body as it does for our personal body, dedicates itself to using our improved health and vitality to protect our bodies and our planet. We *know* that we deserve to live in a healthy and happy environment, and we are willing to fight for our planet's right, just as we fight for our own.

Because the River of Light runs through our root chakra and down into the earth via our legs and feet, we have the expanded power to know what the land needs to become more fertile, identify which minerals are missing or in abundance, know where to find water, predict earthquakes, and feel the areas that are filled with love and those that are filled with fear. As we gain our mastery of the Earth, we magnify our ability to transmute fear into love. In this manner, we can actively choose to heal our planet. Just as our personal body has a vast inner healing capacity if filled with love, Gaia can more easily heal herself if we, her people, can share our great force of love with her.

Much as farmers and Native Americans love the land, all of us can establish a deeply personal and intimate relationship with the earth upon which we walk. When we are partners with our planet, it is no longer a thing. Earth is a beautiful being that has offered her body as a home upon which we can learn and grow. With our SELF grounded in our root chakra, we *know* that our Divine Ideal is to be shared with the entire planet. We have taken our first step toward Becoming ONE with our SELF and with our greater SELF, the planet.

SYMPTOMS OF TRANSFORMATION

Once a chakra has accepted the flow of the River of Light, it will receive more prana due to the movement of kundalini and the higher vibration of our Multidimensional SELF and our Divine Ideal. The sudden influx of light may set the chakras off-balance and cause their spin to wobble. At this time, the polarities associated with that chakra will peak out in a desperate attempt to find homeostasis.

All the functions of our personal and planetary bodies are based on homeostasis, which is a relatively stable state of equilibrium. Our body searches for this centered state, traversing back and forth between the extremes as it gradually hones in on the center point of equilibrium. This process is much like a pendulum that swings back and forth to the right and left before it stops in the center.

The change in the influx of prana or light affects the chakras much like water influences an old-fashioned waterwheel. When the river or stream dries up, the wheel does not turn. Conversely, when the current of the water is extremely rapid, the water wheel will turn rapidly and almost out of control. If there is a flood, the waterwheel may even break. The same holds true for the chakras and the flow of prana. A sudden burst of prana into a chakra would be like a flood to the waterwheel. It is at this time that we experience the symptoms of transformation, which are the two opposites trying the find the center.

An example of a symptom for the root chakra would be the polarities of being so grounded in mundane life that we feel heavy and bored, or the opposite of being so ungrounded that we are spaced out and unable to take care of the responsibilities of daily life. When the high frequency of the fourth-dimensional River of Light floods into a chakra, it flushes out the darkness and fear that has been hiding in certain behaviors, hormones, and parts of our body ruled by that chakra.

A hormonal issue for the root chakra would be too much adrenalin, which would make us hyperactive, combative, and angry. On the other hand, too little adrenaline would make us lethargic, timid, and unfocused. The fearful energy, over which we have no control, is the challenge that we will face in our process of becoming a master of energy. To gain mastery, we must learn to listen to fear, determine if there is a warning in it, then release the fear and choose love. In this manner, we gain a feeling of control.

For us to gain mastery, we must be able to see through illusion to *know* truth. Fear is a restrictive, dispersive energy that binds us to the limitation and separation of the third-dimensional illusions. A commander who leads his or her warriors with fear will only command loyalty if the warriors are sure they cannot escape the situation. Conversely, warriors who have been unified with love for their cause, their family, and themselves will stay loyal to their commander through every condition. Love commands trust, whereas fear breeds deceit.

To become a master of the Earth energy and the physical world of our first chakra, we must be willing to face our fears regarding living fully in our body and committing to our personal and planetary rights. When we don't believe in our self enough to stand firm and fight for our rights, we run from persons, places, situations, and even things that cause us fear.

Because life is a pass/fail system, we cannot run from the fear inside of us, as the re-creation of each fearful situation is projected out into our reality again and again until we get it right. Of course, not every situation will be spun out, only those that are in our way. When we look into the face of our SELF, we see all that stands in the way of becoming our SELF. Fortunately, we have awakened our inner warrior, who can proudly decree:

"I *now* take *all* power
I have ever given to any person, place, situation, or thing
and I *own* it for my SELF!"

If we can feel the unconditional love, forgiveness, and acceptance emanating from the spark of our Multidimensional SELF, which we have now accepted into our root chakra, we can begin to love, forgive, and accept ourselves *unconditionally*. Change happens when we love ourselves enough to forgive all past situations, accept ourselves for exactly who we are right now, and love ourselves unconditionally. It is then that we can truly commit to improving our behavior. It takes great self esteem to change, and self esteem is based on loving ourselves enough to own our many victories.

On a physiological level, weaknesses, toxins, infections, and/or injuries will be amplified by the increased vibration, just as the weakest link is the one to break when a chain is pulled. This process can be quite uncomfortable, but if we can be honest with ourselves, we will see how the problem has been a long time coming, and we have chosen not to heal it. We have been too busy to take our earth vessel in for maintenance. If we treated our cars the way we treat our bodies, how long would they last?

Even if we have been very conscious with our bodies, we are putting a 200 watt light bulb into a circuit that is meant for only 60 watts. Luckily, our Soul/SELF is becoming the captain of our vessel and is more than capable of making any appropriate adaptations to our vessel. However, first we must surrender all control of our physical body to our Soul. We will experience more difficulty with certain chakras, which are usually the areas of our body and our life that have chronically been an issue. It is helpful to remind ourselves, "I am not *having* a problem. I am *releasing* a problem."

THE ILLUSION OF SEPARATION

Our Multidimensional SELF is in constant unity with the ONE of the fifth dimension and beyond. In the ONE, the polarities that exist in our physical world are blended into the unity of oneness. It is these third-dimensional polarities that create the illusions of separation. For example, the polarity of good people and bad people creates the illusion of separation in the spectrum of behavior. The reality is that all people's behavior covers the entire spectrum from good to bad within the same moment. Also, there is good in the worst of us and bad in the best of us.

When we live in a land filled with fear, we create categories of behavior as a form of protection so that we can stay away from "the bad people" and stay with "the good people." This can be quite confusing, as sometimes the "bad people" act like they are "good," and the "good people" act like they are "bad." Our Soul/SELF perceives the world from a multidimensional perspective and knows that both good and bad are behaviors, not people.

Because of the third-dimensional paradigm of separation and limitation, each chakra has its own polarities. Hence, as our Soul/SELF becomes integrated into each chakra, the illusions of separation are released and the polarities blend into ONE. Since our root chakra rules our first steps towards individual consciousness, the polarity of *I am/we are* is blended into ONE as our Soul/SELF is innately united with all life.

BLENDING POLARITIES, FIRST CHAKRA
I AM/WE ARE

The third-dimensional filter in our first chakra creates the illusion that we are an individual entity who is completely separate from everyone else. In the early days of Earth, humanity believed that all reality was interwoven into a common tapestry. The "primitive" tribal people saw each person in their tribe as an extension of themselves. Even modern day children are not fully aware of their individuality until they are about two years of age. As we grow up in today's world, what is it that so convinces us that we are separate from others?

The main thing that happens is *fear*. Something and/or someone frightens us, and our first instinct is to *separate* ourselves from the source of the fear because it gives us a sense of safety. Whenever we believe that we are separate from someone or something, a wall goes up in our mind and in our heart. Then we truly are separate.

Now, with our Multidimensional SELF in our root chakra, we are more able to perceive the realities that were filtered out of our third-dimensional awareness. As we recalibrate this chakra to accept our SELF and our Divine Ideal, our ability to perceive higher-dimensional realities is increasing at the speed of light, and everything around us is changing so fast that we often feel as though we can hardly keep up with our SELF. If that is not enough, fear constantly threatens us. Fortunately, our inner warrior is determined to ground our power and initiate the life we *know* we deserve.

As we fulfill our decree to live a happy life, we discover many things that we cannot, and will not, tolerate any longer. It is not that we hold a judgment; it is just that our multidimensional perspective allows us to release fear and choose love. As we release our addiction to fear, we can feel that something shifts deep inside of us. The third-dimensional world of struggle and work still exists, but we have the ability to choose to *not* participate in that vision of reality. Gradually, we are learning to be in the world, but not of it.

The old world of fear, struggle, and strife is much like a parallel reality going on around us. We see it and it sees us, but even though the old reality and our new reality are both "here," it appears that we see that world through the glass darkly. It seems as though our new reality is a half of an octave above the old one. Because of this, we have less emotional connection to the old reality of struggle and strife. Hence, we are neutral, not connected by *any* emotion. We feel this way because our resonance is rising and our attention is filtering out fear and filtering in love.

We are beginning to realize now how emotions bind us to a certain reality. Once we disconnect emotionally, it is as if we are not really "there." Instead, we are observing "there," and living "here." Unfortunately, because we want our new life *so* much, we may still have doubts about the validity of our higher-dimensional perceptions and therefore doubt our new experiences. Fortunately, our desire for a life filled with love is something that beckons us, because our Soul/SELF reminds us that we deserve it.

As we believe that we deserve our new life, we can use that desire as a homing beam, a compass in a starless night. The only thing that gets us off course is self-doubt and its best friend, fear. When we stay out of doubt and fear, our desire for love pulls us along, as we journey deeper and deeper into our SELF. Even though the world around us is the same, our place in it is vastly changing. Our life may not seem different to others, but it feels different to us because our illusions are rapidly being unveiled.

Our desire for love, our inner compass, is the only thing that we can trust as being real. Why does our life, our reality, feel so different when it looks the same? The answer is that we are pioneers, spiritual warriors, who are constantly navigating between doubt and fear to find our *way*. We sense that something is ending, yet we simultaneously know that *we* are beginning. Both options are correct, both are real! It is the old concepts of our ego/self that are ending, as the new concepts of our Soul/SELF are beginning.

We are learning a new *way* to deal with our personal relationships, as well. We can fake our appearance for others but not for those who know us intimately. They probably wonder why they see us in another way when we look the same. On the other hand, most of them are also changing so much that they may be too distracted to even notice our transition. Our male and female energy polarities are more intermingled now, and any gender roles we once had are scrambled. We are aware of our Multidimensional SELF inside us, rather than above us, which makes us feel more androgynous. At the same time, we also feel more feminine and, concurrently, more masculine. With the integration of our Soul/SELF into our root chakra, instead of being who "*I am*," we are *being* who "*we are*."

We observe ourselves wishing to project our fear out to our mate; after all, what is a relationship good for if not for having someone to blame? We were not as conscious of this behavior before, but now that our male and female energies are blending into one, we can no longer blame our mate for what we are hiding from our self. We can no longer say, "It's not *my* fault," as everywhere and everyone is an expression of *our* reality. We can no longer say, "He [or she] did ___ to me." "He/she" and "you/me" are becoming the same. The tactics of blaming another no longer works as *I am* and *we are* blend into ONE.

Of course, that does not mean that our ego does not try to repeat old behaviors; it is just that we are conscious of them and realize how ineffective they are. Fourth- and fifth-dimensional relationships are not the same as third-dimensional ones. In the fourth dimension, it is much more difficult to hide from each other, and in the fifth dimension, hiding is impossible. However, in order to let go of hiding from our mate, we must be willing to let go of hiding from our SELF.

As more light from our SELF enters our being, more inner darkness is also revealed. We would love to project that darkness out, but it cannot leave us now, as there is no *out*. All is *in*. There can be no victim in higher-dimensional relationships as there is no separation. Without separation, there can no longer be the "him vs. her" or the "you vs. me" dynamic. Only "us" and "we" exist. Therefore, "I" must take full responsibility for the reality that "I" create *alone*, for that is the reality that "*we*" create *together*.

BLENDING SOUL/SELF WITH EGO/SELF

Our relationship with Soul is no longer separate. Our Soul/SELF is in our human form, and our human form contains our Soul/SELF. Therefore, we are beginning to realize that conflict is actually a projection of our inner fears that we have externalized to be "out there" so that it appears to be separate from us. Our inner Soul/SELF now reminds us that *nothing* is *separate*, not even what, or whom, we hate, judge, fear, or love.

Once, it was easier to project our darkness out of ourselves rather than dealing with it in ourselves. Now, the opposite is true. When we externalize our Dark Side away from our SELF, it takes on a life of its own. Once outside our spiritual responsibility, our Dark Side merges with similar emanations that others have projected out to create new and improved versions of victimization, which are then projected into our mundane life to create new disasters in both our personal and planetary bodies. Then we feel victimized and separate from our environment, as it is "out there" and beyond our control.

However, we can only be a victim if we are separate from the world around us. With *I am* blurring into unity with *we are* and *you* blurring into *me*, there can be no victim or victimizer. There can be only the reality that *we* choose to create and share with *them*, the other members of the reality to which our consciousness is presently vibrating. The filter of separation in our root chakra has been altered by our recalibration of our Multidimensional SELF and by our rising kundalini force.

Once we had to learn the rules and balance our karma. Because our root chakra contains the flow of now, we realize that we are creating our own rules and karma is the cause and effect of our immediate reality. Our Soul whispers to our heart, "It is *all* perfect, for this is the reality that *we* (ego and Soul) are creating." Our Soul/SELF and ego/self are entering into a partnership, just as we are entering into a partnership with Gaia, the consciousness of Earth.

The child of this partnership will be the manifestation of our Divine Ideal, which we promised to *be*, express, create, and live before we took our present earth vessel. As we blend the polarities of Soul and ego, the limitations of our ego are replaced with the all knowing of our Soul. That which was impossible for our ego is simple for our Soul. Therefore, the ideal that was impossible to manifest through our ego can easily be manifested through our Soul. With our Soul/SELF as captain of our root chakra, we have planted the seed of our Divine Ideal.

"It is *all perfect*, for this is the reality that *we* are creating," whispers the voice of our Soul/SELF. This message gives us comfort and direction through the chaos of our transition and a better sense of being in control of our life and the earth vessel in which we live. Our ego is attached to being a victim and has gained a sense of control from believing "it's not *my* fault." No, it is not our *fault*. It is *our creation*. Would we rather take responsibility for our life and gain power, or would we prefer to be a victim and allow "them" to have our power? Our Multidimensional SELF is reminding us that there is no person, place, situation, or thing outside of us onto which we can project our fear and darkness. When we find our self habitually giving away our power to hide our fear, we can instead say:

"I now take back all power I have ever given
to any person, place, situation, or thing
and I *own* it for my SELF!"

The illusions of separation and limitation are blurring into ONE. The time is *now*, the place is *here*, and *we* are becoming ONE with our SELF, our Divine Ideal, and our planet.

A MESSAGE FROM GAIA

Beloved People of my Planet,

I, Gaia, am joyous to be your partner. Now that you have begun to integrate Soul/SELF into your earth vessel, you are able to share your expanded consciousness with me, Gaia, the consciousness of planet Earth. In fact, as you continue your process, your personal consciousness will expand to embrace humanity's collective consciousness, then my planetary consciousness, in which you are connected with *all* the elements of my planet.

Once you have stabilized your planetary consciousness, you will no longer feel that you are the most evolved being on my planet. Instead, you will *know* that you are partners with all the planetary life forms, from the first-dimensional Mineral Kingdom to the fourth-dimensional Elemental Kingdom and beyond.

To initiate your planetary consciousness, you will calibrate your personal chakras with my planetary chakras. Both personal and planetary chakras are polarized to provide a balance of outflow/male energy and inflow/female energy. Do not think of these energies as a gender, but instead as external light directed in (inflow/female) and internal light directed out (outflow/male). My planetary chakras display this process with the first, third, fifth, and seventh chakras, which are outflow/male, as mountain peaks.

On the other hand, the second, fourth, and sixth planetary chakras, inflow/female, are female archetypal environments. For example, the second chakra is the Amazon jungle, with abundant trees and water, and the fourth chakra is a volcanic crater on an island in Hawaii. Since the sixth chakra represents my higher consciousness, it is a mountain environment, the Himalayan Mountains. However, instead of being one peak, as in my masculine chakras, it is an entire mountain range representing how the feminine energies join in families.

People are not that dissimilar from my planet. We are both multifaceted, with many personalities and traits within our total being. Most important of all, both person and planet are returning to the glorious beings that we have always been in the higher dimensions. The concept of merging person with planet may be new to some of you, but it is a normal concept to me. You see, dear ones, I have *always* been merged with you.

For those of you who choose to merge, person and planet, I wish to take a moment to tell you how much I appreciate you. You have opened your consciousness to mine. In return, I pledge to be available to you. I see you, my people, as a portion of my greater SELF. You are like my fingers and toes. You are my windows into the experience of individuality in third-dimensional form. Through what you touch, where you walk, what you do, and who you love, or who you hate, I am with you and feeling it all. Is it any wonder why my weather is a reflection of your thoughts and feelings?

Now, I ask you to be as conscious of me as I am of you. We are a team, you know. Without my life forms, I would be a barren planet, and without my earth body, you would not have a planet upon which to experience third-dimensional form. Yes, being third-dimensional has been quite an experiment. We, the beings of Earth, wanted to know absolute separation from other life forms and the limitations created by our loss of unity. It has been difficult, but it has also been splendid, spiritually inspiring, and expanding. I thank all of my humans for the interesting show that you have given me.

However, we are awakening now. I am remembering that *I am* a star, a galaxy, and a universe. In the same moment, you are remembering your true SELF, as well. You no longer need to believe that you are alone—the only humanoids in the universe. You are expanding your minds to embrace your solar and galactic consciousness, and you are remembering your friends, loved ones, and other aspects of your SELF on other planets, galaxies, and dimensions.

What a wonderful experience we shall all have as we rejoin other members of our SELF. Let us begin this process by merging person into planet and planet into person. As we merge our personal and planetary chakras, it is my wish that you, the people of my planet, will again feel unified with me. I ask that you *feel* your body in my chakras, as you also *feel* my chakras in your body. As we review each chakra, allow the essence of my planetary chakras to merge with the essence of your personal chakras. Hence, we will initiate the blending of person into planet. We shall begin with the first chakra.

I am with you always. How could I not be, for I am your planet,
Gaia

BECOMING ONE WITH THE PLANET

FIRST PLANETRY CHAKRA
Mt. Sinai, Middle East

The first chakra is the root of both personal and planetary masculine energy. It has an outflow orientation, which is symbolized by its location in a mountain peak. Mt. Sinai is the root of Gaia's kundalini, the alpha and omega of her experience of form. Many great cycles of change have begun on this mountain. It is her base camp, the seat of her power. It is where Gaia gathers her vitality and initiative, just as the root chakra is where we gather our vitality and initiative. There is a major energy vortex in this area of Gaia's body, which has greatly influenced her evolution as a planet, as well as the evolution of humanity.

Our Western society has traveled so far into third-dimensional individuality that many of us have lost sight of the fact that we are members of a greater whole, the planet. Our forgetfulness closed our root chakra, separating us from our planetary consciousness, and limited us to a small fragment of our SELF, which is the ego/self of our current earth vessel. When our first chakra is closed off from the first chakra of Gaia, it is difficult for us to share our prana with Gaia and for Gaia to share her prana with us.

Just as a lamp flickers when it's not sufficiently plugged into the socket, prana cannot efficiently circulate through a body that is not plugged in. Hence, we are like many small lights living on top of a huge socket. When we can plug in to Gaia, we can become ONE huge light of power and *love*. Just think what personal and planetary healing that union could create!

One the other hand, when we are ungrounded, we also feel disconnected from our Mother Earth and cast adrift on a hostile planet. The adrenal glands of our root chakra release adrenaline to activate our fight or flight consciousness, which assists us in surviving the often harsh environment of third-dimensional reality. Too much adrenalin can leave us feeling anxious, nervous, and angry, whereas too little adrenalin can make us feel as frightened as a small mouse on an open meadow.

However, the hawks are not flying in the sky above us. They are in the office, in the line at the store, in the car next to us, and in the many crowded places where we must live and work. Fortunately, when our first chakra is opened and connected to the planet we can experience a sense of protection through our unity with all life. The most powerful way to fully merge into the oneness of Gaia is to blend our personal chakras with the planetary chakras.

There are several maps of Earth's chakra system. One of them is:

Earth's seventh, or crown, chakra in Mt. Fuji, Japan

Earth's sixth, or brow, chakra in the Himalayas, Tibet
Earth's fifth, or throat, chakra in Mt. Shasta, California, USA
Earth's fourth, or heart, chakra in Haleakala, Maui, Hawaii
Earth's third, or solar plexus, chakra in Mt. Kilimanjaro, Africa
Earth's second, or navel, chakra in the Brazilian Amazon
Earth's first, or root, chakra in Mt. Sinai, Middle East

MERGING CHAKRAS MEDITATION

Inhale a long, slow, deep breath into your first chakra at the base of your spine. As you exhale, send your roots down deep into Gaia's Earth body. Visualize yourself sitting at the base of a tree; connect the base of your spine to the base of the tree, and lay your back flat against the trunk. Look up to see the light of the sun entering the leaves. Track the light with your awareness as it travels through the leaves, twigs, branches, limbs, and into the trunk.

As the light moves down the trunk, it will meet the crown of your head. At this junction, allow some of that light to enter the crown of your head and travel down your spine as it simultaneously travels down the tree trunk. Eventually, the light will reach the base of the tree, and the base of your spine, as well. Feel your roots travel down from your spine to merge with the roots of your Tree of Life, which are planted deep in the earth.

With your first chakra fully grounded, allow your consciousness to continue to travel down into the Earth and wrap your essence around Gaia's essence in the center of the planet. Extend your awareness now to imagine that you are slowly returning to the surface at Mt. Sinai. With your essence merged with Gaia's, you can feel the ancient and all-persistent planetary unrest. The first chakra rules the physical element and the sense of smell. Personally experience the physicality of your planetary body.

As you return to the surface, you are at the foot of Mt Sinai. Feel the calm stability of the Mineral Kingdom within you, and the detached yet compassionate expression of the second-dimensional Plant Kingdom and their partners, the insects. Feel the wavering of the grassy fields and the constancy of the giant forests. Experience the flow of the many bodies of water, from small streams to vast oceans. Feel the valleys as they dip into your body and the heaviness of the mountain ranges. Feel the many life forms that have grown upon, crawled over, or stepped upon the land, flown in the air, or swam in the waters. Merge with all this physical life in the first through third dimensions.

Smell this mountain world, the bushes, the desert, the wind, and the campfires of visiting humans. Allow your primitive sense of smell to take you into an ancient memory of this area. You are now climbing Mt. Sinai to gain illumination. The journey seems long and difficult. You feel the hard rocks under your feet and the hot sun beating on your head. As you continue your climb, you feel the ancient and persistent third-dimensional planetary unrest intermingled with your own ancient and persistent personal unrest.

Exhausted from your climb, you take a few moments to relax in a darkened cave. You lie against the cave's cool stones and close your eyes. Instantly, you are traveling through the base of the mountain and, once again, deep into my core. Once there, you see a huge, inter-dimensional portal. You *feel* your root chakra resonating to this portal to awaken your long-latent personal inter-dimensional portal. As soon as you recognize your own portal, it begins blending with Gaia's. Your personal stargate swiftly becomes merged with the planetary stargate.

You awaken from your meditation feeling grounded and illumined. As you return to your climb, you feel the calm stability of the mineral world within you as well as the detached, compassionate expression of the plants that grow on the slopes and the insects that buzz around your ankles. You feel connected to each plant, each insect, each rock, and each of the creatures that have taken refuge on the rocky slopes or flown in the sky above them.

You and Gaia, person and planet, are ONE. You are an ancient mountain that has survived, again and again. You are solid and patient and have seen and lived through much. Many people have sought refuge and enlightenment within the cave-homes of your body. You, the mountain, were always connected to the flow of Spirit through your body. You, the mountain, are the stargate, the portal, of the first and the last. You are the Alpha and the Omega. You started this cycle, and you, the mountain, will close it.

By the time you reach the peak of the mountain, nothing frightens you, because you have seen it all. You are infinitely patient, because you have outlived it all. You feel the grounding of Spirit at the base of your mountain, while you also experience the world from the peak of your mountain. You stand upon the highest peak of the mountain that you are, and shout to the world below:

"I *am* as ancient as a mountain.

I *am* solid and patient, for I have survived, again and again.

I ground my Spirit in the matter of the planet.

I *am* a vortex of transmutation!"

MESSAGE FROM OUR MULTIDIMENSIONAL SELF

You have done well with the conversion of your first chakra from "ego-operated" to "Soul-operated." Your kundalini energy is calibrating your root chakra to integrate me, your Multidimensional SELF, and *our* Divine Ideal into your earth vessel and your everyday life. Your grounding force and main power house, your root chakra, is in the process of reconstruction.

Therefore, you will likely have some symptoms of transformation. Hence, I ask you to be patient with your self. Also, as I integrate into each of your chakras, I will re-assign your ego/self to other duties so that I can captain your earth vessel, which can also cause confusion and even anxiety. You are being asked to change the way you operate your entire life.

I realize the challenge that you are undertaking and commend you on your great courage. On the other hand, your daily life will be greatly enhanced by your decision to allow the flow from the ONE to enter your body and to share that flow with Gaia. With my entry into every chakra, ego/self will be asked to surrender control of your earth vessel so that it can be recalibrated to receive and integrate the flow of the River of Light from the ONE, which will gradually and safely transform your life.

Your life issues, the problems that have been recreated over and over, will be the most time-consuming and challenging for me to transform, but I will do just that. We may have to repeatedly return to these body issues, thoughts, emotions, and/or behaviors. Please remember that these life issues are your teachers. When your lessons are learned, the teacher, (the "problem"), will depart. Listen closely to these "problems" as they will greatly assist you in your transformation.

Listen also to your body. What does it need you to do, or change, so that it can heal and transform? Do not be dismayed; for I am within you now, healing you/us from the inside out. Be conscious of your thoughts in order to determine the reality which they are creating and re-creating. Feel your emotions in your everyday life. Do not judge or amplify them. Simply say, "Oh, I am releasing the emotion of_____." Notice how your consciousness expands and contracts, and how your behaviors change when your consciousness changes.

Again, do not judge your behavior, or it will be too problematic to consciously view it. Instead, pull your focus into me, your SELF, so that you can observe your behaviors with detached compassion. Feel how I can unconditionally love, accept, and forgive you. I wish to congratulate you on your progress and thank you for your commitment to both person and planet. The lithosphere and hydrosphere of Gaia, the foundations for Earth, will also be transformed due to your expanded commitment to protect the land upon which you trod, have your home, and raise your family. You deserve to create a life with a healthy planet, as well as a healthy body. Now with your root chakra blended with Gaia's, the illusion of separation between person and planet is diminishing more each day.

In closing I wish to say that I am extremely proud to be your Soul/SELF. I shall kindly and gently remind ego that it has completed a job well done and can now focus on grounding *our* earth vessel into the body of Gaia.

I am your SELF

CHAPTER FOURTEEN

GESTATING OUR NEW REALITY

THE SECOND CHAKRA

LOCATION: The second chakra is located at the navel. The navel was once our umbilical cord. This cord was our attachment to our first physical home, our mother, and the nurturing that she provided. The second chakra also represents our attachment to Mother Earth as well as all the plants and creatures that call her home.

PETALS: This chakra has six petals or spokes. In numerology, six is the number that represents the responsibility and nurturing for family and community, as well as finding balance and harmony with our environment.

NOTE & MANTRA: The note for this chakra is D and the mantra is "vam" or "o" as in home. Chanting these mantras in the key of D while focusing our attention on this area of our body can enable us to more consciously access the second chakra.

COLOR: The color of this chakra is orange. Orange is the color of emotion. In the Hindu chakra system, the color orange is associated with death of the old. This "death" refers

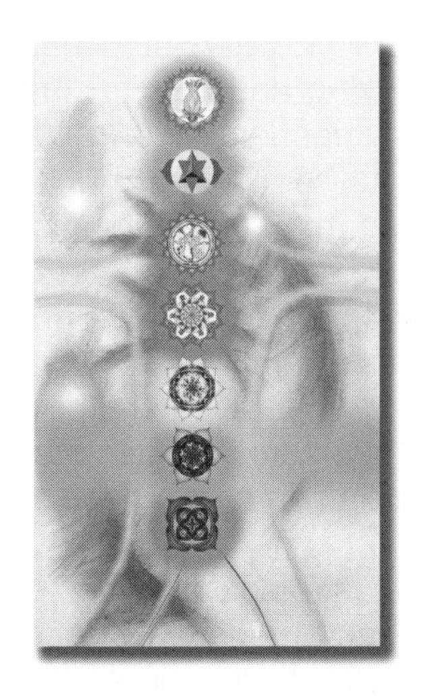

not only to physical death, but also to the death or total liberation of painful emotions that have been repressed. This "death" also refers to the discharge of the defense mechanisms that we created in order to survive those emotions as well as the situations that caused them.

RULES: The second chakra rules our vital, sensual body. This chakra governs sexuality for the purpose of reproduction, emotions, instincts, food, and the general feelings in our body. The second chakra rules the feminine component of sexuality, whereas the first chakra rules the masculine component of sexuality. The second or navel chakra is more sensual than sexual. It tells us how we feel about sex and having children, whereas the first chakra rules sex that is for enjoyment and/or power.

Besides reproduction, the second chakra also governs other kinds of creativity. Swimming, hiking, and gardening make use of the second chakra's connection to nature. Sculpting and carving use materials and objects of nature as a medium, and nature is often the subject of painters and photographers. With dancing and martial arts, the navel area is seen as the base, the hara center, the area to be kept in alignment with the Earth so that perfect balance can be maintained.

Like the first chakra, the second chakra governs survival, but from the perspective of the feminine polarity. The first chakra governs the fight for survival, whereas the second chakra rules the instincts for survival. The first chakra urges us to battle for and protect, whereas the second chakra aids us in using our instincts to find a safe place to hide, to live, and to rear our young. Like the first chakra, the second chakra also rules money, but again, in a different manner. The first chakra rules money and the power that it holds, whereas the second chakra rules money and the security that it brings.

SENSE: The sense of taste is related to this chakra. The sense of taste is important for identification of edible vs. non-edible food and for the enjoyment of eating, which is also ruled by the second chakra. Taste is a very emotional experience and is the basis for the nurturing and comfort that eating provides. Suckling forms the important first bond between mother and child and serves as comfort as well as nutrition. These feelings are often carried into the communion of eating with others.

Preparing and serving food is often an act of love and community, and family meals bind the family together. Eating and food are very culture specific. For generations after a family immigrates to a new area, family members maintain their preference for the food of their culture because of the security and sense of belonging that it provides.

ASTROLOGICAL SIGN: The astrological sign of Cancer is associated with the second chakra because Cancer is the sign of mothering, nurturing, emotions, receptiveness, and fertility.

ELEMENT: Water is the element associated with the second chakra. Our first physical home in the amniotic sac was one of water. This chakra reflects how we feel about being in or near the water. Psychologically, water is the metaphor and symbol for emotion. The second chakra deals with gut instincts, basic emotions such as fear, rage, and joy, and basic interpersonal emotions that are often unspoken.

The second chakra also rules the kidneys, which is where we eliminate our water. This chakra rules our second-dimensional self, which is represented by the Plant Kingdom and less evolved creatures such as fish. Both plants and fish must have water to survive.

CONSCIOUSNESS: The second chakra depicts our emotional consciousness, our animal instincts and our tribal consciousness. This chakra represents the mammalian portion of our brain where the limbic system rules our emotions and short-term memory. The limbic system is an important center for creativity and learning because it is where emotion and memory combine. We all know that it is easier to learn when we are emotionally engaged than when we are bored. Also, a deeply loving experience is usually imprinted in our conscious mind. However, an extremely frightening experience is often banished to our unconscious mind, as the memory of it is too painful.

Higher mammals such as dogs and monkeys remember what they are taught because they have an emotional relationship with the teacher, or because the food that is given as a reward makes them feel happy and nurtured. Humans also use emotions and food as a means of reinforcement and reward.

PERSONAL TIMELINE: The second chakra represents ages 2 to 4 when the child is going beyond basic survival and is beginning to develop his or her position in the family. It is also a time when they are creating their own sense of individuality, but they are still dependent on their "tribe." It is at this age that children are beginning to associate their emotions with specific events, but they are dependent on their caregivers for interpretation and guidance. Emotional events that occur during this age are often unconscious to our adult self, but they form the basis of many of our core beliefs about ourselves and our abilities.

SOCIAL TIMELINE: Anthropologically, the second chakra represents the time when civilization advanced beyond living in caves and was able to settle into tribes. At this time, many tribes began agriculture and animal husbandry. Since the people lived off the land, they worshiped the Goddess with ceremony and sacrifice.

ENDOCRINE GLAND: The endocrine glands for the second chakra are the gonads, which consist of both male and female sex organs. These include the ovaries, testes, and prostate gland. The prostate gland is also ruled by our first chakra. Hormones have a strong influence on mood, as any woman with PMS will confirm. What is not as often noted is the interaction between testosterone and adrenaline. When a man's fight or flight syndrome is activated, the adrenaline in his system interacts with the testosterone to create an explosive combination. Steroids also create strong emotional reactions.

Healthy male and female sexual organs make our personality radiant and magnetic as well as our eyes sparkling and luminous, and they also give us an air of self-reliance. The inner warmth of vibrant sex glands prevents the tendencies for inflexibility, hardening, and stiffening that can come with aging. In fact, a healthy and active sex life can bring a vitality and balance to life even in our old age.

NERVE PLEXUS: The second chakra is located at the lumbar plexus, which rules the reproductive system, abdomen, and lumbar region of the back.

CLEAR: When the second chakra is clear, we feel patient, enduring, nurturing, and secure. We feel intimate with our family, friends, neighborhood, and planet. We feel at home in our bodies and are able to communicate with our SELF. Our emotions are balanced, and we are able to trust our instincts and gut feelings.

Our sex life is natural and loving, and we are able to balance both the male and female components of sexuality. We eat the healthy food in the correct amount for our bodies' needs and enjoy the comfort and nurturing free of any addictive behaviors. Our elimination of waste material is regular and our sex organs, bladder, and kidneys are healthy.

UNCLEAR: When the second chakra is unclear, we feel impotent, frigid, or over-sexed. We may not be able to enjoy sex or we may use it as an addiction to cover what we are really feeling. We may feel disassociated from our friends and family and ill at ease within our home. Our eating and drinking can become addictive in that we eat or drink to comfort ourselves and to cover emotions that we don't want to consciously face.

Fear and anger are just beneath the surface of our awareness, which makes us anxious and/or depressed. Old core beliefs of limitation and fear sabotage our behavior and keep us in survival mode. Life feels like a day-to-day struggle, and we feel as though we are living hand-to-mouth because we are unable to make enough money to feel comfortable in our home and secure in our family life.

EARTH'S CHAKRA: Mother Earth's second chakra is in the Brazilian Amazon. This is a fitting place for her second chakra because it is a paradise of fertility and growth—that is, if we humans do not continue to destroy it.

DIMENSIONS: The second chakra rules our second- and third-dimensional bodies. This chakra, more than any other, represents our humanoid "animal." Animals have emotions, just as we do; ask any pet lover. It is through conscious, third-dimensional awareness of our second-dimensional emotions that we are able to become the protectors of Mother Earth, rather than her destroyers. If we feel the warmth and protection of a tree, if we can honor the food that we eat and the water that we drink, we will not want to pollute or destroy our planet who provided them for us.

However, if we harbor repressed emotions of terror and rage, we will see the world around us as an enemy, which we must conquer. When we can heal our past pain, we can feel our connection to the Earth and all her creatures. It is vital that we love our own bodies, for when we can truly love and respect our own body, we can love and protect the Earth whose body we call home.

THE VOLCANO

There was a feeling, like a slow, bubbling volcano,
rising up from deep inside.

What was this feeling?
Where did it come from?
Why was it coming out now?

The answer was hiding through a thin, misty veil
that threatened to be removed.

What if this revelation,
this expose of SELF,
this true-raw emotion,
without edit,
without guilt,
without the limitations of
how one SHOULD feel
how one SHOULD act
actually escaped?

What if ALL barriers were released
and the pure essence of SELF,
that has always hidden inside,
was openly and eagerly displayed and lived on the outside?

*Slowly, the lava reaches the mouth of the volcano.
Gradually, it crests the peak and begins to
ooze down the outside slope.*

NOW that that which has been hidden is being uncovered,
what will happen?

Will others also open their secret selves,
break down their barriers,
pull down their walls,
push aside their veils?

What if there was no place to hide?
What if every thing,
every thought,
every feeling,
every fear,
and every dream
were revealed?

Then, the inside world would be totally displayed to the outside
world.

Then, there could be no lies,
no secrets,
no coercion,
no deceit.

Then, there would be
only TRUTH
only SELF,
pure and undiluted Self.

Thank you!

Thank you for the veils,
the barriers,
and the walls,
for they have given safety to our inner self where
feelings are too real and thoughts are too honest.

Hiding feels safe, familiar, known.

To take the risk to open the floodgates and expose the truth is UNKNOWN,
and the unknown creates FEAR.

But can an erupting volcano be stopped?

BECOMING ONE WITH SELF

When we were children our ego was very small and the combination of Soul and ego seemed natural. However, the third-dimensional world trained us to attend to our ego and ignore our Soul. Often, when we expressed the experiences of our Soul/SELF, we heard statements from authority figures such as, "Oh, it is just your imagination," "You must have dreamed that," "Don't be conceited," or "You are too full of yourself." Because of this, we ignored our Soul/SELF more and more and placed our attention on the reality of our ego/self.

As the awareness of our true SELF descended deeper into unconscious, our reality changed from the glorious, light-filled childhood realm of discovery, attention to Faeries, and talking to animals into the doldrums of doing chores, finishing homework, and "being good." However, to us it didn't feel good, it felt lonely. We missed playing with the Faeries and talking with our animal friends. Most of all, we missed being filled with our SELF.

It seemed that we had to sacrifice our brilliant imagination so we could "be good" and fit into a reality that was denser, slower, more fearful, and boring. But we had to give up our SELF so "they" would like us, love us, notice us, and let us into their world. We came to this dimension awake, alive, and connected. Then we had to put more and more of our beautiful Soul to sleep. Hence, bit by bit, we died to our true SELF and disconnected from the ONE.

Our second, or navel, chakra is the portal to our fourth-dimensional Emotional/Astral Body and governs our many hidden emotions. Hence, this chakra is ruled by our unconscious mind. When we judge an emotion as "bad," we shove it away from our awareness and into the same archives of our unconscious mind in which the glories of our inner child are stored. Unfortunately, these emotions that are hidden from our conscious awareness are the first ones to be displayed when we are tired, sick, or afraid.

As we integrate our wondrous Soul/SELF and Divine Ideal into our second chakra, we gradually reawaken, rebirth, and reconnect with our magical inner child, who is the physical manifestation of our divine child. Our divine child has remained awake to our Soul and waited for this moment since we put that part of us to sleep. However, before we can connect with our inner child, who is still awake to our divine child, we must first feel and release the many uncomfortable emotions that we have stored in the deepest archives of our unconscious mind along with our wounded child.

Fear has forced our inner child to hide from us, and only love and forgiveness (for that which they *believe* they did wrong) can reconnect us with the glorious imagination, purity, and innocence of the child who lives within. Perhaps if we read our child a story, he or she would feel safe enough to return to our conscious mind.

Once upon a time, so very long ago
There was a special place, where you'll never go
There was a land with ivory towers
Mystical sand and diamond showers

At rainbow's end, was a pot of gold
And in the market, love was sold
It was a land of beauty and peace
And the joy there seemed to never cease

The fairies frolicked in the light of day
And the elves came out when they went away
The people drank and were, oh, so merry
On apple wine and fairy sherry

Never was there a day of grief
For peace and love was the people's belief
Then one day an omen came
And all good things were not the same

The flowers died
And the people cried
For all the joy was taken away
On that dark and awful day

A dragon came to ravage the land
And peace was gone from the mystical sand
A Wizard lived in a city, deep under the sea
Where the people went, to give their plea

"Help us please, you noble man
"You are the only one who can
"A dragon has come to destroy our peace
"And we fear our misery will never cease

"He eats our cows and burns our crops
"With all the fire that he drops
"Help us please, we need your skill
"To save our homes and make this kill."

The Wizard listened to their cry
Finally, he answered them with a sigh,
"Oh my people, I need you to see
"It's hard to slay a dragon, even for me

"For to a dragon you cannot lie
"And dragons are extremely sly!
"They're older and wiser, and have great fame
"If only I knew this dragon's name

"For when you know a dragon's name
"They can no longer play their game
"You'd have them trapped to do your will
"But to find their name would take great skill

"I'll do my very best, I swear
"So you will not live in such despair."
That night he went into his room
Where his wife weaved upon her loom

He had no idea what to do
To make that wretched dragon shoo
Then, all that night he had these dreams
That stitched together all the seams

He dreamt of his young apprentice days
And of a dragon's wily ways
He remembered a day he was hiking around
He also remembered what he had found

He found himself in a slimy cave
With a stench his nose would forever save
The site he saw before his eye
Was enough to make a grown man cry

Before him was a baby dragon
About the size of a horse-drawn wagon
His mother was slain and his brothers all dead
Covered with slime and stained blood-red

But, the baby he saw was still alive
And with some care, could still survive
The baby was hurt fairly bad
And seemed to be so very sad

As he touched the baby, he remembered a day
When he'd learned to heal in a dragon's way
If he could sing in a dragon's tongue
He'd heal the dragon with the song he sung

The first song healed the dragon's sore
But, just to be sure, he sang some more
The dragon, now, would not be lame
And, in return, he gave his name

The dragon left the wizard, never to return
And vowed that HIS land, he would NOT burn
The Wizard awoke with a thought in his head
This could save the village from all its dread

That must have been him, for there is no other
His brothers are dead, along with his mother
He said he was the last of his kind
And no other dragons could one find

The next day the wizard went on a quest
For he had to talk to this horrible pest
When he saw him, he called his name
There was no other, they were the same

The dragon turned and gave him a glance
Then stood there in a stupid trance
"In the name of all that's love and peace,
"Stop this terrorizing, you foolish beast!

"You were banished once, never to return
"Now it is MY land you ruthlessly burn
"What was it that made you go back on your word?
"What happened to the vow that I once heard?"

The dragon gave an awful cry
For now he knew he could not lie
This childhood friend who knew his name
Could make the dragon die of shame

How could he forget his loving friend
Who'd sang to his leg to make it mend?
"What a foolish dragon I must be,
"As you can very plainly see

"I've ravished your land and caused you great strife
"Cause no other dragons are left in my life
"I was so lonely and always so sad
"I guess it turned my life to the bad

"What can I do to change what I've done
"To remove the dark clouds, and bring back the sun?
"I swear upon my name and Soul
"I'll bring this land from its deathly hole."

The dragon did do all that he could
To return the land back to being good
He gladly helped out all the people
And so they gave him a house with a steeple

The dragon no longer was lonely or sad
And never again would his life change to bad
AND, when he turned the land back to how it was
His retched slime turned into to furry fuzz

The Fuzzy Dragon, became his name
And throughout the land, he gained much fame
And up until this very day
His memory lights the Dragon's Way

The moral of this story
As you can clearly see
Is a dragon also needs love
Just like you and me

So, if someone's acting angry
It may be cause their sad
Forgive them for their actions
Even if they're bad

Forgiveness is a healing
That you might need some day
Then you will be so happy
That you learned the Dragon's Way

(story written by Julie Jordan at 11 years of age)

Our negative emotions are actually stored in our Lower Astral Body in the Lower Astral Plane, which stands at the threshold to the Emotional/Astral Plane of the fourth dimension. This plane is much like the mythical dragon who creates havoc in our lives by recycling back into the reality that we are re-creating all the fear, anger, and sorrow that we have hidden in our unconscious. If we can face our dragon and name the secrets we have hidden from our conscious memory, we can reunite with the purity and innocence of our inner child, who has become lost to us due to the fear, anger, and sadness that we have suffered.

By merging with our inner child, we will awaken to the great imagination and creative power of our Astral Body. Our Astral Body is also known as our Emotional Body and our Desire Body. The deep desire of our Astral Body is the first step to regaining our innate creativity, for it is the force of our desire that reminds us how we *want* to fulfill our Divine Ideal and be our true SELF.

Our Divine Ideal gestates in our navel chakra, patiently awaiting birth. The gestation of our ideal continues when we keep our dreams alive with the power of our attention and desire. Furthermore, our inner child, who never forgot our SELF and the Divine Ideal that we promised to manifest, fills our life with wonder, innocence, imagination, and creativity.

To unite with our inner child, we must travel into the Lower Astral Plane to carve a path of light through the layers of old fears. Otherwise, it is the shame, sadness, anger, and fear of our past that recreates our past over and over until, at last, we are healed. Fear is the lowest frequency emotion and sits at the lowest level of the Emotional/Astral Plane like sludge at the bottom of a pond. Beneath that sludge is the hidden treasure of our divine, inner child.

THE SHADOW POND

I walked beside the murky pond and felt a chill deep in my bones. The sky was dark and looked like rain. I knew that I must hurry to shelter, but somehow I could not pull myself away from the foreboding pond.

There was something in there; I felt its presence. It frightened me, but I did not wish to run. I had learned that fear is like a shadow and every time I ran from it, it grew bigger.

"I am going to stay and face it," I said to myself. "Whatever happens, it can't be worse than running away. I have run and run and the shadow at my back only grows. Whatever I have created, it is time to look it in the face."

I turned with the conviction of my final words and planted my feet to awaken my inner courage. It felt good. At least now, I felt in control. At least now, I was the warrior, rather than the victim.

Now, I felt strong enough to face this fear, come what may. I walked to the rim of the pond to see what secrets lay hidden in the gloomy water, but all I could see was a grim reflection of my self.

Oh, it is too dark today and soon it will rain, I thought with a shudder. I will come back on a clearer day. Perhaps then a sunbeam may find its way into the depths of the pond to expose its secret.
I turned to walk away, but with my very first step I knew that I must stay. If I could not see what was in the pond, maybe I would have to feel it. Maybe I would have to actually enter the pond and feel its dark waters upon me.

The thought of entering the murky water made me cringe. Should I keep my clothes on as some meager attempt at protection or should I enter the water as naked as the day I was born?

I knew the answer. I must face the depths without any external protection. I must find my protection in the courage that it would take to enter the murky pond. Courage, which was deep within my core, would be my only protection to face the darkness and the secrets that it held.

I shed my clothes quickly, before I lost my nerve, and jumped into the foreboding pond. I held my breath and immediately dove to the bottom. I navigated with my arms, as I was not quite ready to open my eyes.

When I touched the bottom of the pond, I knew that I must open my eyes while I still had enough air in my lungs to remain at the bottom. A vision of muck and grime awaited my opening eyes. But what was that—just over there?

Something golden was sparkling against the surrounding filth. Oh, it must be rescued, I thought. It does not belong here. This golden thing is different from the dirt that surrounds it.

I swam to the golden sparkle and wiped the mud from its surface. The dark mud hovered in the water, waiting to again cover the golden object. I reached for the treasure with the intention of bringing it to the surface, but I found that it was held fast to the bottom of the pond. I pulled and pulled, but it did not budge.

Finally, I stood on the silt-covered bottom to gather enough resistance to free the bit of gold. My toes squished into the sticky mud and my struggle filled the water with silt. I had to close my eyes to protect them and pulled upon the golden object while I pushed against the floor of the pond.

Yet nothing worked and I was running out of oxygen. Would I have to abandon the treasure that lay hidden in the murky pond's depths? I stood still for a moment and released my hold on the golden object. It instantly sank back into the mire.

Only a small portion of it glistened through the filthy water. With shame, I realized that I could not free the treasure. Then I remembered that it had been my intention to feel the water. Yes, now I felt it. It felt like shame and guilt, and most of all, it felt like fear.

The fear permeated every rock and every atom of the pond. No wonder that which was beautiful could not be freed. As I stopped my struggle, the mud that had filled the water began to settle onto me.

I felt it clawing at my skin reminding me of feelings that I had felt outside of the dark pond. *No!* I must leave these depths and the feelings that they aroused in me. I could not save the treasure. I would have to leave it in the murky depths.

Besides, I could hold my breath no longer. I must return to the surface. The thought of escape felt good and necessary. I swam to the surface with a mixture of relief and sadness, relief that I could free myself from the silt and sadness that I could not free the hidden treasure.

My head bobbed above the surface of the pond and a cool rain rinsed the dirt off my face. I swam to the edge of the pond and pulled myself onto a rock. Standing, I allowed the gentle rain to cleanse my body. The feel of the fresh water upon my skin rejuvenated and calmed me.

The mud of the pond was easily cleared, for it was never mine. I realized then that the filth of the pond was something that I had temporarily taken on, temporarily experienced.

I looked at the pond again. It seemed clearer now. The mud that I had stirred up had again settled to the bottom. I remembered the bit of gold that was still trapped there. How could I free it?

I would have to again enter the murky pond and swim down into its darkest depth. Could I remember my own purity, even when the mud clung to my form? Could I find the bit of gold hidden beneath the silt and bring it to the surface?

"*Yes!*" I cried to the sun that was breaking through the clouds. "I shall find what has been lost. That which has been buried and forgotten shall be found and returned.

“Something of great value is lost in the depths of the darkness, and I must retrieve it."

Once we have dedicated ourselves to clearing our personal darkness, our navel chakra is free to create our reality based on our instincts, our empathy, the things that make us feel good, and those things which are *fun* and carefree. Also, as we liberate our inner child, the part of us that has delayed its development by remaining in a constant state of immaturity can expand our consciousness beyond the victim consciousness of the dependent into independent and even into the group consciousness of being dependable.

When our consciousness can resonate to being dependable, we feel mature enough to release our inner child into our daily life. Just as children who know they are children playing at being adults, adults who *know* they are adults can play like children and still behave like adults. It is in our childlike playfulness that we can recapture our imagination, innocence, and joy, as well as the happy memories that were buried beneath our fear.

SECOND CHAKRA MEDITATION

You may wish to prepare your space with candles, incense, music, privacy, and peace. Since the second chakra rules the element of water, you may wish to sit near water, turn on a water fountain, listen to an environmental CD of water, or meditate in the tub or after a shower. As you begin this meditation, hold the memory of the feeling of water on your body.

Imagine that you are floating in water…

Experience the *flow* as the water follows its current…

without resistance…without question…

without fear…

Feel this *flow* of fluid under and within you as it feeds and heals you…

The second chakra rules our personal *and* planetary home.

Visualize yourself sitting in your favorite place in nature…

Align your second chakra with your first chakra…

Feel your SELF at home in your body…

Feel your body at home on Mother Earth...

The physical sense of the second chakra is taste.

Think of your favorite foods and the memories of enjoying them…

What is your emotional attachment to eating?

What memories are linked to your family meals?

To begin the meditation, align your third-dimensional body with your fourth-dimensional bodies, as well as the fourth-dimensional bodies of Gaia.

Align the base of your spine—*first chakra*—with your
Etheric Body and Gaia's hydrosphere
and your physical body and Gaia's lithosphere.

Align your navel—*second chakra*—with your
Emotional Body and Gaia's biosphere.

Align your solar plexus—*third chakra*—with your
Mental Body and Gaia's troposphere.

Align your heart—*fourth chakra*—with your
Guardian Angel/divine child and Gaia's stratosphere.

Align your throat—*fifth chakra*—with your
Causal Body and Gaia's mesosphere.

Align your brow—*sixth chakra*—with your
I AM Presence and Gaia's ionosphere.

Align your crown—*seventh chakra*—with your
Multidimensional SELF and Gaia's exosphere.

The navel chakra resonates to the color orange.
Close your eyes and take three long, slow, deep breaths.
See yourself as a small orange light in the center of your brain…
Slowly, allow that light to fall down your spine like a feather…
As you travel down past your brow…
past your throat…past your heart…
past your solar plexus…
and into your navel chakra…

REMEMBERING

Breathe into your second chakra…
Allow memories of your youth to come forward…
With each memory, you become younger and younger…
Feel the emotion that is attached to each memory…

With each memory ask, "What did I learn from that experience?"

Store the pleasant memories in your heart...
Release the unpleasant memories with a loud exhalation...

Visualize your child-self standing in front of you...

How old is this child?
What is he or she wearing?
Do you recognize the place he or she is in?

Thank your child-self for hiding your negative feelings when you were a child and were not prepared to deal with them.

Release your inner child from that duty now, as you are mature enough to clear these emotions.

What does your inner child say to you?

LIFE BEFORE BIRTH

Imagine yourself as an infant and still the pure essence of your divine child.

Remember, your imagination is *real*!
Visualize yourself becoming younger and younger until you are in the womb.
Feel the sensation of floating in your mother's womb.
What emotions are you feeling?

Imagine yourself floating in the womb of Mother Earth.

Feel how you are ONE with her.

Imagine your Spirit Essence before you were born.

From this perspective, look down at planet Earth...
See your Earth Mother and your human mother awaiting your birth...
What emotions and memories are you having?

See your Soul/SELF around you as you await your birth...
As you begin your re-birth:

Invite your Soul/SELF, who has recalibrated and entered your first chakra, to move both down from your Spirit Essence and up from your root into your navel.

Feel your Multidimensional Soul/SELF as it assists you to *release fear and choose love*.

As you do so, feel the expansion of your consciousness, as the dense, constricting and separating emotions of *fear* are replaced by the expanding, unifying emotions of *love*.

As your Soul becomes captain of your second chakra, the innocence of your inner child and the wisdom of your divine child assist you in beginning to remember the Divine Ideal you volunteered to fulfill before you were born...

MANTRA:

I am remembering my Divine Ideal.
I gestate my Divine Ideal in my navel chakra
and nurture it
until it is ready for birth.

With the memory of your Divine Ideal in the forefront of your consciousness, establish a constant communication with your inner child.

Allow the inner child of your navel chakra
to unite with you in the Guardian Angel of your heart chakra
to give your inner child the everlasting gift of
unconditional love and divine protection

THE PRESENT

The small child very much wanted the
brightly wrapped present.
But, somehow, she felt she didn't deserve it.

Each time it was given to her
she retreated in shyness and lowered her eyes.

How could that lovely prize be hers?
How could she accept it?

"Just take it," spoke a loving presence.

"There are others who know more than you.
Even though you cannot see all that has brought this to you,
know that it is yours."

The child did not understand.
But she trusted the kindly being and timidly reached for her prize.

But, as she touched it, it disappeared.

"Where has it gone?" cried the child.

"Why, it is yours now," spoke the being.

"It is no longer something that you must reach for.
It is something now which you must own."

GAINING MASTERY

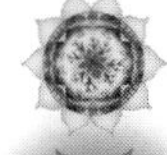

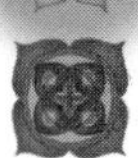

As the multidimensional light of our Soul/SELF fully integrates into each chakra, we can complete our divine intention by becoming masters of the elements and of the portions of our life ruled by these elements. The second chakra rules the third-dimensional element of water and the fourth-dimensional Water Elementals known as the Undines. Since water is the energetic correlate to emotions, when we secure mastery of water energy we gain emotional mastery, and visa versa. This process of gaining mastery is fulfilled through learning the lessons and facing the challenges of the navel chakra.

Water is an element that easily transmutes into higher frequencies. Hence, when we have mastered the flowing element of water, our consciousness greatly expands. For example, ice is the lowest frequency of water, which when heated transmutes to the higher frequency and more flowing expression of liquid. Finally, under continued heat, the ice, which has transmuted into water, transmutes into steam, its highest frequency. Metaphorically and energetically ice is frozen emotions, such as the lost emotions hidden in our unconscious mind. Like these emotions, ice is cold and not pleasant to hold.

However, once our emotions rise in vibration to a more fluid expression, we can more easily allow an intimate expression of our true feelings. As our emotions leap in vibration to steam, they transcend beyond emotion and into the realm of consciousness. Hence, it is through releasing pent-up emotions and expressing them in an intimate manner that we can expand our consciousness. In the case of the navel chakra, we expand our consciousness from the personal consciousness of being independent to the group consciousness of being dependable.

In order to gain mastery of our emotions, we must take full responsibility for the emotions that we allow to remain in our bodies and in our consciousness. Since at infancy our bodies are comprised of up to 70 percent water (which decreases with age), our earth vessels store emotions until we can transmute them into consciousness. Then our emotions are stored in our consciousness. Nonetheless, as long as we have a physical body, we will continue to store and express our emotions through our bodies. Gaia's planet Earth is also 70 percent water, and our language uses many earth-based metaphors to describe emotions, such as an angry sea, frigid waters, and a flood of emotions.

COMMUNING WITH THE WATER ELEMENTAL

Our biosphere, which is the correlate of our fourth-dimensional Emotional Body, is largely dependent on water for survival. Remembering that Gaia is the consciousness of all Earth, including humanity, it is easy to understand how our human emotions impact the waters of our planet. As an example, when we hold fear in our body, our personal Elementals feel restricted and constricted, or they feel a need for fight or flight. Our personal Elementals are then obliged to out-picture and share with the planetary Elementals the separation and limitations of fear, as well as the random and violent movements of fight or flight through our planetary waters.

Fortunately, we can commune with our fourth-dimensional Water Elementals by raising our consciousness into Alpha or Theta Consciousness and focusing our attention to the many forms of water flowing through our earth vessel. We can then take a long moment to bless each Water Elemental as it circulates the flow of fluid throughout our body. We can then *feel* this inner current and assist our Elementals to share our blessing with Gaia's Water Elementals. Then, together and in unison, our personal and planetary Undines can out-picture our blessing into our environment.

As we take full responsibility for how we feel about our body and our interaction with others, we also take responsibility for how we feel about our planet and how we interact with it. Therefore, we can take a moment to assist our Water Elementals in clearing the tainted waters of our fearful emotions. Just as we can no longer poison our bodies with toxic emotions, we can no longer poison our waters with toxic waste.

In this manner, as our emotions evolve to expressions of our consciousness, we become increasingly aware of our unity with all life and with our planet. The love that we have found within our SELF and within the gestation of our Divine Ideal is spread out into our surrounding environment via our fourth-dimensional personal Elementals who are in constant contact with the planetary Water Elementals. It is this emotional mastery that displays the higher abilities of great sages to calm the waters.

Our emotions are also receivers of the vibrations of inner and largely unused instincts and empathy. Empathy is the ability to feel the emotions of other people. However, in order to understand our empathic messages, we must first have an intimate knowing of how our own emotions feel in our body. In other words, we must be conscious of how our body registers fear, anger, sorrow, and love.

When we are empathic, we feel others' emotions inside of our own body. If we have not taken full responsibility for our own emotions, we will not be able to differentiate between our own emotions and the emotions of others. With the integration of our Soul/SELF into our navel chakra, our gut instinct will also become multidimensional, and we will be able to more easily tune into Gaia's first-, second-, and fourth-dimensional beings.

Our emotions not only tell us how we feel, they tell us what we want. Our navel chakra rules our sensate pleasure and the joy of getting what we want. As we gain mastery of our emotions, we learn that *we* are the creators of our life. We first form the template or matrix for our manifestation with our thoughts, but it is our emotions that give life to that creation.

It is our conscious intention that gives us the patience and endurance to hold our desire until it is ready to be born into our physical reality. This creativity extends beyond our personal self and into our planetary self, as we realize it doesn't matter what we have if we don't have a planet on which to enjoy it. The secret to finding peace with our desires is learning that happiness is not getting what we what. Happiness is wanting what we have!

SYMPTOMS OF TRANSFORMATION

Many of the symptoms, which must be balanced and centered for the navel chakra, are emotional. For example, we may have very erratic and childish tantrums one day and then feel emotionally shut down and even depressed another day. Sometimes the shift in our emotions can happen several times within one day. Since the genitals are ruled by this chakra, our sexuality and attitudes towards sex and intimacy may vary greatly each day, and/or our bodily symptoms may be centered on our sexual organs.

As we fully integrate our Soul/SELF and settle into our increased vibration, our emotions become calm and our consciousness peaceful. We begin to see our self as a lover, not a fighter. We want our world to be a safe nest for our young, and we see Earth as our mother and our *home*.

Just as we enjoy the sensate pleasure of other humans, we begin to deeply appreciate the many sensate pleasures of feeling the sun on our face; the sand, dirt, or grass between our toes; and the many wonderful aromas of nature. Since the planet is our home, we begin to treat our planet with the same respect as we do our house and the entire biosphere as members of our family. Since we fully realize that we share the Earth, our attitudes about Gaia's many creatures shift. We also realize that we cannot *own* the land, but instead we share and protect it for future generations to enjoy.

We may suffer physical symptoms of flashes of heat that arise from within our body. These heat flashes denote the resistance of our ego/self to the rise in frequency as our Soul/SELF slowly and safely takes command. Fatigue also accompanies this process of changing the guard. Our physical body is not accustomed to the frequency of our Soul/SELF and becomes exceedingly tired in its effort to integrate the higher frequencies.

During this transition, time alone and inside our SELF is vital so that our mundane consciousness can be aware of and accept our process of transformation. As we integrate our Soul into our earth vessel, it is vital that we keep the grounding cord of our recalibrated root chakra connected with the core of Gaia. This grounding cord allows us to assist Gaia and to accept her assistance in return.

BLENDING POLARITIES, SECOND CHAKRA
I HAVE/WE HAVE

With the integration of our Multidimensional Soul/SELF and Divine Ideal into our second chakra, the vibration of our reality is raising at the speed of light. Because of this, everything around us seems to be changing so fast that we can barely catch up with ourselves. There are also many things that we find we can no longer tolerate. We are trying to not judge, but the third-dimensional reality of separation and limitation, work and reward, no longer excites us or gives us comfort. The external reward of *having* something is becoming less important than the internal reward of *being* someone.

The recalibration of our first and second chakras is creating an immense shift deep inside of us. The "regular" world still exists, but we are less emotionally charged by it. Consequently, we are less emotionally attached to the many external dramas and illusions, as we are deeply involved in the internal spectacle of our own transformation. Our growing detachment from the dramas of third-dimensional life is allowing us to gradually raise our resonance above the mundane, physical reality. With this rise in resonance, we often look at life from the perspective of the observer.

With our androgynous, Multidimensional SELF integrated into our root and navel chakras, our male and female polarities are more intermingled now and our gender roles are scrambled. Hence, we have had to learn new ways of dealing with our personal relationships. With our Soul more inside us, rather than above us, our increased inner intimacy allows an inner *trust* so that we can be more intimate with our outer love relationships and inner-circle people.

As our Soul is less separate from our ego, our consciousness is beginning to expand beyond its normal limitations. From our new, expanded consciousness, the old tactics of blaming others for our problems no longer functions. Of course, our ego may try to repeat this old behavior, but it is not as satisfying as it was before.

The third-dimensional illusions of separation are leaving our reality, and we are realizing our role and responsibility in all our dealings. With the blending of the polarities of *I/we*, we no longer believe that there is a "they" who can limit us. Hence, we must take full responsibility for the reality we have created.

EXPANDED PERCEPTIONS

As the polarity of "I" becomes "we," and "I have" alters to "we have," our sense of ownership encompasses not only what is "mine," but also what is "ours." With the return of our primitive self and inner child, we remember that Earth is a living being. Now that our consciousness has expanded beyond the confines of our small, physical earth vessel, we feel that we are a component of that great being. In the same way as our fingers and toes are components of our physical being, every rock, insect, fish, plant, animal, human, Elemental, Faerie, Deva, and Angel are components of the being who is planet Earth.

When we shift from *I have* a body to *we have* a planet, we begin to experience a unity with all life, which activates our multidimensional perceptions. Thus, our ability to perceive the aura of a friend, the life force of a plant, a higher-dimensional being standing beside us, the Faeries in our garden, and the subatomic molecules which connect all life increases. Hence, we are no longer separate from or limited in our ability to intimately *know* and commune with the reality that *we have*. More often now our expanded sense of SELF can see someone or something in the corner of our eye that disappears when we turn our head to look straight on.

We are also learning to focus our hearing to hear the overtones and undertones of sound. Our communication with the first- and second-dimensional world is steadily growing to the point where sometimes we find we can listen to the quiet, communicate with a rock when we hold it in our hand, and touch a tree or lean against it to allow the tree to tell its story. Trees have much to say, because they have their roots deep in Mother Earth and the life force of their branches and leaves is high in Father Sky.

We are expanding our once-limited consciousness to be receptive to the many different frequencies of multiple dimensions all within the same moment of the *now*. Because of this, we may often feel tired, as our third-dimensional consciousness strains to accept these expanded perceptions. On the other hand, from our "primitive" first and second multidimensional consciousness, these new perceptions seem natural because Gaia and her inhabitants are included in our mundane thoughts and decisions. Gaia is well aware of our contribution and adds her expanded frequency to our process. The partnership has begun. Person and planet are becoming ONE.

In fact, we have so immensely expanded our consciousness that it can no longer be housed in one small earth vessel. Our awareness is expanding to fill the entire Earth, which is why we can perceive and commune with Earth's creatures. However, in order to be conscious of these experiences, we must trust the inner silent voice of our new captain, Soul/SELF, who is translating our multidimensional perceptions so that our third-dimensional sensory organs can understand them.

Gradually, as each chakra integrates our Soul/SELF, the organs, nerve plexus, and endocrine glands that are governed by that chakra will also be recalibrated to resonate to the frequency of our SELF. As the inner mechanisms of our earth vessel are recalibrated, our earth vessel will begin its slow and steady transformation. Some of us will experience that transformation in our bodies first, and others will experience it in our lives first. Eventually, we will experience it in both.

Either way, it is best if we don't try to foresee who we will be, what we will do and create, or what we will look like, for we are not yet free of the influence of our ego/self and may want to compare ourselves to or compete with others. It is helpful if we remember to surrender *all* control of our physical body to our Soul!

Our awakened ability to commune with *all* life is breaking down the final barriers of limitation and separation that once held the third-dimensional illusions in place; and the solid world around us is beginning to waver and flicker in and out.

Just for a second, the second in which we are able to calibrate our consciousness to our awakening multidimensional preceptors, our reality of *I am* blends into *we are*. We then realize that "I" and "we" are ONE. Therefore, what *I have* and *we have* are ONE, as well. Within that moment, the polarities of *I have/value/desire* merges with *we (family, community, nation, planet, Gaia, solar system, galaxy, universe, all that is) have/value/desire*.

EGO BLENDING WITH SOUL

One of the first missions of the new captain of our earth vessel, Soul/SELF, is to embrace our suffering ego/self and give it the comfort, validation, acknowledgement, and success that it has always wanted. Then our ego/self no longer needs to *have* the money, fame, and success of the third-dimensional game because it *has* its true essence once again. As our ego merges with our Soul, we can easily remember that we can manifest anything we want to *have* by focusing our thoughts and emotions through our intention.

With the blending of the polarities of the ego and the Soul, the ego's personal desire cannot be used to harm or conflict with any other separate person's desire, as *nothing* and *no one* is separate. Our Desire Body is being recalibrated to synchronize with the desires of our expanded consciousness, as well as the expanded consciousness of Gaia and her inhabitants. Within the higher vibrations of our Soul/SELF, we no longer need to work hard.

All we have to *do* in order to *achieve* is to choose to calibrate our desires with the frequency of that reality. In other words, if we want abundance, we calibrate our consciousness to the feeling or frequency of abundance, or if we want love, we calibrate our consciousness to the feeling or frequency of love.

If we monitor our thoughts and listen to our emotions, we can keep positive thoughts and loving emotions, which resonate to a higher frequency than negative thoughts and fearful emotions. In that manner, we can more easily allow that reality into our conscious perception. Myriad realities function within the same time and space. In order to choose our reality, we choose the resonance of our consciousness. In that manner we will be able to remain consciously engaged in that version of reality.

BECOMING ONE WITH THE PLANET

SECOND PLANETARY CHAKRA
The Brazilian Amazon

The second chakra is female/inflow energy. It is the place in our body where we connect to our emotions, and *feel* our gut instincts. Gaia's second chakra, the Brazilian Amazon, is also where she can best *feel* her body, the planet. Whereas Mt. Sinai is Earth's base, the Brazilian Amazon is Earth's womb. It is the cradle of all life. All of the elements of earth, air, fire, and water are abundant there and freely interact with each other in this womb of Gaia's biosphere. This paradise of undiscovered miracles is being sacrificed due to greed and poverty, as daily, more of Gaia's beloved Amazon dies.

The second chakra, ruled by our reproductive organs, is a fitting match for Earth's second chakra, as the Brazilian Amazon holds myriad secrets of fertility and growth. Our navel chakra is where we connected to our mother via our umbilical cord. This cord was severed at our birth. Now we will connect that cord again, except this time, it will be connected not to our birth mother but to our Earth mother. We take a moment, to *feel* Mother Nature as we connect our umbilical cord to her womb in the Brazilian Amazon.

Our second chakra, as well as Earth's second chakra, is the area which most exudes passion, gestation, birth, and rebirth. Ruled by the element of water, our navel chakra also represents sensuality and creativity. One of the foundations of our immense creativity is our sensual sensitivity, which registers our emotional reactions to life. If we remain intuitively tuned in to both our second chakra as well as to Earth's, we will reconnect with our personal and planetary instincts, intuitions, and ancient traditions.

BLENDING CHAKRAS MEDITATION

Travel again into the core of Gaia's body to reconnect your essence with hers. Down, down, down you go into the very womb of the Planetary Body. The further into Gaia's core you travel, the further back in your childhood you go. At last you are in Mother Earth's womb, as well as in the womb of your birth mother.

As you slowly rise to the surface, you are rising up through the birth canal. At last, you are born again, this time deep in the heart of the Brazilian Amazon. Breathe in the many aromas that hang in the damp air of the jungle. Listen to the sounds of the creatures and see the myriad plants, many of them unknown to science. Feel the humid heat on your body as you grow into maturity.

At last, you are again adult, only you are transformed. Earth is your mother, and you are a child of nature. As you walk through the dense jungle and along the many rivers, you feel at ONE with your environment. You listen to the sounds and voices of the jungle's creatures, and you *feel* the sense of *now* in which these many life forms live. You hear the rain tapping on the roof of the distant canopy above as you move along the jungle trails.

Feel your self alive amongst the blossoming goddess, as your own creativity is ignited by the fertility of the world around you. Welcome all that you are experiencing into your physical body. Feel the creativity and glory of the Brazilian Amazon within your own navel chakra, as you allow your ancient memory to recollect the many secrets for healing that hide in this vast jungle.

Take a long moment to experience your Planetary Body. Sense the gestation of the spark of your Multidimensional SELF and the seed of your Divine Ideal within your second chakra and the second chakra of Earth in the Brazilian Amazon, as you say:

“*I am* creation. *I am* fertility.

Through the *power* of the Amazon

I patiently gestate my Divine Ideal

to be expressed through my

Multidimensional SELF!”

MESSAGE FROM SOUL/SELF

Hello dear child,

I am your Soul, here to play with you again. Do you remember how I was with you when you were a child? I want to thank you for clearing out the old, emotional memories so that I can awaken within you again.

Sister Gaia is also happy that you can again play with her Faerie friends, talk to the animals, fly like the clouds, and imagine yourself in other times, places, and realities.

I promise that I will tend your Divine Ideal, which you have carefully planted in your root chakra and loved into gestation in your navel chakra. Our partnership is growing now as you are remembering me—that is, as you are remembering your SELF.

It feels so good to be awake within you again. Continue dear warrior and wise child. I am with you!

Your Faerie, your Soul, your SELF

CHAPTER FIFTEEN

EMPOWERING OUR NEW REALITY

THE THIRD CHAKRA

LOCATION: The third chakra is located in our solar plexus, which is between the sternum and the navel.

PETALS: There are ten petals in the third chakra, which when spinning, may appear like a vortex. In numerology, the number ten is reduced to the number one, which symbolizes the beginning. And all communication and action begin with a thought. This chakra rules analytical as well as psychic thinking. It also rules contact with and travel to the fourth-dimensional Astral Plane.

NOTE AND MANTRA: The note for this chakra is D and the mantra is "ram" or "aum."

COLOR: The color of this chakra ranges from yellow to gold. When seen in our aura with astral vision, the color yellow represents intellectual thinking. The color gold represents identification with our Soul qualities. A predominance of yellow in our aura represents our attachment to our ego's rational thought. On the other hand, the predominance of gold in our aura represents an ego that has surrendered its control of the physical earth vessel to the Soul.

On a physical level, the color yellow stands for caution. Yellow is between the red of "stop" and the green of "go." Great caution is needed to integrate our physical and astral selves. The road to spirituality is paved with cautious patience.

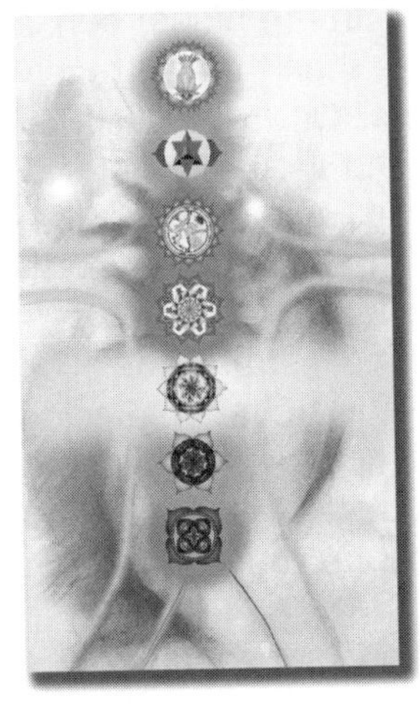

RULES: The third chakra rules the *mental* portion of our consciousness and governs thinking, psychic abilities, and the power, control and/or freedom that is gained by our minds. This chakra is our power chakra. It governs our sense of self, the power that we have within and over our destinies, the power that we have over others, and the power that others have over us.

If a person is too yin (female energy), then he or she may feel no power within. On the other hand, if a person is too yang (male energy), then he or she may need to have power over others. The third chakra relates to the liver, gall bladder, stomach, spleen, and pancreas. This chakra also regulates how well our mental facilities and our ability to be self-motivated intermingle—in other words, whether or not we can we follow our thoughts with actions.

The projections of our ego and our vital energies are both influenced by this chakra, because it rules how well we can maintain our sense of self when in a power struggle with another. The battle between egos is difficult to win if we are children and our opponent is our parent. Therefore, this chakra holds the secrets of the many power struggles that we fought and lost with our parents and other authority figures when we were children.

The third chakra is known as the gateway into the Astral Plane of the fourth dimension. It therefore rules our psychic emotions. However, these emotions are very different than physical emotions that we feel through our second chakra (which rules emotions of survival and instincts). The emotions of the third chakra are intertwined with our thought process.

They can also be emotions that we have psychically and unconsciously picked up from others.

These more cognitive emotions are felt as reactions to others and as reactions to our desires and goals. It is this combination of thought and emotions that opens our gateway into the fourth dimension. Once opened, this portal can begin to blend our third-dimensional perceptions with the higher senses of our physic, intuitive consciousness. It is then that we receive emotional and mental images from others. On the other hand, some of us were born with that ability, and if we did not have guidance, this ability most likely caused us great fear and discomfort because we didn't feel we had control over the process.

The integration of our physical and astral bodies can create yet another control issue for the third chakra. Besides the control issues of different egos attempting to assert their personal power over one another, we struggle with the internal control issues of our thoughts vs. emotions, our intuition vs. intellect, and our yin vs. yang.

SENSE: The third chakra rules our sense of sight. It rules the physical sight of our third-dimensional consciousness as well as our second sight, or fourth-dimensional astral vision.

ASTROLOGICAL SIGN: Leo is often associated with this chakra. Ruled by the sun, Leo symbolizes our warmth and strength as well as our striving for recognition, power, and social status. Astrologically, our sun represents the ego system that we embody within this lifetime.

The third chakra represents the struggle of that ego system, first with others and then with our Soul. When we find our power within ourselves, we no longer need to struggle against others. Then our ego must learn to recognize the still, small voice of our Soul and learn to surrender control of our earth vessel to this superior captain.

ELEMENT: Fire is the element associated with this chakra. Fire represents the electrical/neural portion of our third-dimensional physical body. Electricity is associated with our ability to consciously rule our behavior by our thoughts because it is the electrical firing of our nervous system that allows our cortex to choose our behavior.

When we have gained the will power to choose our behaviors, actions, words, and attitudes, we are consciously in control of our life. On the other hand, if we do not consciously choose our behavior, actions, words, and attitudes, we are reacting rather than responding. Then, we feel as though we are *not* in control of our life because we are unable to choose a response that empowers us.

The third, or solar plexus, chakra rules the Animal Kingdom of which humanity is said to be at the top of the hierarchy. This determination is made by the size of our cortex and our supposed ability to control our own destiny. However, that control is not based solely upon the size of our cortex. Whales and dolphins have larger cortexes than we do, and dolphins actually have more speech mechanisms than humans. However, whales and dolphins have been at the mercy of mankind's violence for many years.

Humans have also harmed, killed, and enslaved other humans as well. The third chakra is the chakra that deals with both inter- and intra-species' struggle for power and dominance. The ability to communicate our thoughts and feelings through speech has always been an important factor in that struggle.

CONSCIOUSNESS: The area of the brain associated with this chakra is the neo-cortex, which is the beginning of higher mental functioning. The third chakra represents our third-dimensional consciousness, as well as how our fourth-dimensional Astral Body influences our physical world. If we disallow any conscious influence from our astral self, we limit our reality.

PERSONAL TIMELINE: This chakra represents ages 6 years to adolescence. This is the time frame when the child begins to go to school and moves away from the constant influence of the family. From the ages of 6 through 12, children are interacting with teachers, friends, and their friends' families, but their primary influence is still their home.

Children of this age increasingly become aware that they are different from their parents. This awareness drives them to find their own identity within the family, especially as they move into early adolescence. From age 12 through adolescence, the focus switches from the family to friends. If these young adolescents are able to develop a sense of self while living in the family system, they will have an easier time when they repeat that process outside of the home.

SOCIAL TIMELINE: Anthropologically, the third chakra represents the civilizations of about 5,000 years ago when the great empires of Egypt, Syria, Greece, and Rome existed. These societies became dominant through having power over their opponents. The rise and peak of these civilizations marked the expansion of humankind's cognitive abilities. Within these civilizations, at least some members of the society had time to pursue something beyond survival. The people of most of these societies worshiped multiple gods and goddesses as well as animals.

ENDOCRINE: The endocrine gland for the third chakra is the pancreas. The pancreas plays an important role in the digestion of food. The pancreas secretes the hormone insulin, which regulates the level of blood sugar in the system and the metabolism needed for digesting carbohydrates. Enzymes that are secreted by the pancreas are important for the balance of fats and proteins.

This endocrine gland is thrown off when too much sugar is taken into the system. This is often because the person wants more sweetness in his or her life and does not know how to get it. Alcoholic beverages instantly convert to sugar, and diabetes can result from alcoholism. Again, this person does not feel like he or she has the power within to face life and must take a substance to comfort himself or herself.

NERVE PLEXUS: The solar plexus, which is located just beneath the ribcage, is associated with this chakra. Areas of the body associated with this chakra are the lower back, abdomen, digestive system, stomach, liver, spleen, gall bladder, and autonomic nervous system.

CLEAR: When the third chakra is clear, we have a strong sense of personal power and self-motivation. Our power struggles with others are minimal because we accept responsibility for the creation of our own reality. Therefore, we do not feel victimized or controlled by others. If we have a problem in our life, we realize that if it comes to us, it is ours to deal with. We have keen decision-making abilities, a strong will power, and a good self-image.

Since we take charge of our lives, we have good health and vital energy. When we can balance yin and yang, thoughts and emotions, intuition and intellect, will power and surrender to Soul, we can be conscious of the many messages that come to us from the Astral/Emotional Plane. We are able to shield ourselves from the psychic pull of others, as we are able to discriminate our emotions from the emotions of others. We can do this because we have listened to our own astral world as it communicates with us through our dreams and imagination.

UNCLEAR: When the third chakra is unclear, we feel powerless. Since we feel that we have no ability to gather what we need when we need it, we can be reduced to greed, doubt, anger, and then of course guilt. Our bodies respond to the constant tension by developing ulcers, jaundice, hepatitis, diabetes, hypoglycemia, and gallstones. Our sense of powerlessness in the world causes excessive worrying, hypochondriac pain, irritability, and procrastination. We are overly sensitive, cry easily, feel fatigued, and are often anxious and/or depressed.

Our inability to integrate the inner call of our astral life with the outer world creates an over sensitivity to the psychic world of others. Other people's fear, which is the "loudest" emotion to be felt in our third chakra, piggybacks onto our own fear. It then becomes increasingly difficult to be with others or in groups. Our mind races against us with obsessive thoughts and worries, and our negative emotions then amplify our negative thinking and keep us in a constant state of turmoil.

The power that we lost in our past must be regained so that we can live in the present. We must go back to find the negative core beliefs that we hold against ourselves. These beliefs constantly remind us that we are inadequate to face life's challenges and that we do not have the personal power to be happy and successful.

EARTH'S CHAKRA: The earth's third chakra is Mt. Kilimanjaro in Africa. Mt. Kilimanjaro is one of the largest freestanding mountains in the world. The other largest freestanding mountain is also in Africa, the heart of our first great civilizations. Mt. Kilimanjaro reminds us of the power that we can gain to stand alone by finding our power within.

DIMENSIONS: This chakra represents our third- and fourth-dimensional bodies. The third chakra is the gateway to the fourth dimension. Unfortunately, this gateway is often first experienced in our bodies by uncomfortable feelings in the third chakra area of our bodies. In order to avoid being a victim of the psychic world of others, we must gather our own fourth-dimensional power. When we have come to peace with our inner world, as well as with the thoughts and feelings that originate in that world, we will find our true power to stand alone in the outer world.

THE PENNY

The small child was very excited that he had found a penny. The adults smiled because they knew that a penny was not worth much. But the child did not know that. He was as proud of his find as an adult may have been of a hundred-dollar bill. Every day he polished his penny and returned it dutifully to his pocket. Some days he had no pocket so he carried it in his shoe. But always he carried it.

It became a talisman—an omen. He knew that it meant that something special would come to him. It even made him believe that he was something special—special because *he* had discovered the penny. The adults thought he was being cute.

Until *it* began…

No one could say when it first began or even how, but slowly—very slowly— the penny began to glow. At first, everyone thought it was because the child polished it so much. But gradually, it became evident that no ordinary penny could glow like that, no matter how carefully it was polished. And furthermore, the glow began to change. Some days it was gold, other days it was blue or orange, and sometimes the colors flickered in and out like rays of the rainbow.

Everyone was surprised and shocked, except for the child. He had known all along that the penny was special and that he was special for finding it. Unfortunately, life being as it is, someone (and we won't say who) coveted this penny so much that this person sought to steal it from the child.

One night, when the child was sleeping, the culprit crept into his room, took the glowing penny away, and put it in *his or her own* pocket. However, that night the child had a dream. In the dream a wise old man came to him and said,

"Someone seeks what you have and will steal it from you while you sleep."

"No, no!" cried the child. "That cannot be! I need that penny!"

"Oh, no, my child you are very wrong. You see, the penny is just an ordinary penny, but you made it special because *you* are special! The glow comes not from the penny, but from you. The penny was just something that you could cherish outside of yourself because you did not yet know your own inner worth. The penny is gone now because you no longer need it."

"But *I do* need that penny!" the child replied.

"Here," replied the kindly man, "take this one. This is a penny that came from inside of you and it is the symbol of your inner self-worth."

"But it is only a penny! It can't be worth much!" said the boy.

"Only a penny! Have you been listening to others instead of your self? Even the largest tree grows from a small seed. If the seed is loved and nurtured from the very start, the tree will grow healthy and tall. This penny is like your seed. It is a special penny because it is *yours*."

The child awoke with only the memory of a tree. He grabbed the penny from its sleeping place and went about his day.

Now, the one who stole the penny was riddled with guilt and could not understand how it was that the child was not upset. Finally, the guilty party said,

"How is your penny today?"

The child smiled and reached into his pocket. He pulled out the glow that was stronger than ever. It was so strong that no one could see a penny through it. At once, the wily adult ran to the stolen penny to see what could have happened.

There the penny was, but alas, *without* the glow!

The voice of guilt whispered into the culprit's ear,

"You see? You can steal someone's penny,
but you cannot steal someone's *glow*!"

BECOMING ONE WITH SELF

Our child-self is maturing now, and more than anything, our solar plexus chakra represents our *glow*. Our third, solar plexus, chakra is our inner sun, the core of our power within. This power within is maintained by clear, centered, positive thinking. We are our own greatest champion, as well as our greatest enemy. As our Multidimensional SELF and Divine Ideal enter this chakra, our thinking gradually becomes multidimensional and our innate abilities of telepathy, clairaudience, clairvoyance, and clairsentience skirt the edges of our consciousness and/or come into full bloom. Our core beliefs will dictate whether or not we can allow ourselves to believe in our higher senses.

Since the fourth-dimensional body correlating to this chakra is our Mental Body, our thinking goes under the microscope, and thoughts that were once unconscious reveal themselves in our daily life. Because of this, it is vital that we learn to hear the thoughts that pollute our minds. Furthermore, as we expand our consciousness to encompass Gaia, we realize we must also take responsibility for the pollution of Earth's troposphere.

The solar plexus chakra rules our transition from being unconscious to being conscious of our thoughts, emotions, actions, decisions, and choices. The spleen, ruled by this chakra, is a major port for the flow of the fourth-dimensional River into Unity. Hence, as the flow enters this chakra, we experience conscious, inter-dimensional journeys. We may well have had these journeys as children, but they were likely dismissed as just our imagination. As our Soul/SELF integrates into this chakra, we remember that our imagination is fifth-dimensional thought.

At first, when we have not yet realized the extent of our innate power, we believe we are talking to spirit guides (who may actually be higher-dimensional aspects of our SELF) or those who have crossed over, i.e. ghosts. Communicating with the newly departed is the primer for interdimensional communication, as they are just beyond the threshold into the fourth dimension. The danger of interacting with these beings, however, is that they will not know more just because they have crossed over. Also, communication with those who are trapped in the Lower Astral Plane is not likely to be beneficial, as these beings are likely filled with fear, sorrow, or anger. Fortunately, our integrated Soul/SELF will protect us from that negativity until we have released the need for the excitement of fear.

These adventures in consciousness prepare us for the expansion of consciousness from the independent, individual consciousness of the first chakra and the dependable, group consciousness of the second chakra into the telepathic communications of collective consciousness here in the third chakra. As we develop our collective consciousness, we can tune into the general trend of thoughts and emotions of the humans of this planet. Usually, it is best if our intellect is adequately developed before we expand our consciousness to this extreme, because we need our left brains analytical, sequential thought to balance and ground the right brain's interdimensional experiences.

Our interdimensional ability to tune into the collective consciousness, which arises from the entry of the fourth-dimensional River of Light into our solar plexus chakra, activates a great expansion of our reality. First, we can tune into the collective consciousness of our local area. Then, we gradually expand our consciousness to encompass our state, country, hemisphere, and world.

Simultaneously depending heavily on logic and independent thought will keep us at the helm of our traveling earth vessel. In this manner, we are not easily led by any entities who introduce themselves as our leader. Being our own leader is a vital component of finding and maintaining our power within. It is only through having a strong sense of our individuality that we are able to enter the collective consciousness and remain fully grounded in our SELF.

The integration of our SELF into this chakra will create a huge increase in our Beta brainwave intellect and our Alpha brainwave psychic perceptions. With practice and connection with our power within, we can also activate our Theta brainwaves, which guide us into expanded intellectual endeavor and higher frequencies of interdimensional travel. Our power within comes primarily from allowing our Soul/SELF to have power over our ego/self.

THIRD CHAKRA MEDITATION

Close your eyes and focus your awareness on your solar plexus, which is in-between your naval and your heart, just behind your stomach and slightly to the left.

Take three long, slow, deep breaths to breathe yellow light into and out of your solar plexus.

Solar means the sun and a plexus is a structure of interlaced parts combined to create a network. Hence, your solar plexus is the network that creates your *inner sun*.

For your first breath, *inhale* the frequency of brilliant yellow light into your solar plexus…

Exhale this light down through your navel chakra where the frequency of yellow light blends with the frequency of the orange light of the second chakra…

Exhale this light down through your root chakra where the frequency of yellow light blends with the frequency of the red light of your first chakra…

Exhale through the root chakra and down, down into the core of the planet…

With your second breath, *inhale* up from the planetary core, up through your root, your navel, your solar plexus and into your heart…

Exhale the blessing of Gaia's breath out through your heart…

For your third breath, *inhale* the frequency of the green light into your heart chakra…

Exhale slowly, as you merge the green light with:
The yellow light of your solar plexus...
The orange light of our navel…

The red light of your root…
And deep into the core of the planet…

In this manner, you blend the energy of your lower chakras with your heart and with the heart of Gaia…

To begin the meditation, align your third-dimensional body with your fourth-dimensional bodies, as well as with the bodies of Gaia.

Align the base of your spine—*first chakra*—with your
Etheric Body and Gaia's hydrosphere
And your physical body and Gaia's lithosphere.

Align your navel—*second chakra*—with your
Emotional Body and Gaia's biosphere.

Align your solar plexus—*third chakra*—with your
Mental Body and Gaia's troposphere.

Align your heart—*fourth chakra*—with your
Guardian Angel/divine child and Gaia's stratosphere.

Align your throat—*fifth chakra*—with your
Causal Body and Gaia's mesosphere.

Align your brow—*sixth chakra*—with your
I AM Presence and Gaia's ionosphere.

Align your crown—*seventh chakra*—with your
Multidimensional SELF and Gaia's exosphere.

You are ready to begin your meditation.

You will now calibrate your third chakra to accept your Soul/SELF and to activate multidimensional power within.

Allow a picture to enter your consciousness of an area of your life where you feel or have felt *power within.*
How does your body feel?
What emotions are you experiencing?
What thoughts are in your mind?

Allow this *power within* to send down a tail past your navel, through your root and deep into the Earth.

As you travel back up from the core, connect this tail to your inner warrior in your first chakra, your divine child in your second chakra, and the *power within* of your third chakra.

Visualize your Soul/SELF taking that tail of light and connecting it into your inner sun, which is the *network* for your *radiance*.

As your Soul/SELF plugs in the light, your Soul steps into your *inner sun*.

As your Soul enters your *inner sun*:

Allow a picture to enter your consciousness of an area in your life where you feel that there is or there was *power over* you.

How does your body feel?
What emotions are you experiencing?
What thoughts are in your mind?
How does this *power over* limit your behavior?

What third-dimensional illusions of separation and limitation trap you in this *power over* situation?

Feel the tension of these illusions in your body.
Feel the tension of your emotions.
Feel the tension of your thoughts.

Allow the *power within* of your Soul/SELF to:

Sweep up this wounded self as you *fall into* the flow and allow the flow to *fall into* you.

You hear the inner voice of your Soul saying:

You have come to the current of the flow believing it will cleanse you. The flow looks like water, but it is actually liquid light. It has taken great courage for you to take this first step into the flow, but now it will be simple. Won't it?

All you have to do is relax into the flow and release… but, release what? Perhaps you aren't sure. Nonetheless, you settle into what you imagine must be the flow. It is not physical, so you cannot be sure as you may not totally trust your intuitions. Pushing your doubt aside, you settle into the current of the flow expecting it all to be easy.

However, as the flow begins to pull old portions of yourself to the surface, another force counters it by pushing your secrets back into hiding. This force is resistance to change, resistance to the truth. You can feel the flow beginning to move through your body, releasing the stress and strain of your life. However, once again, there are places that are afraid of change—any change.

You feel nervous and uncomfortable, as part of you wants to come to the surface, while it also wants to stay hidden. You know that you have to use your power within to participate in your own healing in order to allow the flow into these hiding places of your powerless, wounded self.

What would be the sense in hiding from your self, from others, or from the truth?

You have always sought the truth. Haven't you? But what if the truth reveals something you don't like, some aspect of your self, some emotion or thought that you are not ready to confront?

You can feel the resistance, but your power within has the courage to face what lays hidden behind this resistance. Can you allow yourself to love even the wounded self that hides behind it? Yes, only love, unconditional love of your own wounded self, will give you the power to accept your resistance as a part of the change, accept that which you are resisting, and then surrender it all to the flow. What do you have to lose?

"You can lose sorrow," says a small, distant voice as you allow the flow to pull your sorrow to the surface.

"Yes," you hear your thoughts say, "But first I know I will have to accept and love it. How can I accept sorrow? How can I love it?"

"Your sorrow has taught you to seek comfort," murmurs the voice.

You know that to be true. Can you take the risk of accepting an old enemy? Can you stop resisting your sorrow, love it free, and release it into the flow? Years and years of sorrow fill your memory until you have no choice. You can hold it no longer. You have to release it, forgive it, and love it. You have to love it free.
"I love you sorrow," you cry into your heart. "You have taught me to seek comfort."

With your words the sorrow leaves you. Your tears join the current of the flow and float away. Comfort now lives in the place that was once filled with sorrow, comfort from the power within that it took to release it. It worked. You loved your sorrow and surrendered it to the flow. However, you know that there is more that you can lose. You listen for the next voice.

"You can lose confusion," says a nearby voice, as the current travels in circles about you. Your thoughts swirl like a flooded river and you almost lose your footing. You will have to surrender your confusion to the current, as you can no longer live with it. But what has it taught you?

"It has taught you to seek clarity," the voice loudly responds.

Without the pent up sorrow you can listen more easily to voice that seems to be gradually moving deeper and deeper into your core.

"I love you confusion," you sing into your mind. "You have taught me to seek clarity."

Because of your love and willingness to surrender to the flow, your confusion is washed from your thoughts. You find that you can more easily relax into the current of the flow. It seems to have a direction now. At last!

"You can lose pain," continues an inner voice as the flow pushes against your body.

Yes pain, the sum-total of your inability to find happiness. You can lose that. But what has it taught you? Yes, you know.

"I love you pain, you have taught me to seek happiness," you say as your arms embrace your body, protecting your wounded self.

Your body's ego/self relaxes as a life of pain is pulled to the surface of your consciousness and released into the flow. Your arms open now and float on the surface of the current, allowing your heart to release all its pain, as well.

"You can lose fear," cries your entire being.

You know the answer and respond. "I love you fear. You have taught me to love," you call to your fear as it floats down the flow with the current.

Then, all that is left is *love* and the power within that you gained by surrendering to the flow. However, one last question taunts your mind.

"What is the flow?" you call into the very current that surrounds you.

"It is I," answers the voice of your Soul. "*I am* the flow of your true SELF. Because you have surrendered to me, we are now ONE."

MANTRA

I *now* take *all* power that I have ever given to any

person, place, situation, or thing

and I hold it *within* my SELF!

MESSAGE FROM GAIA

LAYING DOWN THE MATRIX

Beloved and powerful people of my planet,

You have now re-calibrated your third chakra to face any and *every* person, place, situation, or thing from the perspective of your *power within*. Call upon the new captain of your earth vessel, your Soul/SELF, to assist you in *remembering* this fact. In the days ahead, many things will come to pass, and pass they will. In fact, as you have become translucent to the darkness and receptive to the light, the darkness will pass through you, while the light will pass into you.

You have calibrated your consciousness to the frequency which filters out the vibration formerly known as the darkness, and you have detached your attention from the battles and illusions around you. Now, all that remains is the Power of *truth* that resonates from inside your SELF. The outside world is recognized as a reflection of your inner world cast upon the matrix of the third dimension.

You are a sovereign being, the source of the reality that you share with the others who play on your stage of life. And yes, the drama of the third dimension has taken on epic proportions. However, just beyond the drama is the peace that you so dearly crave. You yearn to feel the soft morning breeze on your face and hear the chirp of the birds as they roost in the nearby tree of life. You wish to feel the warm sun and the cool moon beams on your transforming body. Your greatest desire is to laugh, love, and create. So create that world. Create it *now*!

Appreciate the third-dimensional world that you are creating, for soon it will be transformed. Then *all* of you will remember your Divine Ideal and how you are to *do* and *be* it. Idea by idea, step by step, you will empower your Divine Ideal as you walk your path and lay down the matrix of transformation for *our* planet and for your self. Then *we all* shall *be* ONE, and the planet, the solar system, and the stars shall be your family. Your consciousness is expanding far beyond the confines of your physical body, which is now perceived as the present third-dimensional grounding point for your Soul/SELF.

Your grounding point is the vessel through which you are planting your multidimensional essence into my heart, the heart of Gaia, to share my reality and expand the light of people and planet joined into ONE. It is through the thoughts and desires of your third chakra that you find the power within to complete your ideal. I remind you now to ground all three of your lower chakras into my core. In this manner, you can bring down your greatest power without harm to your earth vessel and join your sweet essence with mine.

I take this moment to thank you for foregoing your personal victories long enough to remember that you came here to participate in the flow of planetary transformation together, as ONE BEING.

Your mother, your SELF,
Gaia

GAINING MASTERY

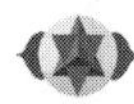

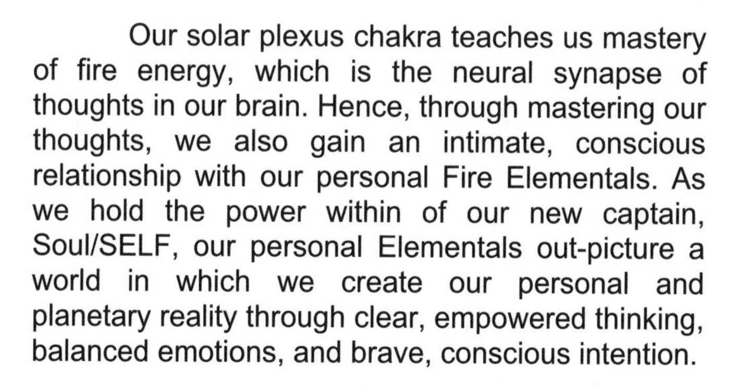

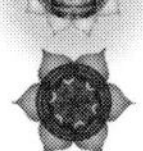

Our solar plexus chakra teaches us mastery of fire energy, which is the neural synapse of thoughts in our brain. Hence, through mastering our thoughts, we also gain an intimate, conscious relationship with our personal Fire Elementals. As we hold the power within of our new captain, Soul/SELF, our personal Elementals out-picture a world in which we create our personal and planetary reality through clear, empowered thinking, balanced emotions, and brave, conscious intention.

COMMUNING WITH FIRE ELEMENTALS

We take a moment now to raise our consciousness enough to commune with our Fire Elementals. We begin by consciously hearing a thought and using our great imagination to observe the flash of neural energy that accompanies that thought. If the thought is positive, it likely ignites our inner sun, but if it is fearful, it likely dims our inner light. We choose now the thoughts of fulfilling our Divine Ideal and living the life of your Multidimensional SELF, as we observe how these thoughts flash our inner sun into its full brightness. We then use the power within our sun to project our fulfillment out into our reality.

In this manner, we have set the matrix for our personal Fire Elementals to out-picture the reality we choose to create. In this manner, our personal Elementals can work with the Earth Elementals to place a similar matrix into the collective consciousness. We close our eyes and open our telepathy and clairaudience to hear the new core belief resonating in the collective consciousness saying, "We can fulfill our ideal and live from the core of our SELF."

As we have joined our great force with the collective consciousness, we feel courageous enough to openly display our innate expanded perceptions. We refuse to allow the fear of others, wrought from ignorance and superstition, to limit the full expression of our SELF. We have aligned the matrix of our Divine Ideal with Gaia's Divine Ideal to create a worldwide matrix of peace and love. Furthermore, through our interdimensional travels and connection to Earth, we are seeing how our personal puzzle piece connects with the planetary puzzle of healing and transformation.

Furthermore, we have consciously connected with our personal Elementals of Earth, Water, and Fire. Because of this, we are also consciously connected to the planetary Elementals of Earth, Water, and Fire. We now realize that we are not just one. *We* are ONE! As the empowered ONE of Earth, we shall endeavor to transform our self and our planet.

SYMPTOMS OF TRANSFORMATION

Since the solar plexus chakra rules our stomach, pancreas, spleen, and gallbladder, problems with these organs may develop as the high frequency light of our Soul/SELF and kundalini flush out our inner darkness. Just as our thoughts digest what happens in our life, the organs of the third chakra digest what happens in our body.

Stress, which is actually low-grade fear, is often displayed in our bodies through problems with heartburn, acid reflux, hypoglycemia, imbalance in blood sugar, and digestive problems. The spleen, our inner sun, is taking in prana or light of a higher frequency, and our bodies are trying to digest this vibration.

Our behavior may be unpredictable as we confront situations in which we have allowed others to command power over us. We are no longer willing to be anyone's victim. We have activated our inner warrior and are willing to fight for our rights. Furthermore, we have learned that a degree of mastery over our emotions assures us that we will not lose our power through hysterical or erratic displays of emotion. We are now able to think the situation though, realize that *we* are the creators of our life, and take full responsibility for what is happening to us.

Yes, sometimes the only part of our life that we can control is our thoughtful responses, but that is one of the primary lessons of this chakra. Thought precedes actions. Neil Armstrong was once asked, "If you were out in space, the hose to your air supply broke, and you had only ten seconds of oxygen left, what would you do?" He replied, "I would think for nine seconds and act in the tenth." With our Soul/SELF as our guide, we are able to think from a multidimensional perspective, which puts us at a great advantage in every situation. As the polarities blend within our SELF, they also blend in our world.

BLENDING POLARITIES, THIRD CHAKRA INDIVIDUAL THOUGHT/ COLLECTIVE CONSCIOUSNESS

As we integrate our Soul/SELF into our earth vessel, and into the body of Gaia, the polarity of individual thought is blending with the opposite polarity of collective consciousness. When we no longer think of ourselves as a separate being, we can accept the responsibility that *we*, the collective consciousness of the inhabitants of the third dimension, are the weavers of *our* third-dimensional matrix.

The third-dimensional matrix is created by weaving together the horizontal, subatomic strings of molecules of matter and the vertical, subatomic filaments of Spirit. If we look with our multidimensional vision, we can actually see these filaments. The vertical filaments of Spirit are glistening, transparent strings of white light (all colors together). On the other hand, the horizontal strings of matter have gone through the third-dimensional prism and have been separated into the seven different octaves or colors of light.

It is through weaving together the strings and filaments of Spirit and matter that we, all the inhabitants of Gaia, create the third-dimensional matrix upon which the hologram of our reality is projected. Our separate self is a small segment of our true, Multidimensional SELF. Just as one could cut a hologram into many fragments and each separate piece would display a vision of the whole, our individual, third-dimensional self can also be used to present a vision of our whole, personal, and planetary SELF.

In order to create a hologram, an object (in this case, a thought-form) is photographed (held in our thoughts and emotions and focused by our intention), and then bathed in the light of a laser beam (the vertical spiritual filaments). Then a second laser beam (the polarized material filaments) is bounced off the reflected light of the first, and the resulting interference pattern (the area where the two laser beams commingle) is captured on film or third-dimensional matrix (the third dimension).

When the film is developed, it appears as a meaningless swirl of light/spirit and dark/matter lines. But as soon as the developed film is illuminated by another laser beam (the perceptions of the third-dimensional observer), a three-dimensional image of the original thought-form appears. A thought-form is different from a thought in that a thought-form resonates in the fourth and fifth dimension, as well as the third dimension.

Each culture has many iconic thoughts about people, rulers, and places that carry such enormous emotional charge that they become thought-forms. Thought-forms are collective thoughts that have received so much attention from the collective consciousness that they have taken on form in the fourth dimension. These fourth-dimensional, etheric forms act as windows into the third dimension through which multidimensional beings can easily observe the workings of the physical world. It is through these windows that members of the physical plane can also observe the higher dimensions.

Many of these windows are spiritual teachers who have crossed over. These beings no longer resonate to the fourth dimension, as they were able to return to their Multidimensional SELF and travel through the universe. However, they have left fourth-dimensional thought-forms of themselves so that their followers can use them as windows into the higher worlds.

WEAVING THE MATRIX

We weave our third-dimensional matrix much like we crochet or knit. The separate filaments of matter and Spirit are the strings of yarn. We unconsciously weave in the patterning that is in the genetic code of our body and the beliefs that were given to us as children. Our genetic coding is also the way we are tied to our family members and the family of humanity.

Since we have connected to the collective consciousness, we can see how our Divine Ideal fits into the ideals of others and the Divine Ideal of Gaia. In the third dimension, the conflict between fear and love is the yarn of our weaving. The filaments of matter/fear, and Spirit/love, are woven together with our crochet hook or knitting needles.

At times, fear and love work together with two different hooks to catch the thread. At other times there is fear *or* there is love. In those cases, you choose, consciously or unconsciously, whether to use the fear hook or the love hook. At times we choose the fear hook because it is fast, and we don't have to confront the truth. However, fear exists only in the past or in the future. Therefore, we end up creating what we have already experienced, or what we fear *will* happen. With the love hook, we can only be in the *now* to make the strings catch. To do that, we need to release old core beliefs of the past, as well as worries and fears for the future.

We must be very still inside to catch the *now* of the present. This *now* is in the *forever*-present. Hence, we travel through what appears as time to others, yet it eternally feels like *now* to us. When we choose two hooks to create our matrix, the love hook and the fear hook, it is much like a beginner's knitting, because the tension of the strings is not the same. The fear part is tight and worrisome; whereas the love part is loose and hopeful. Every so often, we are so completely enmeshed in one area of our life that we create our reality with only the love hook *or* the fear hook.

Creating only from love is a divine experience, but it is difficult to maintain. That is why it is enjoyable to be away from others in a natural setting where the collective consciousness of nature is louder than the collective consciousness of people bustling through their busy lives. In this stillness, it is easier to create *only* from love. Also, while in nature, we can go on our own body clock. We can rest when tired, eat when hungry, and create when we are rested and nourished. In the midst of our working life, external parameters dictate what we must do and when we must do it.

To weave a happy, loving third-dimensional experience, it is best to cease all creation done in fear. What we create in fear produces the experience of fear; whereas what we create in love produces a loving experience. The best way to cease creation from fear is to be a conscious creator. Of course, few are *always* conscious creators, even though that may be the goal. If we are always conscious of our SELF, we would never choose to create a fearful experience. We would not choose to use the fear hook, because we would know that fear only comes back to its creator. For this reason, we are in the process of surrendering our life to Soul/SELF, who has now integrated into our first three chakras.

Our Soul is well aware that there are some on this planet who chose to be the fear creators of the third dimension, but our Soul/SELF knows that it is best to neither fear nor judge them. These people have made a great sacrifice to carry that fear banner so that others can play the third-dimensional polarity game. It is our love and light that will neutralize their fear and darkness and bring this conflict to an end.

When enough inhabitants of Earth tire of judging, fearing, fighting, resisting, and externalizing fear, the fear creators will retire and return to their true, Multidimensional SELVES, just like everyone else. As they do so, the collective consciousness of Earth will be more able to embrace a multidimensional reality. Each person who awakens to their Multidimensional SELF contributes to the developing transformations, which will one day reach critical mass and pilot all of Earth into a planet of peace and love.

THE DIFFERENCE BETWEEN LOVE AND FEAR

It is only our separate ego/self that experiences the difference between love and fear. Our wounded ego/self still needs to believe that everything is separate so that it can separate from what is fearful. Our ego has access to only third-dimensional perceptions. Therefore it cannot consciously perceive the subatomic particles that actually join all that is manifest (horizontal filaments of matter) with all that is not manifest (vertical filaments of Spirit). While limited to our third-dimensional consciousness, these subatomic filaments cannot be perceived.

On the other hand, our Soul/SELF, who is now becoming the captain of our earth vessel, consciously perceives the sub-atomic particles that connect all third-dimensional life. Our Soul also experiences and interacts with the many different dimensional realities resonating to the higher frequencies that are *now* a component of our present reality. From the perception of our SELF, there is no space or time in-between these multidimensional realities, as there is *no* in-between in realities without separation. There is only *here* and *now* in the realities that resonate to the ONE.

From the perspective of our ego/self, the dimensions are separated into layers of experience so that we can more easily integrate multidimensional information into our physical brains. Our ego/self uses only about 10 to 15 percent of our physical brain, as it is restricted to the familiar logical, sequential order that we have always thought of as reality. In order to consciously perceive the true, multidimensional reality, we must have a steady expansion of our consciousness and belief systems.

To suddenly awaken to the true, multidimensional world with all frequencies and dimensions intermingled and instantly available for us would be quite overwhelming. Third-dimensional order provides us with the illusion of the progression of time while we prepare for the rest of our life. The collective consciousness has chosen to take this time to prepare so that sufficient numbers of people can awaken enough to have the unified power within to transform the entire planet.

CONSTANT COMMUNICATION

We are becoming increasingly unified via our technology of cell phones and the internet. Now, we can instantly communicate our thoughts with anyone, anywhere in the world in real-time. Eventually, we will be awake enough to drop our technological crutches and realize that we are already united in the collective consciousness. Then all we need do is think that we would like to communicate with someone, and instantly our consciousness will be connected with the other person's. That person can choose to check his or her "caller ID" and decide to pick up the phone, so to speak, to answer the call (our thought) or not. However, because we are united, we will know that the other person made that choice. With no separation, there can be no lying and no deceit.

Within the *flow* of a multidimensional reality, the layers of frequencies/dimensions are as thin as gauze and quickly become obsolete as we become our Soul/SELF in our everyday life. Then, each dimension turns into a camera lens through which we calibrate our perceptions to the frequency of that reality. This calibration is necessary, as all realities are right *here* in the *now*. However, we are not actually calibrating our senses; we are calibrating our consciousness. Once we calibrate our consciousness to a certain frequency, our perceptions naturally abide by that calibration.

While functioning from our Soul/SELF, we are aware of the surrounding frequencies of reality and our unity with *all* of them. Just as the radio or television has many channels that are broadcasting at the same time, we only experience the channel to which we calibrate our attention. With the television or radio, we push a different button on our remote control to change the channel. The recalibration is done inside of the machine. However, when we change the channel of our attention, *we* are the machine. Hence we must calibrate our brainwaves to a vibration that can receive from that frequency of reality.

For example, Beta brainwaves cannot calibrate our consciousness to experience interdimensional travel, as these brainwaves are not capable of receiving that frequency. Because of this, we must calibrate our consciousness to Alpha brainwaves to travel and communicate with the fourth dimension and to Theta brainwaves to travel and communicate with the fifth dimension and beyond. While only using 10 to 15 percent of our brains, we find it difficult to choose our brainwaves. Fortunately, our Soul/SELF handles that challenge with ease.

REALITY SHOPPING

Calibrating our consciousness to our chosen reality is as familiar to our Soul/SELF as shopping in a mall is to our ego/self. When we are shopping in a clothing store, we see many racks of clothes. We know that the experience of wearing each of these clothes will present a different self when we look into the mirror. We could wear many different articles of clothing at one time, or we could wear only one simple outfit. We are also aware that we can change clothes whenever we desire.

When we look around the store through the eyes of our Soul/SELF, we see others who are also shopping. From our ego's point of view, these people appear to be separate. However, our Soul sees that we are connected to all of them by subatomic molecules. The mall has many other stores, as well. Through our Soul we can pan back until we see the entire mall with all the subatomic particles that connect us to the essence of the mall. As we pan back further still, we see that there are many other malls, with many stores within each one.

These malls are all connected by subatomic particles to the city, the cities are connected with these same particles to the state, the states are connected to the country, the countries to the continent, the continents to the planet, the planets to the solar system, the solar systems to the galaxy, the galaxies to the universe. As we pan back even further, we see that there are universes in many different dimensions, which are also connected by these same subatomic particles.

THE COLLECTIVE CONSCIOUSNESS

We are separate because we choose to perceive or believe that we are separate. It takes time to travel from place to place, because we have chosen to separate our consciousness into an individual, third-dimensional body. However, our consciousness is united with every other individual body in every other separate city, state, country, continent, planet, solar system, galaxy, universe, dimension... through our consciousness.

Once we choose to think in a united collective consciousness fashion, it is very difficult to harm another. It is also not as easy for fear to get a grip on us. If we don't enjoy this store in the mall, we simply calibrate our consciousness to experience a different store, or a different mall. If we cannot achieve our goal in one store, or state of consciousness, we need only change our consciousness. Once we can pan back our lens beyond the illusions of separate stores and separate goals, we will remember that we are all connected to a larger goal, a goal that we do not need to achieve alone.

Furthermore, we don't need to achieve our goal because we are not separate from it. We are not separate from the ONE who is calibrated to the experience of living that goal. Again, *if we want to change our experience, all we need do is change our consciousness.* Once we alter our consciousness, we adjust the filter in our camera lens. We can even choose to expand our consciousness so much that our camera can *see* the inbetween, *listen* to the sounds that make no noise, *feel* the nothingness and *expand* into a larger SELF resonating to an even higher frequency.

We can constrict our consciousness to have the experience of being a molecule, *or* we can expand our consciousness to have the experience of being a galaxy. We can do this by *not* allowing the illusion of our separate, limited body to restrict our consciousness. Our consciousness is *not* in our body. Our body is *in* our consciousness. Only a small portion of our total being is choosing to shop for clothes in this small store. All of our consciousness or essence lives in unity with the ONE, and *all* of our consciousness is united with everyone and everything.

In reality, *we* are not a person, city, state, nation, planet, or galaxy. *We* are a dimension. We are the third-dimensional matrix of this third dimension. We have chosen to shop here for the experiences of separation and limitation. We are no longer a baby, or even a child, and have outgrown the clothes in this store. We are grown up *now*, grown up enough to embrace our true, Multidimensional personal and planetary SELF!

BECOMING ONE WITH THE PLANET

THIRD PLANETARY CHAKRA
Mt. Kilimanjaro, Africa

Mt. Kilimanjaro is the source of ancient, planetary power. This great being witnessed the birth of humanity and has survived as the giant conduit that it is. With its peak in the clouds and its base bonded to hard, rocky soil, the mountain stands proud. Kilimanjaro is the power within Gaia's Soul, her sentry and her guardian. Gaia gains great power from the emanation of this mountain and its ability to protect and guide.

The third chakra is a masculine/outflow polarity, which represents the outflow of our personal power. The challenge of this chakra is to find our own inner light and share it with the world by projecting our inner power in an out-flowing manner. Often, when we are unable to discover our inner power, we become fearful and try to steal another's power through domination and control. Mt. Kilimanjaro represents the power of a peak, standing alone in a barren land. This peak does not need to pull from its environment for strength. Instead, it takes command by projecting its mighty beacon of inner strength gained through the long process of becoming a mountain.

Mt. Kilimanjaro is one of the largest, freestanding mountains in the world. From Earth's third chakra, Gaia can show you how to use our great power within to find the courage to *stand alone*. Our personal third chakra is ruled by our pancreas and governs the many organs of digestion, synthesis, and distribution of the food that empowers our physical body.

This chakra, at our solar nerve-plexus, is also where our spleen receives an abundance of prana to be distributed throughout our system. Prana, or intelligent light, is our spiritual food and one of the primary sources of our inner strength. Hence, our third chakra deals with the digestion, synthesis, distribution, and emanation of our spiritual food, as well as of our physical food.

Our third chakra is also the portal to our fourth-dimensional psychic abilities. Unfortunately, a good deal of the power of our fourth-dimensional abilities was stolen by or given to others when we were a child. Now, as adults, we can learn to protect ourselves from this siphoning of power by consciously guarding our thinking. If we allow any thoughts that we are a victim to anyone or anything, including our own ego/self, we have unconsciously allowed something outside of our SELF to take power over our life.

The third chakra is meant to be the outflow of our personal power. However, because there is so much fear in the third-dimensional world, the fourth-dimensional aura of this fear can piggy-back onto the inflow of prana into our solar plexus. This lower-frequency fear can then enter the unguarded psychic field of our third chakra. However, we can protect ourselves against these fearful emanations by maintaining an outflow of our own inner power that is so strong that no inflow of fear can invade. Remember, love has more power than fear because it unifies us with the power of our Multidimensional SELF, as well as the power of our planet.

It is also helpful to visualize mighty Mt. Kilimanjaro, standing as the sentry at the entrance to our solar plexus, and to allow the power of this mountain to create a frequency net to shield our solar plexus, allowing only the frequency of love to enter. In this manner, the low vibration of fear will be filtered out, while the high vibration of loving prana will be allowed to enter. To assure that we keep our frequency net activated, we call upon our ever-expanding, higher perceptions to perceive any fearful, low frequency, emanations that are attempting to enter our solar plexus.

In this manner, our Soul/SELF, who is far above the fear and darkness, calibrates our firewall so that we can perceive negativity but at the same time, deny its entrance into our body. In addition, by merging with the power of Gaia's third chakra, we have the power to stand free of the influence of the psychic leakage of others. This inner power will give us the ability to face the world with a strong conviction to *be* our SELF. We are then strong enough to look fear in the face and *know* that we are always protected by the power within our true, Multidimensional SELF.

BLENDING CHAKRAS

Once again, travel down into the core of Earth's body to reconnect your essence with the essence of Gaia. Down, down, down you travel into the planet's third- and fourth-dimensional body. As you do so, you remember your entire life on Earth. Allow yourself to feel any darkness that may be attached to any of these memories. Do not fear this darkness, for you shall take it onto Kilimanjaro to be cleansed and released by the mountain's great power. Take a moment, while you are deep in the core of Gaia, to feel the weight and protection of the great mountain above you.

As you slowly rise to the surface, you feel heavy with the psychic attachments that you have gained in your earthly incarnation. These attachments are like viruses in your computer in that they are invisible yet interfere with your ability to process information and communicate with your reality. After what seems like many lifetimes, you find yourself at the base of mighty Kilimanjaro. You experience a rush of excitement as you throw your psychic burden at the feet of the great mountain!

Now, free of old, psychic effluvia and open to your clear, fourth-dimensional psychic abilities, you *feel* your personal power blending with Gaia's planetary power. Be aware of the heat rising from the base of the mountain as you begin your hike toward the mountain peak that is kissing the heavens. Be sure to completely ground yourself by sending your first chakra's root deep into the mountain. Once you are plugged into the mountain, unite the psychic vision of your solar plexus with the wisdom, power and love of your inner, Multidimensional SELF, so that you may *know* the clearest path for your journey.

With strength and determination, climb the mountain. Allow each step upon the body of Kilimanjaro to awaken your power within. Think only of your victory as you approach the peak and the power that it holds. Know that you can only climb this mountain alone, for it is a symbol of the power that you must find within yourself.

Ingest, digest, assimilate, and integrate the planetary power with your personal power. Be ever-confident of your success and guard against any negativity or fearful thinking. *You* are a strong spiritual warrior who is fighting for a peaceful and happy life. Your only enemy is fear. Wash that fear away with the immense outflow of your power within, as you say:

"*I am* the guardian of my SELF *and* my planet.
***I am* in complete control of *my* life.**
I stand alone, yet *I a*m united with Earth."

Hold this emanation of your power within as you walk through your mundane reality. Project that power out into your world, and allow it to clear a path upon which you can stand as majestically as Kilimanjaro.

MESSAGE FROM SOUL/SELF

I, your new captain, wish to address all of the members of my multidimensional earth vessel and crew. Yes, I can directly address my vessel, as it is as alive as the planet on which it is currently docked. Initially, I wish to address the first-dimensional, mineral members of my crew: the cells, atoms, chemicals, and DNA. These members have diligently taken from Gaia's body the necessary elements to create this vessel. I have accessed the control panel on this first deck/chakra and recalibrated all of your chemical markers to begin the transformation of this vessel from carbon-based to light-based.

I have also re-calibrated the control panel for this deck in order to filter in your kundalini force, thereby changing your power source from one-dimensional to multi-dimensional. Hence, the second-dimensional organs of this vessel will now be able to gather fuel, not just from the flora and fauna of this planet that has been your docking station, but also from the light of the entire universe, as well. This advanced power source will allow you to more easily detect and move through the many illusions of your current port. Your new source of fuel also prepares your entire vehicle for its impending lift-off into the higher dimensions.

I commend the first- and second-dimensional crew members who have served me on this deck, and I wish to congratulate you all on your ability to accept change. I would like to introduce you to a new crew member. You will find her within you. Her name is Gaia. Gaia, the planet from whom you have gathered the elements to create this vessel, is also transforming and has kindly offered to join your crew to better assist with the vessel's ongoing transformation. Since Gaia is a multidimensional being, she has no problem serving on many, in fact, on millions of vessels in the same moment of the *now*.

I, your new captain, am also multidimensional. I have not excused your past captain, ego/self, as it is one of the many components of my total SELF. Instead, I have re-assigned this portion of me to be my first mate in charge of grounding the vessel and mundane activities. In this manner, my vessel will be able to continue its tour of being a separate individual forging through the many limitations of third-dimensional illusion. I congratulate you all for your success with this tour of duty. It is because of your great victory with this assignment that I have been able to begin the process of becoming your new captain.

I remind all the crew on this deck that I am always available for any assistance you may need in your transformation or even with your daily tasks. Because of my multidimensional consciousness, I can easily assist each and every one of my crew, individually, within the same moment. Ego, my first mate, will be in constant communication with me. Hence, you may also address me through your former captain, Ego.

Now, I would like to address the second deck/chakra. I also commend you in learning the fine art of partnership *with* rather than domination *by* your emotions. The fuel for this deck, emotion, is a strong power source, but it can also cause erratic functioning or even completely shut down the operating systems. Because of this, I have recalibrated the emotional control panel on this deck to filter out intense, polarized emotion and to filter in the higher dimensional, unconditional emotions.

The divine child, who has now merged with your inner child, has never lost connection with me, and is, therefore, very comfortable with unconditional emotions. Because of this, the divine child has been appointed as the supervisor in charge of emotional operations. The duties of this position include channeling the immense power of emotions towards fulfillment of our chosen Divine Ideal, as well as assisting all crewmembers to deeply enjoy their remaining time in this port.

I wish to commend the second- and third-dimensional members of this crew on your total acceptance of me, you new captain. I realize that your magnificent instincts and intuitions have largely been rejected by the rules of your current port and by the overly intellectual crew members on the third deck. With the recalibration of your emotional network, you will have greater access to these innate powers. Also, you will no longer care if they doubt you, for you will no longer doubt yourself. I ask you all to feel free to share any of your instincts, intuitions, and ever-expanding creative ideas with my SELF or my first mate, Ego.

In closing, I ask that you take a long moment to join your core, your hara center of your navel, with the core of our new partner, Gaia, Mother Earth. Your deck shall be the incubation center of our new light vessel. Hence, send down an umbilical cord into the womb of your Earth Mother for nurturance and assistance with your rebirth. Allow this cord to travel down through the first deck and into the heart of Gaia, who is now a crew member on the first deck. Gaia will then lovingly implant this cord into the womb of her planet.

I move now to the third- and fourth-dimensional members of the third deck/chakra. I have recalibrated your control panel so that your great intellectual ability can merge with your fourth-dimensional intuition. In this manner, the rigid belief systems of your individual third-dimensional reality will no longer limit your great mind or cause you to doubt your inner communiqués.

I commend the fourth-dimensional members of our body Deva and its personal Elementals who have tirelessly served in the healing and reconstruction of this vessel since its conception. You have been very patient with your remodeling while I and the other members of the crew have remained in the vessel of your making. I realize that the overly intellectual crewmembers have not always thought highly of you, if they have thought of you at all. However, they were merely doing their job of operating under the illusions and limitations of this port.

I have re-calibrated the control panel for this deck to filter in the conscious recognition of fourth-dimensional signals. I have also installed a powerful firewall so that unwanted psychic attacks of the Dark Side by the fourth dimension will be detected by our radar screen, yet filtered out before they can do any harm to our *vessel*. These unwanted assaults will no longer be allowed.

Dear third-dimensional, intellectual members of this deck, I would like to introduce you to the fourth-dimensional Elemental members of your crew. You may, or may not, have known of their constant interactions and contributions, as you were focused on your former directive: "*Forget* your Multidimensional SELF." I wish to inform you that your directive has been altered drastically. In fact, your new directive is, "*Remember* your true Multidimensional SELF."

I also wish to commend you, the intellectual crew members, for your ability in playing the third-dimensional game so well that you have come to this point. You have done an excellent job of being individual and living through myriad limitations. I now instruct you to constantly consult with your silent partners, the Elemental crewmembers. Because they operate from a higher dimension, they have been aware of you, while you have been largely unaware of them.

First meet the Earth Elementals, the Gnomes, who have greatly assisted you in the care and maintenance of your hard drive and physical vessel. Next, meet the Water Elementals, the Undines, who have been assisting you in maintaining the flow of all the liquid through this vessel. The Air Elementals, the Sylphs, have kept the space of this vessel clear and filled with oxygen. Finally, meet the Fire Elementals, the Salamanders, who have kept all the electricity and other power sources operational.

I ask now that all third and fourth-dimensional crewmembers of the third deck join in conscious collaboration of duty and responsibilities. I also ask that you remain in constant connection with the first- and second-dimensional crewmembers of the first and second decks. Take a moment now to connect your control panel, or chakra, with the control panel of the second deck, and hence with the umbilical cord within that deck. You will then automatically be connected with the first deck and with Gaia herself. Remember to consult with the instincts and intuitions of the second deck, as well your trusted partner, Gaia, on the first deck.

I am very proud of your ability to begin this major transformation. I know that it is the most difficult for the lower decks to alter their operating systems, for they have been functioning within the old system for eons. I will now move to the bridge on the fourth deck/chakra, which is the heart of our dear vessel. I know that I will be warmly welcomed, as this deck has been calling to me for quite some time.

My communiqué with you, the lower decks, is now complete, and I leave you in the trusted hands of my first mate, Ego. I will continue my recalibration with the higher decks, but since I am multidimensional, my attention will also be continually with you. Therefore, I will be able to instantly respond to your every question or request.

Again, *I am* Soul/SELF, the new captain of this vessel,
Your captain

PS
I look forward to continuing our process in **Volume Two** of ***Becoming ONE, People and Planet,*** as does Gaia, our dear planet.

CONGRATULATIONS

You have completed the first half of your process of becoming ONE with your Multidimensional SELF and your Multidimensional Planet. Your journey toward personal and planetary transformation continues in Volume Two of *Becoming ONE, People and Planet.* The following outline maps your future journey:

To Order Volume Two call
1-800-247-6553
or go to Multidimensions.com

VOLUME TWO OUTLINE

SECTION FIVE

When we *love* all creation,
we can *create* love.

CHAPTER SIXTEEN

Conscious Creation

Choosing Our Thoughts, Emotions and Intentions

CHAPTER SEVENTEEN

The Fourth Chakra - Breathing Life into Our New Reality

Integrating our Soul/SELF into our heart chakra and sharing our process with Gaia's fourth charka, the Haleakala Crater in Maui, Hawaii.

CHAPTER EIGHTEEN

The Fifth Chakra - Manifesting our New Reality

Integrating our Soul/SELF into our throat chakra and sharing our process with Gaia's fifth chakra in Mt. Shasta, California.

SECTION SIX

As we become *ONE* with our SELF we become *ONE* with the Planet.

CHAPTER NINETEEN

Superconscious Creation

Living in Surrender

CHAPTER TWENTY

The Sixth Chakra - Mastering Our New Reality

Integrating our Soul/SELF into our brow chakra and sharing our process with Gaia's sixth chakra in the Himalayan Mountains in Tibet.

CHAPTER TWENTY ONE

The Seventh Chakra - Expanding our New Reality

Integrating our Soul/SELF into our crown chakra and sharing our process with Gaia's seventh chakra in Mt. Fuji, Japan.

SECTION SEVEN

The reality we choose to *perceive* is the reality we choose to *live*.

CHAPTER TWENTY TWO

Opening the Third Eye

Entering our Sacred Triangle and performing our Mystical Marriage to activate our whole brain thinking and expand our perceptions.

CHAPTER TWENTY THREE

The Portal of the Third Eye

Perceiving reality as a hologram and awakening the latent potential in our *junk* DNA.

Becoming a Master of Energy

APPENDIX ONE

DEFINITIONS

ANGELS: Angles are beings who live in unity with the ONE and serve to bring love and higher dimensional light to the third dimension. Archangels are the most evolved of the Angelic Evolution.

ARCHETYPE: An archetype is an original model or prototype that serves as a pattern for other things of the same type. It's like an ice cube tray in that whatever liquid is frozen in the tray will have the same "archetypal" form.

ASCENDED MASTERS: Ascended Masters are humans who have expanded their consciousness enough during their Earth lives that they were able to consciously step into the higher dimensions at the close of those lives. These ascended beings serve in the fourth and fifth dimensions to assist earthbound humans in their spiritual growth. Ascended Masters are the most evolved of the Human Evolution.

BRAINSTEM: The brainstem forms the base of our brain. Together with the area immediately above it, this part of the brain is called the Reptilian Brain, as all creatures from reptiles to humans possess this structure. For reptiles, this area is their entire brain, but for humans it is merely the base, or stem, of their brain. The brainstem is associated with the first chakra, which rules our survival consciousness and most primitive self.

BRAINWAVES: Electrical activity emanating from the brain is displayed in the form of brainwaves, which are measured by an electroencephalogram (or EEG). Brainwaves, like all waves, are measured in two ways. The first is frequency, cycles per second (cps), or the number of times a wave repeats itself within a second. The second measurement is amplitude, which represents the power of electrical impulses generated by the brain.

Beta brainwaves: Beta brainwaves, in which our brainwaves pulsate at between 13 and 39 cps, are associated with day-to-day wakefulness.

Alpha brainwaves: Alpha brainwaves, in which our brainwaves pulsate between 8 and 12 cps, are associated with focused concentration on one thought, emotion, or activity that is usually creative in nature or thoroughly enjoyable.

Theta brainwaves: Theta brainwaves, in which our brainwaves pulsate between 4 to 7 cps, are associated with shamanic experience, moments of illumination, and scientific and/or creative discovery.

Delta brainwaves: Delta brainwaves, in which our brainwaves pulsate between .5 to 4 cps, are involved with our empathy, as well as our interaction and connection to our full multidimensional perception. To our mundane mind, a Delta brainwave would likely denote a state of coma.

Gamma brainwaves: Gamma brainwaves, which resonate around 40 cps, are thought of as the harmonizing frequency. They are associated with the brain function that creates a holographic synthesis of data stored in various areas of the brain to fuse them together into a higher perspective.

New brainwaves: EEG researchers are noticing extremely high brainwave frequencies (even higher than Gamma) of up to 100 cps that they have titled **Hyper Gamma brainwaves** and even higher brainwaves at 200 cps titled **Lambda Brainwaves**. Conversely, extremely low brainwaves that are lower than Delta waves at less than 0.5 cps are titled **Epsilon Brainwaves**. All of these "new brainwaves" are associated with higher states of SELF-awareness, the ability to access superior levels of information and insight, psychic abilities, and out-of-body experiences.

CENTER CURRENT: The center current, or fulcrum point, is the place of neutral charge where neither the negative emotional charge of "conditional" nor the positive emotional charge of "unconditional" exists. Within this current, there is no polarity and no imbalance. When we live our lives in the flow of the center current, we fuse the opposite polarities into ONE, and the third-dimensional charge is neutralized.

CHAKRAS: Chakras are small vortexes that rest on the surface of the Etheric Body. Our chakra system serves as the portal through which our Etheric Body downloads the higher-dimensional light into our physical body. Both our physical body and the body of Earth have seven primary chakras. Auxiliary chakras also exist that are not covered in this book.

CONSCIOUS INTENTION: We use our conscious intention when we choose to harness our positive thoughts and loving emotions and project them via our will power to strongly determine that we will follow a certain inner directive.

CONSCIOUS: We are conscious when we are aware of and able to attend to stimuli within our own dimension. Our third-dimensional self is conscious only of what can be perceived by the five physical senses of sight, hearing, touch, taste, and smell. We can expand our ability to be conscious by releasing the victim role in our life and taking responsibility for how we create our reality.

Unconscious: We are considered to be unconscious when we are unaware of and unable to attend to internal and/or external stimuli within our own dimension, let alone within other dimensions. Third-dimensional humans are largely unaware of their first-, second-, fourth- and fifth-dimensional selves. The human unconscious is an archive of all the forgotten and repressed memories and experiences of our lives so far. Our unconscious mind is best accessed through our physical body, introspection, dreams, and meditation.

Superconscious: Our superconscious is a higher order of consciousness that is innately multidimensional. Our third-dimensional self can become conscious of the superconscious through meditation and prayer and by surrendering to the perceptions of the higher-order consciousness.

CONSCIOUSNESS: Our consciousness represents the magnitude of our awareness of our self and our environment via all our senses. When we are not very aware of our self or our environment, we have a limited consciousness. On the other hand, when we are extremely aware of the many aspects of our self and of our reality, we have an expanded consciousness.

Individual Consciousness: Individual consciousness is the ability to perceive ourselves as independent individuals in our third-dimensional reality. Third-dimensional consciousness is based on the precept that we are separate from everyone and everything.

Collective Consciousness: Collective consciousness is the ability to perceive ourselves as members of the sum total of all human consciousness interwoven into ONE.

Planetary Consciousness: Planetary consciousness is the ability to perceive ourselves as members of the sum total of all consciousness of all beings, including the being Gaia, interwoven into ONE.

Solar Consciousness: Solar consciousness is the ability to perceive ourselves as members of the sum total of all consciousness of our solar system.

Galactic Consciousness: Galactic consciousness is the ability to perceive ourselves as members of the sum total of all consciousness of our galaxy.

Cosmic Consciousness: Cosmic consciousness is the ability to perceive ourselves as members of the sum total of all consciousness of our universe.

DEVIC EVOLUTION: The Devic Evolution refers to the spiritual forces and beings behind nature and encompasses all the holders of form from the highest evolution of Elohim to the lowest evolution of Elementals. The Devic Evolution also works from the Mental Plane to translate thoughts into physical forms.

Elementals: Elementals are the lowest expression of the Holders of Form or Devic Evolution. The Elementals are the fourth-dimensional counterpart of the third-dimensional elements of earth, air, fire, and water, which serve as the building blocks of third-dimensional form.

Deva: The term Deva refers to the fourth- and fifth-dimensional group Elementals who unite, supervise, and direct many individual Elementals to hold the form for physical creations such as mountains, forests, and buildings. We also have a body Deva who is the supervisor of the individual Elementals of our physical body.

Elohim: The highest expression of the Keepers of Form or Devic Evolution. Elohim have a male and a female aspect and are the creator gods and goddesses. Just as Angels specialize in emanating love, the Elohim specialize in holding form as they work with their divine complements to carry out their cosmic service.

DIMENSIONS: Dimensions are a means of organizing different planes of existence according to their vibratory rate. Each dimension has certain sets of laws and principles that are specific to the frequency of that dimension.

DIVINE CHILD: Our divine child is the crystal core of our true SELF, which is gradually and steadily covered with the dust of our many life experiences. Our divine child represents our multidimensional SELF, and he or she has a consciousness that expands from our first-dimensional, cellular self to our highest-dimensional, Spirit SELF.

DIVINE COMPLEMENT: Our divine complement, also known as our twin flame, is the other polarity of our Multidimensional Soul/SELF, who was limited to one gender when we took embodiment in the third dimension. Once our Soul becomes the captain of our earth vessel, our consciousness becomes androgynous and our masculine and feminine polarities become balanced and equal, in spite of our body's gender.

ELECTROMAGNETIC SPECTRUM: The electromagnetic spectrum is the range of frequencies of electromagnetic waves of light entering Earth's atmosphere. The longer wavelengths are the lower frequencies and the shorter wavelengths are the higher frequencies. The electromagnetic spectrum ranges from the lowest frequency radio waves to microwaves, infrared rays, optical rays, ultraviolet rays, X-rays, and finally gamma rays at the highest frequency of the spectrum. The light visible to the human eye is only a very narrow region within this spectrum.

ELEMENTS: The elements are building blocks of form in the third dimension: earth, air, fire, and water.

ENDOCRINE GLANDS: Each chakra is associated with a different endocrine gland. Just as there are seven chakras, there are seven endocrine glands. Both the chakras and the endocrine glands are located along the spinal cord. The endocrine glands manufacture hormones and supply them to the bloodstream. These glands are called "ductless" because they do not have ducts to any specific part of the body. Instead, hormones are released into the bloodstream where they are carried by the blood to every organ and tissue to exert their influence on all functions of the physical body.

Adrenal Glands: The endocrine glands of the first chakra are the two adrenal glands, each one located on top of one of the two kidneys. The release of adrenaline, brought on by real or imaged danger, is vital for the survival of every species.

Gonads: The endocrine glands of the second chakra are the gonads, which consist of both male and female sex organs. These include the ovaries, testes, and prostate gland.

Pancreas: The endocrine gland of the third chakra is the pancreas. The pancreas plays an important role in the digestion of food and secretes the hormone insulin, which regulates both the level of blood sugar in the system and the metabolism needed for digesting carbohydrates.

Thymus Gland: The endocrine gland of the fourth chakra is the thymus gland, which is the core of our immune system and vital for our healing.

Thyroid Gland: The endocrine gland of the fifth chakra is the thyroid gland, which produces hormones that influence essentially every organ, tissue, and cell in the body. Thyroid hormones regulate the body's metabolism and organ function, affecting heart rate, cholesterol level, body weight, energy level, muscle strength, skin condition, menstrual regularity, memory, and many other conditions.

Pituitary Gland: The endocrine gland of the sixth chakra is the pituitary gland, which is about the size of a pea and is located behind the center of our forehead, between our eyes. The pituitary gland is known as the master gland because it acts as a main control center that sends messages to all the glands.

Pineal Gland: The endocrine gland of the seventh chakra is the pineal gland, which has photoreceptor cells that regulate the secretion of the hormone melatonin. Melatonin regulates our circadian body rhythms of waking and sleeping and our state of consciousness in our outer and inner realities.

ETHERIC DOUBLE: The Etheric Double, also known as the Etheric Body, is a faintly luminous violet-gray mist that interpenetrates and slightly extends beyond the physical body about one-quarter of an inch. The Etheric Body is not separate from the physical body, nor does it have a separate consciousness. It serves solely to receive the vital forces of prana that emanate from our third-dimensional sun and our Multidimensional SELF.

EXPANDED PERCEPTIONS: As we expand our consciousness beyond the strict confines of the third dimension, our perceptions also expand so that we can consciously perceive beyond the limits of our third-dimensional reality. Some of the expanded perceptions that we will activate are:

Empathy: Empathy is the ability to feel another person's emotions.

Instincts: Instincts are an innate knowing and ability to tune into the planet and our environment.

Intuition: Intuition is the ability to combine our earthly instincts with perceptions of the fourth dimension and beyond.

Telepathy: Telepathy is the ability to read or have a knowing of another person's thoughts.

Precognition: Precognition, seeing into the future, is the fourth-dimensional ability to move beyond the constraints of third-dimensional time and into the mutable time of the fourth dimension to see a possible reality.

Telekinesis: Telekinesis is the ability to move and change objects with the force of our mind.

Clairvoyance: Clairvoyance is the ability to see objects that resonate to the fourth dimension and beyond.

Clairaudience: Clairaudience is the ability to hear sounds from the fourth dimension and beyond.

Clairsentience: Clairsentience is the ability to see, hear, sense, and know about the fourth dimension and beyond.

Illumination: Illumination arises as we surrender our ego to our fifth-dimensional Soul/SELF to become ONE with the NOW of the higher dimensions.

GAIA: The name Gaia means "the consciousness of the planet;" it was given to the planet Earth in early Greece.

GODDESS SHAKTI: Shakti is a Hindu goddess representing the kundalini energy at the base of the spine, believed to be the divine complement of Lord Shiva. As we awaken our kundalini, the goddess Shakti sweeps up from our root chakra and ascends chakra-by-chakra to join her divine complement, Lord Shiva, in our crown chakra. This mystical marriage of our inner male and female not only initiates the process wherein we are freed of the polarities of the third dimension, but it also greatly amplifies the frequency rate of our cerebrospinal fluid and the potential voltage of our entire nervous system.

KUNDALINI: The word "kundalini" is derived from the Sanskrit word "kundal," meaning coiled up. It is the primordial dormant energy, also known as the sleeping serpent, present in three-and-a-half coils at the base of our spine in a triangular bone called the sacrum. Whereas our personal kundalini energy rests at the base of our spine, the planetary kundalini energy rests in the core of Mother Earth. The goddess Shakti is also known sometimes as the goddess Kundalini.

LIGHTBODY: Our lightbody is the form of our Multidimensional SELF in the fifth dimension and beyond.

LORD SHIVA: Lord Shiva is a Hindu god believed to be the divine complement of the goddess Shakti, also known as the goddess Kundalini. Lord Shiva waits in the crown chakra for his bride, the goddess Shakti, who is brought to him by the rising kundalini force.

MANIFEST DESTINY: Manifest Destiny is a 19th-century policy of U.S. territorial expansion westward to the Pacific Ocean, which was defended at time as necessary and benevolent because it was generally viewed as the right and duty of the country.

MERIDIANS: In acupuncture, meridians are invisible channels through which qi (or chi), another term for prana, flows. Each meridian is related to and named after an organ or function. The main meridians are the lung, large intestines, spleen, stomach, small intestine, heart, liver, gall bladder, kidney, urinary bladder, pericardium, and san jiao.

MERKABA: Also spelled "merkabah," this is the divine light vehicle allegedly used by the enlightened to connect and commune with the higher dimensions. "Mer" means light. "Ka" means Spirit. "Ba" means body.

MULTIDIMENSIONAL BEINGS: A multidimensional being is a life form, whether a person, animal, or planet, that has a form on more than one dimension. Their form may likely be different on each dimension, as form follows frequency.

MULTIDIMENSIONAL CONSCIOUSNESS: Our ability to be conscious of more than one dimension within the same moment is referred to as multidimensional consciousness. It allows us to be aware of our potential to expand our perceptions to dimensions above and below the third dimension.

PLANE OF EXISTENCE: A plane of existence, sometimes called simply a plane or a dimension, is a region of space and/or consciousness inhabited by evolving beings in different stages of consciousness consistent with the frequency of that plane or dimension. The physical plane, the third dimension, is an example of one plane of existence.

PRANA: Prana is a Sanskrit word that means "to breathe." Prana, also known as chi, is the energy or life force of our bodies and of the universe. Prana emanates from and is directly relational to the sun, entering our Etheric Body as well as the physical atoms that float in the earth's atmosphere.

RAINBOW BRIDGE: The Rainbow Bridge is the frequency bridge that connects the ONE of the fifth dimension and beyond with the third and fourth dimension.

REALITY: Reality is a term used to define an individual, collective, and/or planetary perception of an individual or group experience.

REALM OF FAERIE: The Realm of Faerie is the fourth-dimensional reality in the Emotional/Astral Plane, just beyond the Lower Astral Plane.

RESONANCE: When the vibrations produced by one object come into alignment with those of another, it is called resonance.

RESONATE: If we were to play the note C on a piano with a violin next to it, the C string of the violin would also vibrate, or resonate. When something resonates with us, we recognize that its vibration, its pattern of energy, is compatible with our own.

RETICULAR ACTIVATING SYSTEM: The reticular activating system is the physiological and anatomical mechanism that filters stimuli to certain areas of the brain. The word "reticular" means "net-like," and the reticular formation itself is a large, net-like, diffuse area of the brainstem. Since, the brain's reticular activating system controls arousal, attention, and awareness, which are core elements of consciousness, it is instrumental in managing how we interpret, respond to, and react to both internal and external information.

THE FLOW: The *flow* is the term used to denote that we are surrendering to the center current of the ONE. While living in the *flow*, we are in harmony with all life and follow our inner directives regarding all decisions and actions.

THE ONE: The ONE is the state of consciousness in which all are intertwined in a cosmic dance of unity, with *no* separation in consciousness across all galaxies, solar systems, planets, and dimensions.

THE THIRD EYE: The third eye is the unification of our sixth and seventh chakras and is located between our eyes, in the center of our forehead. It is often used as a focal point for meditation. The third eye is opened when the rising kundalini force enters the brow (or sixth) chakra and joins essence with the crown (or seventh) chakra through the combining of the workings and secretions of the pituitary gland of the brow chakra and the pineal gland of the crown chakra.

THOUGHT-FORM: A thought-form is an individual or collective thought that has been imbued with so much emotion and received so much attention that it has taken a form in the fourth dimension.

TRANSMUTATION: Transmutation is the transformation of a person, place, situation, or thing by raising its vibration. In other words, the object, thought, emotion, planet, etc., is not replaced. Instead, it is converted.

WHOLE BRAIN THINKING: Whole brain thinking is the ability to simultaneously use our left, analytical/sequential-thinking hemisphere of our brain and our right, holistic/creative hemisphere. This synchronized and unified thinking can allow us to access more than the usual 15 percent of our brain as well as activate our expanded perceptions. Opening our third eye accelerates this type of thinking and expands of the use of our brain's potential.

APPENDIX TWO

Dimensional Charts
Qualities of the Five Dimensions

Quality	First Dimension	Second Dimension	Third Dimension	Fourth Dimension	Fifth Dimension
Awareness	point	point & line	point, line, length, breadth, height, & volume	point, line, length, breadth, height, volume & time	point, line, breadth, length, volume, time & spirit
Primary Consciousness	mineral kingdom	plants, biological creatures w/o self-awareness	higher animals & humans	higher human astral body	androgynous lightbody
Self Awareness	none	none	individual awareness & ego	awareness of self & all 3D lives	awareness of self, all 5D lives, all 4D lives & all 3D lives
Human's 5 Physical Senses	conscious to external senses unconscious to internal senses	conscious to external unconscious to internal	conscious only to CNS 5 senses indicate reality	unconscious to this plane until awakened doorway is body & dreams	unconscious to this plane unless awakened
Portions of Physical Body	mineral, water, genetic coding	lower brain autonomic NS life support + all the above	entire humanoid form + all the above	etheric & astralform + all the above	light matrix & meridians of physical form + all the above
Time	no awareness of	instincts & body clock	time/space past, present & future	time/space is mutable & different from 3D	no time or space only Nowness Hereness & Beingness

Quality	First Dimension	Second Dimension	Third Dimension	Fourth Dimension	Fifth Dimension
Laws and Principles	no awareness of	survival of species	polarization of light and dark cause/effect time/space & work	still polarization of light & dark still cause/effect & time/space	no polarization unconditional love, & forgiveness
Travel	no travel except within physical body	instinctual only	use will to take time to travel across space	desire location and fly or morph reality to get there	desired location & experience instantly manifest or floating/flying
Creativity and Sexuality	slow metamorphosis into form	procreation for survival of species nest building & some tool making	procreation to love making thoughts & feelings slowly create reality	sex for magic and lovemaking reality quickly created by thoughts, feelings & magic	sex is merging with Twin Flame reality instantly created by thoughts & feelings
Service	foundation for physical planet and body	life, beauty food chain	guide to lower beings & balance Earth's	guide to 3D self assist newly dead	Higher Self to 4D & 3D selves balance
Sub-planes within the dimension	mineral atoms to crystals	single cells to mammals	higher animal to dependable self-realized human	lower astral to causal plane	5 D threshold threshold to Soul

THE THREE LEVELS OF CONSCIOUSNESS		
Humans are Usually Conscious of	Humans are Usually Unconscious of	Humans are Superconscious Aware of
1. external inhabitants of first dimension i.e.: rocks and crystals	1. internal components of first dimension i.e.: water, minerals, genetic coding of body	1. all inhabitants of 3D-5D simultaneously
2. external inhabitants of second dimension i.e.: plants and insects	2. external components of second dimension i.e.: life support of autonomic nervous system	2. all inhabitants of 3D-5D simultaneously
3. animals in external world	3. animal component of 3D self	3. all inhabitants of 3D-5D simultaneously
4. intellect and reason	4. instincts and intuition	4. the "knowing"
5. ego/outer self	5. inner self	5. Soul/SELF
6. willful thoughts and reactive emotions	6. self-talk and repressed emotions	6. every thought & feeling because it is instantly manifest
7. pertinent information relayed to brain by central nervous system i.e.: conscious, willful movement, & information about survival	7 nervous system stimuli that is not consciously attended to i.e.: reflexive movement, & information from autonomic nervous system	7. all information relayed to all members of 5D Unity Consciousness
8. reality that is observed with 5 senses	8. realities that are not observable with 5 senses	8. collective reality chosen to be experienced
9. memories of conscious experience i.e.: experiences attended to when they happened	9. memories of unconscious experiences i.e.: experiences not attended to when they happened	9. all memories of all experiences of 1D to 5D simultaneously
10. memory of past experiences i.e.: pleasant memories	10. memories of past experiences i.e.: repressed, unpleasant memories	10. memories of all past, present,& future experiences of 3D & 4D
11. some emotional needs of present self	11. many emotional needs of past & present self & inner child	11. emotional needs instantly manifest into reality

THE THREE LEVELS OF CONSCIOUSNESS		
Humans are Usually Conscious of	**Humans are Usually Unconscious of**	**Humans are Superconscious Aware of**
12. locations which were consciously attended to while traveling there	12. locations that were NOT consciously attended to while traveling there	12. each location that is thought of is instantly experienced
13. cause and effect of conscious action	13. cause and effect of unconscious actions	13. cause & effect are merged into instant experience
14. physical need for sex	14. emotional need for sex	14. sex is a need to merge into One
15. intentional effect upon lover	15. unintentional effect upon lover	15. all love is intentional & unconditional
16. goals achieved by "work"	16. goals achieved by intention & desire	16. surrender to Soul/SELF
17. present, ego based desire for goal	17. past,emotionally based desire for goal	17. NO ego-based desires, emotions instantly manifested
18. "hard work" creates reality	18. that thoughts & feelings create reality	18. reality perceived is reality lived
19. some sensations of physical body	19. unconscious physical body sensations, etheric double, astral body, higher human	19. sensations of all 3D-5D "bodies"
20. some dreams & their meaning	20. most dreams & their meanings	20. dreams are 4D way of communicating
21. purposeful intention	21. imagination, instincts, latent creativity	21. Divine Ideal
22. information from 5 physical senses	22. information from higher, inner senses i.e.: ESP, psychic ability	22. information of all 3D, 4D & 5D lives
23. communication via hearing & some visual input	23. communication by telepathy, empathy, intuition & visual cues of body language	23. communication via merging into an experience of ONE
24. present	24. past lives, past deaths	24. all 3D, 4D past, present & future

THE THREE LEVELS OF CONSCIOUSNESS		
Humans are Usually Conscious of	Humans are Usually Unconscious of	Humans are Superconscious Aware of
25. physical guides & mentors	25. spiritual guides & mentors	25. guides & mentors 1D to 5D and beyond
26. physical body	26. etheric & astral body	26. Multidimensional SELF
27. present physical time	27. time/space paradigm	27. the NOW
28. individual consciousness	28. collective consciousness	28. Unity Consciousness
29. separate individuals	29. Communication with the One	29. Oneness with All That Is
30. limitations of everyday life	30. freedom from physical limitation	30. freedom from all limitations
31. concept of God	31. Reality of God/Goddess/All That Is	31. merging with the ONE
32. physical mate in 3D world	32. Divine Complement in 5D world	32. merging with Divine Complement
33. outer identity of human mate	33. true identity of human mate	33. awareness of 5D self of all human mates
34. conditional love, conditional forgiveness, conditional acceptance i.e.: I will love you if you	34. true love, true forgiveness, true acceptance i.e.: I love you truly	34. Unconditional Love, Unconditional Forgiveness, Unconditional Acceptance for others & for self
35. awareness of this 3D life,	35. awareness of 3D and 4D reality	35. awareness of all 3D, 4D, & 5D lives
36. awareness of human self	36. 1D, 2D, 4D & 5D selves	36. Multidimensional SELF

APPENDIX THREE

CHAKRA INDEX

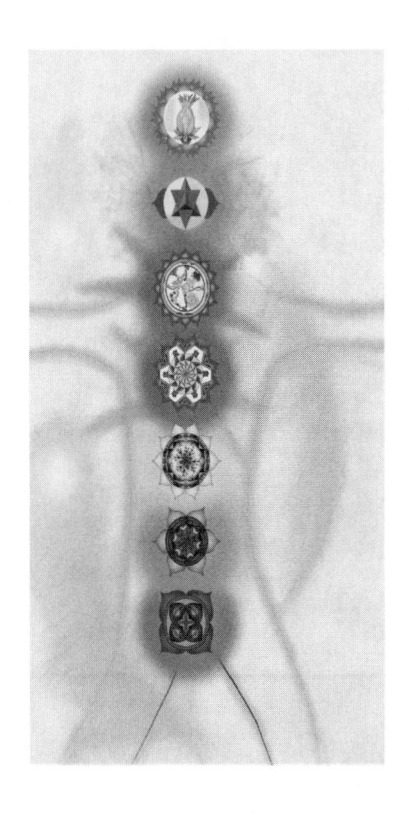

BIBLIOGRAPHY

The 11th Hour. (the film) Dir. Leila Conners Petersen. Warner Independent, 2007.

Anderson, Mary. *Numerology: The Secret Power of Numbers*. New York: Samuel Weiser Inc., 1979.

Anka, Darryl Bashar. *Blueprint for Change*. Seattle: New Solutions Publishing, 1990.

Archangel Ariel, channeled by Tachi-ren, Tashira. *What Is Lightbody?* Livermore, Ca.: Oughten House Publications, 1995.

Arntz, William; Chasse, Betsy; and Vicinte, Mark. *What the Bleep Do We Know!? Discovering the Endless Possibilities for Altering Your Everyday Reality*. Deerfield Beach, Fl.: Health Communications, Inc., 2005.

The Ascended Masters Write the Book of Life. New York: The Bridge to Freedom Inc., 1974.

Avalon, Arthur. *The Serpent Power: The Secrets of Tantric and Shaktic Yoga*. New York: Dover Publications, Inc., 1953.

Bernard, Helene. *Great Women Initiates, or the Feminine Mystic.* San Jose, Ca.: Supreme Grand Lodge of AMORC, 1984.

Besant, Annie, and Leadbeater, C. W. *Thought-Forms*. Madras, India: The Theosophical Publishing House, 1925.

Braden, Gregg. *Awakening to Zero Point: The Collective Initiation.* Ann Arbor, Mich.: Braun – Brumfield, 1993.

Brother Philip. *Secret of the Andes*. Bolinas, Ca.: Leaves of Grass Press, 1976.

Budge, E. A. Wallis, translator. *The Book of the Dead, The Hieroglyphic Transcript of the Papyrus of Ani in the British Museum*. New York: Bell Publishing Company, 1920.

Currie, Ian. *You Cannot Die: The Incredible Findings of a Century of Research on Death*. New York: Methuen, 1978.

Chaney, Earlyne. *Kundalini and The Third Eye*. Upland, Ca.: Astara Publications, 1980.

Chaney, Earlyne, *Initiation in the Great Pyramid*. Upland, Ca.: Astara Publications, 1987.

Dinnage, Rosemary. *Annie Besant*. New York: Penguin Books, 1986.

Doreal, M. (translation and interpretation). *The Emerald Tablets of Thoth the Atlantean*. Sedalia, Co.: Brotherhood of the White Temple, 2002.

Gore, Albert. *An Inconvenient Truth: The Planetary Emergency of Global Warming and What We Can Do About It*. (the film) Emmaus, Pa.: Rodale, 2006.

Greene, Brian. *The Elegant Universe*. New York: W. W. Norton, 1999.

Griscom, Chris. *Ecstasy Is A New Frequency, Teaching of the Light Institute*. New York: Simon & Schuster, 1987.

Grof, Stanislav. *The Holotropic Mind: The Three Levels of Human Consciousness and How They Shape our Lives*. San Francisco: HarperSanFrancisco, 1992.
Gross, Darwin. *You Can't Turn Back*. Oak Grove, Or.: Darwin Gross, 1985.

Gross, Darwin. *Consciousness in Life*. Oak Grove, Or.: SOS Publishing, 1986.

Gross, Darwin. *Your Right to Choose*. Oak Grove, Or.: SOS Publishing, 1986.

Gross, Darwin. *Power of Awareness*. Oak Grove, Or.: Darwin Gross, 1987.

Gross, Darwin. *The Atom Oak Grove*. Oak Grove, Or.: Darwin Gross, 1984.

Gross, Darwin. *Light is Knowledge*. Oak Grove, Or.: Darwin Gross, 1987.

Gurdjieff, G. I. *Meetings with Remarkable Men*. New York: E. P. Dutton, 1969.

Guru Rinpoche according to Karma Lingpa. *The Tibetan Book of the Dead, The Great Liberation Through Hearing in the Bardo*. Berkeley: Shambhala, 1975.

Hall, Manly P. *Death to Rebirth*. Los Angeles: Philosophical Research Society. 1979.

Hall, Manly P. *The Ways of the Lonely Ones*. Los Angeles: Philosophical Research Society. 1962.

Hodson, Geoffrey. *The Kingdom of The Gods*. Madras, India, and Wheaton, Ill.: The Theosophical Publishing House, 1952.

Hodson, Geoffrey. *The Brotherhood of Angels and Men*. Wheaton, Ill.: The Theosophical Publishing House, 1982.

Hodson, Geoffrey. *Fairies at Work and Play*. Wheaton, Ill.: The Theosophical Publishing House, 1982.

Huxley, Aldous. *The Doors of Perception*. New York: Harper & Row, 1954.

An Inconvenient Truth. Dir. Davis Guggenheim. Based on the book by Albert Gore. Paramount Classics, 2006.

Kaku, Michio. *Hyperspace: A Scientific Odyssey Through Parallel Universes, Time Warps, and the 10th Dimension*. New York: Oxford University Press, 1994.

Kaku, Michio. *Parallel Worlds: A Journey Through Creation, Higher Dimensions, and the Future of the Cosmos*. New York: Doubleday, 2005.

Klein, Eric. *The Crystal Stair: A Guide to the Ascension*. Livermore, Ca.: Oughten House, 1992.

Krishna, Gopi. *Kundalini: The Evolutionary Energy in Man*. Boston: Shambhala, 1971.

Krishnamurti, J. *Freedom from the Known*. New York: Harper & Row, 1969.

Kuhn, Thomas, S. *The Structure of Scientific Revolutions.* Chicago: The University of Chicago Press, 1962.

Leadbeater, C.W. *The Masters and the Path*. Chicago: The Theosophical Publishing House, 1925.

Leadbeater, C. W. *Ancient Mystic Rites*. Wheaton, Ill.: The Theosophical Publishing House, 1986.

Leadbeater, C. W. *The Inner Life*. Wheaton, Ill.: The Theosophical Publishing House, 1978.

Leadbeater, C. W. *Man Visible and Invisible*. Wheaton, Ill.: The Theosophical Publishing House, 1969.

Leadbeater, C. W. *The Chakras*. Chicago: The Theosophical Publishing House, 1927.

Leadbeater, C. W. *The Astral Plane*. Madras, India: The Theosophical Publishing House, 1977.

Leadbeater, C. W. *Dreams: What They Are and How They are Caused*. Madras, India: The Theosophical Publishing House, 1998.

Leadbeater, C. W. *Invisible Helpers*. Madras, India: The Theosophical Publishing House, 1980.

Long, Max Freedom. *The Secret Science at Work: New Light on Prayer*. Los Angeles: Huna Research Publications, 1953.

Maclean, Dorothy. *To Hear the Angels Sing*. Hudson, N.Y.: Lindisfarne Press, 1990.

Muktananda, Swami. *Play of Consciousness*. San Francisco: Harper & Row, 1978.

McKeough, Michael. *The Coloring Review of Neuroscience.* Boston: Little, Brown & Co, 1982.

Vywamus; McClure, Janet; and Harben, Lillian. *Scopes of Dimensions, How to Experience Multi-Dimensional Reality*. Sedona, Ariz.: Light Technology Publications, 1989.

McClure, Sanat Kumara. *Training a Planetary Logos*. Sedona, Ariz.: Light Technology Publications, 1990.

Mishra, Rammurti S. *Fundamentals of Yoga*. Garden City, N.Y.: Anchor Press/Doubleday, 1974.

Mishra, Rammurti S. *Yoga Sutras: The Textbook of Yoga Psychology*. Garden City, N.Y.: Anchor Press/Doubleday, 1973.

Moss, Thelma. *The Probability of the Impossible*. Los Angeles: J. P. Tarcher, 1974.

Moser, Robert. *Mental and Astral Projection.* Cottonwood, Ariz.: Esoteric Publications, 1974.

The Mystery of the Ductless Glands. San Jose, Ca.: Rosicrucian Fellowship, 1980.

Narby, Jeremy. *The Cosmic Serpent: DNA and the Origins of Knowledge*. New York: Jeremy P. Tarcher/Putman, 1998.

Neal, Viola Pettit. *Through the Curtain*. Marina del Rey: Ca.: De Vorss & Co., 1983.

Parker, Derek and Parker, Julia. *Dreaming: An Illustrated Guide to Remembering and Interpreting your Dreams.* New York: Harmony Books, 1985.

Pickover, Clifford. *Surfing Through Hyperspace: Understanding Higher Universes in Six Easy Lessons*. New York: Oxford University Press, 1999.

Powell, A. E. *The Etheric Double: The Health Aura of Man*. Madras, India: The Theosophical Publishing House, 1969.

Rachele, Sal. *Life on the Cutting Edge*. Sedona, Ariz.: Light Technology Publications, 1994.

Raphael. *The Starseed Transmissions: An Extraterrestrial Report*. Kansas City, Mo.: Uni-Sun, 1982.

Raymond, Andrew. *Secret of the Sphinx.* Pukalani, Hawaii.: UNI Productions, 1995.

Roberts, Bernadette. The *Experience of No-Self.* Boulder, Co.: Shambhala Publications, 1985.

Rolfe, Mona. *Initiation by the Nile*. London: Neville Spearman Limited, 1976.

Samuels, Mike, and Samuels, Nancy. *Seeing With the Mind's Eye*. New York: Random House, 1975.

Sannella, Lee. *Kundalini--Psychosis or Transcendence?* San Francisco: Atrium Publishing Group, 1976.

Sapolsky, Robert. *The Trouble with Testosterone*. New York: Simon & Schuster, 1997.

Satir, Virginia. *Peoplemaking*. Palo Alto, Ca.: Science & Behavior Books, Inc., 1972.

Sheehy, Gail. *The Silent Passage: Menopause.* New York: Random House, 1992.

Southern Centre of Theosophy. *Devas and Men: a Compilation of Theosophical Studies on the Angelic Kingdom*. Madras, India and Wheaton, Ill.: The Theosophical Publishing House, 1977.

Steiner, Rudolf. *The Evolution of Consciousness*. London: Rudolf Steiner Press, 1979.

Steiner, Rudolf. *Christianity and the Occult Mysteries of Antiquity*. New York: Steiner Books, 1977.

Steiner, Rudolf. *Esoteric Development*. Spring Valley, N.Y.: Anthroposophic Press, 1982.

Steiner, Rudolf. *Knowledge of The Higher Worlds and Its Attainment.* New York: Anthroposophic Press, 1947.

Steiner, Rudolf. *Egyptian Myths and Mysteries*. New York: Anthroposophic Press, 1971.

Steiner, Rudolf. *Cosmic Memory*. Englewood, N.J.: Anthroposophic Press, 1959.

Stone, Joshua David. *Hidden Mysteries*. Sedona, Ariz.: Light Technology Publishing, 1995.

Suzuki, Shunryu. *Zen Mind, Beginner's Mind*. New York: Walker/Weatherhill, 1970.

Talbot, Michael. *The Holographic Universe*. New York: HarperCollins, 1991.

The Findhorn Community. *The Findhorn Garden*. New York: Harper & Row Publishers, 1975.

Thomas, Eugene. *Brotherhood of Mt. Shasta*. Los Angeles: DeVorss & Co., 1974.

Twitchell, Paul. *The Spiritual Notebook*. Santa Monica, Ca.: DeVorss & Co., 1971.

Twitchell, Paul. *The Three Masks of Gaba*. Menlo Park, Ca.: Illuminated Way Publishing, 1983.

Twitchell, Paul. *Dialogues with the Master*. Menlo Park, Ca.: Illuminated Way Publishing, 1970.

Twitchell, Paul. *The Far Country*. Menlo Park, Ca.: Illuminated Way Publishing, 1988.

Twitchell, Paul. *The Flute of God*. Menlo Park, Ca: Illuminate Way Publishing, 1969.

Twitchell, Paul. *The Tiger's Fang*. Menlo Park, Ca.: Illuminate Way Publishing, 1967.

Van Gelder, Dora. *The Real World of Fairies*. Wheaton, Ill.: The Theosophical Publishing House, 1977.

Weed, Joseph. *Wisdom of The Mystic Masters*. West Nyack, N.Y.: Parker Publishing Company Inc., 1968.

Wolf, Fred Alan. *Taking the Quantum Leap: The New Physics for Nonscientists*. San Francisco: Harper & Row Publishers, 1981.

Wolf, Fred Alan. *Parallel Universe: The Search for Other Worlds*. New York: Simon & Schuster, 1988.

Wolf, Fred Alan. *Mind into Matter: A New Alchemy of Science and Spirit*. Portsmouth, N.H.: Moment Point Press, Inc. 2001.

Wood, Ernest. *The Seven Rays*. Wheaton, Ill.: The Theosophical Press, 1925.

ABOUT THE AUTHOR

Suzan Caroll is a sought-after psychotherapist and a life-long student of metaphysics and world religions. Suzan holds a PhD in Clinical Psychology, an MA in Audiology, and a BA in Speech Pathology. As a licensed Marriage and Family Therapist and a Certified Hypnotherapist, she has been counseling in private practice for more than twenty four years. She has a love of nature, and through her expanded perceptions, she experiences the LIFE in ALL of Earth's creatures.

The yearning to learn more about personal and planetary transformation started when Suzan was a graduate student studying for her PhD in the early 1980s. She began the documentation of this quest in 1999 on her website, Multidimensions.com, which offers an in-depth look at multidimensional consciousness and the journey of awakening to our Multidimensional SELF. Through sharing her theories and experiences in cyberspace via her website and monthly newsletter, Multidimensional News, Suzan has communicated with many other seekers such as herself from all over the world.

Suzan has authored several books on multidimensional consciousness, *The Thirty Veils of Illusion, Visions from Venus, Reconstructing Reality and Seven Steps to Soul, A Poetic Journey of Spiritual Awakening*, and two illustrated short stories, "A Child's Adventure in Faerie" and "What Did You Learn?" She also offers free audio versions of many of the meditations presented in this book through her website, Multidimensions.com.

Suzan lives near the beach in Southern California with her husband and five birds. She enjoys traveling, reading, writing, drawing, meditating, gardening, walking on the beach, and spending time with her two adult children, their spouses, and seven grandchildren.